AFGHANISTAN, WAR AND THE MEDIA: DEADLINES AND FRONTLINES

EDITED BY
RICHARD LANCE KEEBLE
JOHN MAIR

070. 4499581047
KEE

Published 2010 by arima publishing

www.arimapublishing.com

ISBN 978 1 84549 444 5

© Richard Lance Keeble and John Mair

Abramis is an imprint of arima publishing.

arima publishing
ASK House, Northgate Avenue
Bury St Edmunds, Suffolk IP32 6BB
t: (+44) 01284 700321

www.arimapublishing.com

Contents

Acknowledgements

With many thanks for getting this book to market in record time to:

BBC College of Journalism (Kevin Marsh, David Hayward and team)

Coventry University Vice Chancellor Madeleine Atkins

Coventry Pro Vice-Chancellor David Pilsbury

Denise Skinner, Dean of the Business School at Coventry University for "seed" money for the Coventry conference

Journalism.co.uk (Laura Oliver and Judith Townend)

John Ryley, Editor in Chief, Sky News

Jon Williams, Foreign Editor, BBC News

All the contributors, even those who promised but did not deliver.

Our families who lived with the project for three months.

The Editors

Richard Lance Keeble has been Professor of Journalism at the University of Lincoln since 2003. Before that he was the executive editor of *The Teacher*, the weekly newspaper of the National Union of Teachers and he lectured at City University, London, for 19 years. He has written and edited 17 publications including *Secret State, Silent Press: New Militarism, the Gulf and the Modern Image of Warfare* (John Libbey, Luton, 1997); *The Newspapers Handbook* (Routledge, 2005, fourth edition); *Ethics for Journalists* (Routledge, 2008, second edition); *The Journalistic Imagination: Literary Journalists from Defoe to Capote and Carter* (Routledge, 2007, with Sharon Wheeler) and *Communicating War: Memory, Media and Military* (Arima, Bury St Edmunds, 2007, with Sarah Maltby). He is also the joint editor of *Ethical Space: The International Journal of Communication Ethics*.

John Mair is Senior Lecturer in Broadcasting at Coventry University. He is a former BBC, ITV and Channel Four producer/director on a wide range of programmes from daily news to investigative documentaries on *World in Action* to more considered pieces on *Bookmark*. A Royal Television Society Journalism Award winner, he publishes widely in the media and journalism press including the *Guardian* and *journalism.co,uk*. This is his fourth co-written or edited book. For the BBC, he co-wrote *Marx in London*, with Asa Briggs, in 1981.With Richard Lance Keeble, he edited *Beyond Trust* (2008) and *Playing Footsie with the FTSE? The Great Crash of 2008 and the Crisis in Journalism (2009)*, both published by Abramis.

Preface

Huw Edwards

Shortly after my return from Lashkar Gah in 2008, I was confronted by a man on a train heading for London. In a blistering conversation that lasted no more than five minutes, he raised fundamental concerns about the BBC's coverage of Afghanistan. They were all linked in some way to the nature of the British media's relationship with the armed forces.

He had been enraged by our "twisted" reporting, our status as "prisoners" of the forces during our stay in Helmand, and our seemingly wilful refusal to report "the truth". Ah, yes. The truth.

As one author notes elsewhere, it is the journalist's "most elusive aspiration". In war reporting, that elusiveness is taken to even more daunting levels. This book allows some of our leading practitioners of war reporting to have their say. The commentators also have theirs. It is a sobering read, to put it mildly.

Reporting from Afghanistan, as Channel Four's Alex Thomson points out, remains an exceptionally dangerous activity. Embedding is one of the solutions available. Indeed, it is an unavoidable arrangement for most British journalists, but the editorial pressures are clear to everyone. As a result, the desire to push the boundaries of any agreement rarely fades. The Ministry of Defence knows that. The soldiers on the ground know it, too.

In my experience, the visit becomes a daily tussle with "Media Ops". We are there to obtain memorable, newsworthy material and to explore the main challenges. They want to sell the best story and keep us safe. There is a constant tension which tends to militate against any temptation to collude or be complicit.

The task of covering the conflict and discovering "the truth" has become even more complex in recent years. The BBC's Kevin Marsh rightly draws attention to the rock-solid political consensus which propelled us towards war after 9/11. He argues that any failure of journalism to "give a full account" of the war in Afghanistan has nothing to do with "embeds" or questions of access, and almost everything to do with "the failings of editors in London". Those failings have to be seen in the stifling context of 9/11 and the global response to that event.

As the number of British losses rises, government ministers and senior military officers try to make it difficult for journalists to question the true purpose and value of the mission. But question we must. Clearly, the quality of the answers will depend on the merit and variety of our sources. Will Barton makes the point that our information needs to come "from beyond the compounds of the British army".

In an area of increasingly trenchant debate, the last point is one on which we can all come together.

Huw Edwards presents BBC *News at Ten*

Section 1. Frontlines and deadlines

From the poppy fields of Helmand – to the rebirth of "embedding"

John Mair

The war in Afghanistan passes new and grimmer milestones every day. As I write in mid-June 2010, the US/UK/ISAF forces have suffered their worst month of casualties – 29 dead, 10 on one day. To date, more than 1,000 US military personnel have died, the British total has already passed 300. Wootton Bassett, the north Wiltshire market town, will see more sad cortèges pass through its "honour" guard. Helmand is the new Killing Fields. The US has now been involved in the Afghan conflict for one hundred and four months: one month longer than their ultimately disastrous war in Vietnam. The parallels are frightening.

This book explores the journalism coming out of the Afghan war from the frontline and from the greater comfort of the library. It is an unusual hybrid: the testimony of some of the best frontline correspondents of our era, much of it placed in appropriate historical contexts, alongside detailed academic analysis – and much more. It ranges from the poppy fields of Helmand province to New York via the Iraq War and the modern rebirth of "embedding". It mixes action, reflection and analysis and focuses on some of under-reported groups such as women and the humanitarian effort in Afghanistan.

It has its origin in a conference in Coventry in March 2010 put on as part of the university's Coventry Conversations series (with financial support from the Pro Vice-Chancellor and the Dean of Business) in conjunction with the BBC College of Journalism and journalism.co.uk (the website forum for digitally active journalists). All of that conference can be seen and heard on bbc.co.uk/journalism and Coventry.ac.uk/itunesu. Many of the contributors to this book took part in that conference though some extra pieces have been specially commissioned.

3

The war in Afghanistan will soon be coming up to its tenth anniversary. Operation Enduring Freedom started on 7 October 2001 as a response to the 9/11 al-Qaeda attacks on the Twin Towers in New York. Freedom in Afghanistan has far from endured in that decade. There are today 100,000-plus US troops, 10,000-plus British troops and 17,000 from ISAF allies – including Germany, France, Italy, Poland and Canada.

The West is fighting a phantom

US intelligence admit that there are now fewer than 100 al-Qaeda (the reason for invading in the first place) fighters left in the country and that the Taliban could fight on for ever. British Prime Minister David Cameron told the House of Commons on 14 June 2010 after his return from his first official visit to Afghanistan that it was only the presence of the ISAF troops that kept al-Qaeda from returning to Afghanistan in numbers. The West is fighting a phantom and desperately searching for an exit strategy. The trouble is they will leave behind an Afghan government scarred by illegitimacy, corruption and more. The Killing Fields will continue for a while yet. Journalism has escaped comparatively lightly – just nine Western journalists killed in Afghanistan since 2001.

Like all big stories, this war has attracted the cream of British journalistic talent especially the broadcast reporters. TV awards have been won on the field of battle by the new Brahmins – the war corrs parachuted in and out of Helmand. The idea for the conference and for the book took hold when I judged the Royal Television Society News Programme of the Year Awards for 2009. All entries featured front line action from their stars. Many of them have contributed to this book.

Allan Little, the BBC's Special Correspondent, experienced reporting the Gulf conflict of 1991 and it gave him an enduring distrust of embedding. But now, he argues, independent, free-roaming, eye-witness reporting, which journalists used to pursue with such vigour and commitment, faces enormous threats.

Alex Thomson, chief correspondent of Channel Four News and an embed in Afghanistan, says that in future he aims to tweet live from the battlefield. And it is very hard to see how the MoD's media minders can filter this process, he says.

Sky News' Stuart Ramsay, aged just 45, is already a veteran reporter of 16 wars including Chechnya, Sierra Leone, Israel, Gaza, Lebanon, Sudan, Bosnia, Kosovo, Somalia and Afghanistan. Here he argues that the embeds are here to stay. But they owe it to themselves and their viewers, readers and listeners never to let their guard down and always ask this basic journalistic question: are they lying?

Embedded reporting – from both sides

Sky News' Alex Crawford, a Royal Television Society winner at those awards I judged, tells how she manages to combine embedded reporting from both sides of the Afghan conflict. And while a general picture of the conflict may be possible based on time spent with either of the fighting forces, she says much of the truth about how the war is going will be filled in by the civilians at the centre of it all.

Vaughan Smith is the founder of the Frontline Club in London who filmed the only uncontrolled footage of the Gulf War in 1991 after he bluffed his way into an active-duty unit while disguised as a British army officer. Here, he argues that news management by the military is a risky business. Though it might maintain a certain level of support for the war that backing becomes more brittle for the deception.

David Hayward, of the BBC College of Journalism, pulls it all together and draws on the first-hand experiences of frontline journalists to argue that coverage of the Afghan conflict needs to incorporate the views of the Taliban and the views of the local people and politicians as well as the perspectives of the US-led forces

Finally, Hanan Habibzai, a freelance Afghan journalist, highlights the complexities of the conflict which, he says, the Western media largely fail to understand.

In defence of the non-embed

Allan Little's experiences reporting the Gulf conflict of 1991 gave him an enduring distrust of embedding. But now, he argues, independent, free-roaming, eye-witness reporting, which journalists used to pursue with such vigour and commitment, faces enormous threats

In April 2003, I got in my car at the Hotel Palestine, Baghdad, overlooking the broad green curve of the Tigris River and drove to the notorious Abu Ghraib prison on the outskirts of the Iraqi capital. There was a cemetery on the edge of the prison complex. Two young men, Shia Muslims from the south of the country, had come to try to retrieve the body of their brother who had been executed some years earlier. They believed, but did not know, he was buried here.

A cemetery keeper consulted a bulging file, and found their brother's name and its corresponding grave number, and led them to the place where their brother had been interred. I followed them. As we went, the keeper explained that under Saddam Hussein's regime, the condemned fell into two categories: soldiers were executed by firing squad; common criminals were hanged. The second category included political opponents such as the brother we were about to disinter.

I stood on the edge of the grave and watched them dig. A couple of feet into the dry, pliable soil, their brother's remains began to emerge. As they recognised the clothes in which he'd been buried their stillness fell away. They fell on the body and wept and embraced it and howled their grief to the sky. We filmed. They let us film. That was how it was then. There was freedom of movement, pretty much unfettered access to the seismic forces that were changing the topography of this most volatile region.

Political vacuum after Saddam's fall

Within days of Saddam Hussein's statue in Fardus Square, Baghdad, coming down on 9 April 2003, two things were evident. The first was that the coalition forces that had invaded Iraq were not ready. They did not know what was about to unfold and they had made no effective plan. So there was a vacuum.

The second was that very quickly, organised religion moved to fill that vacuum. The Imams were the only trusted public authorities. It was the clerics who put a stop to the looting that had swept the city after the Ba'ath regime had fallen. It was the clerics who organised rotas of men to stand guard at the hospitals to protect the medical staff from lawlessness. It was the clerics who sent the young to busy road junctions to act as traffic cops to keep the city's roads flowing when all the lights were out.

One day, an American arms dump exploded in a residential suburb. Nearby houses that had withstood weeks of allied bombardment were obliterated. Families were wiped out. But what was striking was how quickly public anger was channelled. Within an hour there was a "spontaneous" demonstration of Iraqis – hundreds, perhaps thousands, strong – already with printed placards and leaflets blaming the Americans for deliberately endangering the lives of Iraqis. I went along. I marched with them, interviewed them for television. One man told me, in fluent English, that "the United States of America is the enemy of Islam, it is written so in the Holy Koran". I said in my report for that night's news on BBC1:

> The explosion has ignited an anti-American fury. Within hours that fury was organised. It has not taken long for this to turn into a demonstration of rage against the Americans…Today, nothing the Americans can say will be heard amid the din – the *organised and carefully marshalled chorus* – of anti-American sentiment (my own italics).

But still we filmed. Still they let us film. This happy state of freedom was not to last long.

There had been signs of what was to come. Before the invasion I had decided against embedding myself with a Coalition unit. I had covered the first Gulf War in 1991 from the Iraqi side. I had watched Baghdad night after night as it was slowly taken apart by the precision bombing of a high-tech and largely unseen allied air force.

War as a rudimentary video-game

It was only after the war, when I went back to Jordan, that I saw, for the first time, how most of the world had witnessed it. In those pre-internet, pre-24 hour news days, I had not seen, from my Baghdad viewpoint, the missile nose-cone cameras that had made the war look like a rudimentary video-game. I had seen what those missiles had done when they came into contact with human flesh. My perspective was more visceral – literally. The experience gave me an enduring distrust of embedding alone.

On 13 February 1991, an allied air raid struck a large, fortified structure in a western suburb of Baghdad called al-Amariyah. We were taken there shortly after dawn. This is the report I filed for BBC radio news:

> *It's reported from Baghdad that hundreds of Iraqi civilians may have been killed when a large air raid shelter was hit during an allied air attack. Two missiles or bombs penetrated its reinforced concrete roof exploding inside. Our correspondent in Baghdad, Allan Little, was among a small group of journalists taken to the shelter in a residential area of the city hours after the attack. His report has not been subject to Iraqi restrictions.*

When we arrived, black smoke was still pouring from the shelter. There was chaos. The operation to recover bodies had barely begun. The charred and mutilated remains of those inside were being carried out in blankets and piled into the back of a truck. Some were hardly recognisable as human. Local people said the shelter had a capacity of 2,000. Between 700 and 1,100 had used it every night since bombing began they said, almost all women and children from the middle class suburb of Amariyah.

Crowds of near-hysterical men pushed and jostled their way through to try to find news of their wives and families. Popular army men had been drafted in to assist. Some wept uncontrollably. One young officer pointed to a neighbouring house: seven people from one family had died, he said; the women of the neighbourhood had been wiped out.

We were taken to a nearby hospital. Between 30 and 40 bodies, blackened and twisted, were laid out on blankets. Most were women, but many were children three-, four-, five-years-old. Some curled on their sides as though they'd died instantly in their sleep. No one knows how many have been killed. Civil defence officials here say up to 1,000; others, perhaps 400.

I saw no evidence of nearby military installations.

This attack will send a shockwave through Baghdad, many of whose citizens take nightly shelter in buildings like this, believing themselves safe. Among many Iraqi people, it will further strengthen Saddam Hussein's claim that the allies aim not to liberate Kuwait, but to destroy the Iraqi state and nation.

How the BBC became dubbed the Baghdad Broadcasting Corporation
Within hours, the news had caused a political sensation in the allied countries. In Britain, my BBC TV colleague Jeremy Bowen and I were being denounced as dupes of the enemy. The BBC was the Baghdad Broadcasting Corporation, according to one British tabloid newspaper.

The allies said the building was not a civilian air raid shelter but a military command bunker. Yet we were there, standing among the bodies. A few feet away, a pick-up truck was being piled high with the remains of the dead. As it sped off, the body on the top of the pile fell to the ground a few feet from where I stood. I walked into a grassy clearing a vomited, again and again. Jeremy and I scoured the building for evidence of military or communications facility and could find none. The allies also challenged Iraqi claims about the number of dead. So I went to the morgue and I counted – one, two, three… until I got to a little more than three hundred.

The power of eye-witness journalism

Eye witness journalism is in one sense the purest and best of what we do. It has the power to settle part of the argument, to close down propaganda, to challenge myth-making. It is the first draft in the writing of history and, in itself, a primary source for future historians.

So in 2003 I went to Kuwait to try to cover this second war as an independent, non-embedded reporter. As the invasion began, braver souls than me headed north, unembedded, under their own steam. I stood in the lobby of an international hotel, just after dark, on the first or second day of the invasion. A US Army major was talking urgently into a mobile phone to a journalist who had got lost in southern Iraq.

"These voices you can hear," the major was saying, "are they English or Arabic? Arabic. I see. Then lie flat on the ground. Do not move. Switch off your mobile phone because if it rings it will give away your position. Stay there all night. When you hear American forces arrive, wave something white and put up your hands. Now, is there any message you would like me to pass on to your next of kin while you still can?"

That same day we heard news that an ITN crew had gone north with the invasion forces, unembedded, and was now missing. The correspondent was a friend of mine, Terry Lloyd, whom I had come to know in Bosnia a decade earlier. He was a generous and thoughtful colleague and a welcome friend in any bad place. I'd run into him earlier, we had greeted each other with enthusiasm and punched each other's local mobile numbers into our phones. We promised to stay in touch and swap notes. He was killed the next day as he tried to make his way to Basra, killed in pursuit of being first in to a liberated city.

And so the portents were there for us to read. By 2004 they were unmistakable. The kidnap, in Pakistan, of the American reporter Daniel Pearl in January 2002 was an early indication of how utterly changed the world was for independent reporting. Pearl was beheaded in front of a video camera and the pictures were posted on the internet. A new phenomenon was born – that of the "exhibition killing". It created a market in Western lives, a way for Islamist and other anti-Western or insurgent groups to advertise their own radicalism and attract a global community of support.

In Iraq, the murders of the British contractor Kenneth Bigley, in October 2004, and the British-Irish aid worker Margaret Hassan, in November 2004, and many others turned this phenomenon into an ever-present danger. Also in 2004, two French journalists, Georges Malbrunot and Christian Chesnot, were kidnapped while driving from Baghdad to the southern Iraqi city of Najaf, along a road that had not, until then, been considered dangerous territory. They were held for more than four months, before being released after a massive intervention by the French security services.

Kidnappers – organised and disciplined

On their return to France, a few days before Christmas, they gave a remarkable insight into the organised and disciplined nature of the kidnappers' thinking. Their captors had told him their case would be heard by a high ranking tribunal. There were, they were told, four categories of people who, when captured, deserved execution. These were: foreign combatants; anyone working for the occupying, or coalition, forces; anyone carrying the passport of one of the occupying, or coalition, countries (British, American, Australian, Danish etc); and spies. Malbrunot and Chesnot had satisfied their captors that they did not fit into any of the first three categories. The question of whether or not they were spies was, for months, undecided.

This, broadly, is the state of affairs that prevails. It has required international news organisations to invest in providing security for their reporters. It has placed a screen of security between us and those whose stories we need to hear. What is life like in those great swathes of Afghanistan that are controlled by the Taliban? We can only know a small part of the picture. We can listen to the stories of those who flee to government-controlled territory. But we can no

11

longer get in our cars in Kabul and drive unmolested into the countryside to see for ourselves.

The intrepid, courageous *New York Times* reporter Stephen Farrell tried to do this in September 2009, after a Nato airstrike on two hijacked fuel tankers had caused dozens of civilian deaths near the northern Afghan city of Kunduz. He found his eye witnesses, he was listening to their story, he was piecing together what had actually happened from those who had actually seen it. He was acquiring that vital commodity – evidence, the kind of evidence that writes the first draft of history and which is such an essential tool in combating propaganda and myth-making.

And he was kidnapped. Worse than that. He was held for four days and then rescued in an audacious raid by British forces. Four people were killed in the operation – Farrell's popular and highly respected Afghan colleague Sultan Munadi, one British soldier and two Iraqi women who had the misfortune to get in the way. It is – surely – too high a price to pay. The world is now very hard, indeed, for the kind of independent, free-roaming, eye-witness journalism we used to pursue which such vigour and commitment.

Note on the author
Allan Little is Special Correspondent with the BBC. He covered the Gulf conflict of 1991, the break-up of the former Yugoslavia, was for two years BBC South Africa correspondent, then Moscow correspondent and Africa correspondent. He has won several awards including a Gold Sony Radio Award for Reporter of the Year in 1992 and in 1994 he was named the Bayeux War Correspondent of the Year.

The rough guide to roughness

Alex Thomson, chief correspondent of Channel Four News and an "embed" in Afghanistan, says that in future he aims to tweet live from the battlefield. And it is very hard to see how the MoD's media minders can filter this process, he says

I intend this as a user's guide to embedding as a correspondent, a sort of reality-driven manual perhaps, to what it is really all about and how it is set up and why, in the context of the rather more learned material to be found elsewhere in this book.

But just before we engage with the joys of "MediaOps", the *Green Book*, Bastion, Lash and the joys of embedding with the Brits in their long-running Afghan adventure, can we just nail a large fallacy?

The only thing new about embedding is that rather nasty, ugly Americanism. The thing itself is – like hookers – as old as soldiering itself. Consider if you will, the travails of one Alexander the Great (356-323 BC), far from home and far from happy, in a place which we will call Lashkar Gah – because that's where he was. Mightily pissed off too, with the recalcitrant locals.

The point of this being, not that history repeats itself (though it painfully does in this locale) but that Alexander was good enough to take along scribes who wrote up his observations en route. The embed was – even then – alive and well. Roll forward the centuries and the Pentagon have just come up with a very new nasty word for something very, very old.

Which is why I laughed out loud recently as the retired BBC correspondent Martin Bell pontificated about how he was some kind of "pioneer" of embed reporting when he donned a British soldier's uniform during Operation Desert Storm in Saudi Arabia in 1991. No Martin, sorry. You were, no doubt, a genuine pioneer of many, many things before and after your eminent BBC career. But you were not a pioneer of embed journalism nor anything like it. And if it really is so old – what is the debate all about?

All manner of controversy about war coverage

It seems the mere invention of the neologism "embed" has sparked all manner of controversy about war coverage, bias, impartiality and various other ways in which the modern media might be selling their souls down the highways of Helmand and beyond.

It has though, never been any other way. I don't remember standing in some kind of no man's land when I was in Sri Lanka, Lebanon, Iraq, Somalia, Congo, Burundi, Kashmir (I could go on, but you get the drift...) in order to portray some kind of noble picture of Reithian objective war coverage unsullied by being with either side. If you are lucky enough to have just two sides – but don't get me into Bosnia.

No, to do that would be a rather obvious and bloody method of inviting sudden death by modern high-explosives or high-velocity round. Are there really people alive out there who seem to think you can stand around in the middle and attempt on-the-one-hand-but-on-the-other journalism?

Well, astonishingly there are it seems. Or something like it. Chief among the carpers about embedding, of course, the indefatigable editors at MediaLens who get extremely hoity-toity at the entire concept of embedding. However, ask them how they would cover Helmand if they were off to the main bazaar, Lashkar Gah, at noon next Tuesday and guess what? Total silence, from the normally electronically incontinent MediaLens email service.

Which rather clinches the argument, simple though it is. You cannot stand in the middle on the battlefield for very long without incurring huge risk.

Independent coverage of Operation Desert Storm

That's not to say you shouldn't try and our colleague Terry Lloyd, of course, died doing just that in Iraq at the outset of the last Western invasion of that country in 2003. I covered Operation Desert Storm for thee months in 1991 roving around the deserts of Saudi Arabia, Kuwait and Iraq avoiding any Coalition forces in order to bring some kind of independent coverage to the invasion.

This is vital, critical and essential to all wars – including Afghanistan. As I write, I am putting together some more remarkable images about civilians and the impact on them of current Nato operations, all of it shot outside the embeds' construct, on traditional independent grounds. But it is done by brave and resourceful Afghan journalists. Not by me, for reasons which we shall explore later.

What is critical is that we attempt to do this more and attempt to give more balance of airtime to independent journalism. There is certainly the grave danger that the relative ease of doing embed journalism and in relative safety, means there is simply too much of it and other avenues are not sufficiently explored. And here the critics of the mainstream media have a point.

So it can be done, it should be done and we will all go on doing it. But do not the parties to warfare also deserve to have their stories told? Do not the Taliban, Hizbe-e Islamia, a host of other Afghan militias and Nato have a right to their story, their war, their perspective being told? I know of nobody who says no to this.

Put simply, you should quickly arrive at where we try to be at Channel 4 News at any rate, which is yes, using embeds as and when we need to; talk to and film with the Afghan insurgents and also put local reporters into the civilian picture around places such as Helmand.

The risks of reporting Afghanistan are very high and very real

Don't get me wrong, I would love to go, but as I write a number of French journalists remain hostage in Afghanistan. I have no wish to join them. The risks are very high and very real. Still less, do I wish to be party to a hostage situation in which the Western reporter comes out alive, but his driver and/or translator get their throats slit back to the spine.

Only recently we had the example of a brave, independently-minded *New York Times* reporter who got captured by insurgents whilst trying to investigate a Nato airstrike which had killed civilians. He ended up coming home alive and well. But his translator – himself a hugely respected Kabuli journalist – was killed. That's not all. A British special forces soldier was also killed in his rescue operation.

Be in no doubt that is the reality of war coverage right now in Afghanistan. These are the simple facts of it. Like Iraq, it has simply become so dangerous that even if I wanted to cover the war, neither Channel 4 nor my employer ITN would allow me. The war is – like some other places such as Somalia, for instance – off limits.

Of course that is "wrong", limiting, filters our coverage, imposes a bias in the coverage – of course all of that is patently true. But it is not of our making and as I have said till I'm blue in the face and my keyboard is melting, would that the insurgency in Afghanistan saw the value of journalists as journalists, rather than walking infidel ATMs of great value on the ransom market.

Just pray to whatever god you have or not, that this changes, for we can do little more. Failing that, having courageous and resourceful local film-makers able to get to the insurgents and, indeed, the ordinary Helmandis, are the next best thing and as I write we at Channel 4 News have recently achieved the former with interesting results. And when I've finished writing this I shall be on the telephone to our redoubtable team who have been finding out from Afghan civilians what Operation Moshtarak actually means for them among the poppy fields of the Helmand River valley.

Me? Well I am freshly returned from another embed with British forces. Such things are planned and laid down many months in advance and from the outset there are politics in play. A lot of politics. No point in wrapping this up and anybody who says different has spent too long with their spin doctor.

The MoD has a war to sell

The MoD wants the most positive coverage set before the biggest audience. Obviously. It has a war to sell which is now longer than the Second World War. And it is not going very well. And they want to get out. And...And...They have soldiers dying who were at junior school when the invasion and occupation (for it is both, whatever the spin) began. They have a problem. And the drip drip drip of Wootton Bassett homecomings are not helping, as they also privately acknowledge.

Which means naughty things happen at times of stress. I cannot mention names here because I will never be allowed to by ITN. But pretty clearly the MoD knows who will be the biggest cheerleaders among the television media. Look at any academic analysis of , say, coverage of the invasion of Iraq and you will see it laid out for fact.

Some journalists and some television stations almost in their entirety lose their corporate head in times of war and it shows. The MoD rather likes that, of course. It should not be so in TV news but it is so and from Cardiff University to name but one, the factual proof, the statistics, the evidence is out their in spade loads. The MoD also studies these things rather carefully, I understand.

So our embed for the front end of Operation Mostarak never, ever happened. Promises were ditched. Deals broken. Suddenly other broadcasters were there but Channel 4 News was, well, put back a few weeks.

Now as it happened I was not to bothered because I'd decided – rightly as it turned out – that Operation Moshtarak was never going to be about front-end combat. It would be – critically – about holding the ground which Nato would, initially, occupy in a matter of hours because of overwhelming force. But holding it would be different and it still is. Very different.

Pathetic lack of protest over reporting ban

But I throw this episode out just to illustrate that the "who goes where" is controlled by the MoD and they do it rather bluntly and crudely, for obvious political ends, in terms of selling the war. Should anybody doubt this, please remember that this is the country about to ban all embeds completely during a coming General Election, with, it seems, no hint of embarrassment in Whitehall. And, it should be said, a pathetic lack of protest from the broadcast media and newspapers.

Once decided, this being Britain with its pathology of secrecy, control and censorship, you have to sign up to the *Green Book*. It is essentially a deal between the media and the MoD not to reveal anything that would compromise operational security ("OpSec").

I have yet to meet a journo who had any problem with this and I don't either. But, of course, it is never quite that simple. The military, it is written, cannot and will not censor anything for reasons of politics, taste, decency or embarrassment. Looks good in theory. In practice, though, something which is, say, embarrassing, could impact on morale and thus "Op Sec", could it not?

So you see , within the austere print and rules of the *Green Book*, lie all manner of elephant traps waiting to swallow you up when you get into the Theatre of War.

Or they do up to a point. Of course, in the age of the blog and the tweet in which we now live, all such control systems are frankly rather limited. I can perhaps make a small claim to pioneering in that, during a recent trip to Helmand, I more or less invented the "time-delayed tweet". We were out on a deep patrol with the British Coldstream Guards. It occurred to me that the Thuriya satfone was up and working and I could simply phone over tweets to the newsdesk and be, in tweeting terms, live from the battlefield.

There certainly was fighting all around. In the end I opted to delay the tweets simply because – with no external scrutiny whatsoever – I might not be able to judge that the things I would write might or might not affect "Op Sec".

Brave new world of online twittery

The brave new world of technology and online twittery can be a lonely old place these days. In the end I simply wrote down the tweet messages along with blogs, then relayed them all when I got back. The tweeters out there loved it. The MoD never said anything to me about it either way.

But they must be frantically assessing ways of getting their control systems up to speed to cover this issue. I for one will be trying to push this forward to actual live tweeting from the battlefield at the first opportunity I can get and it is very hard to see how media minders can filter this process.

In fact though, many of the potential pitfalls of the *Green Book* Rule don't actually crop up all that often. In my experience the further down the line you get from Whitehall, the nearer you are to the front line, the less any body gives a toss about censorship. They have a war on their hands. Frankly, they're just chuffed to have someone along who cares enough to tell their story. Soldiers want to be on telly. Officers want to be on telly even more. And some further up the ranks are almost a hazard in their desire to get their mug on screen.

So it is that I spent many weeks setting up a film about the teams whose task it is to defuse IEDs in what has – to a large extent – become the war of the IED: the Improvised Explosive Device or homemade bomb.

It is hard to imagine anything that could potentially be more sensitive to OpSec. Clearly Nato does not want to inform the insurgency just how it goes about its business here. But in the end everything was cleared. I'd suggested the chief Media Ops officer should absolutely fly down from Lashkar Gah to Camp Bastion to see the final cut in person and change anything that could compromise OpSec.

Filming without any media minder whatsoever

But first – to the film. In the end – irony of ironies – we spent our entire time with the IED unit without any media minder whatsoever. This, on the most sensitive news item to have come from Helmand possibly since the Brits arrived there (this time around). It illustrates precisely how all the best-laid Whitehall plans survive no contact with war whatsoever. There may be all manner of *Green Bookery* and other arcane malarkey in London – come Afghanistan and other factors soon somehow crowd it out. And hallelujah for that.

Not least – there's the question of trust. We had pivotal figure on this occasion in terms of the "Media Ops" officer in Lashkar Gah – Lt Col David Wakefield. His job is to somehow match the needs of media teams on the ground downwards, to the demands of Whitehall upwards. You can see how that is as near to defining the impossible as you can get. But he genuinely tried hard and worked effectively to get us what we wanted. He wanted the IED film made and he made sure it happened, after months of organisations asking for access but not getting it.

So much hangs on who your "Media Ops" boss is in Lashkar Gah. You can get people like Wakefield who either instinctively understand what we are about or at least try to. Or you can get people in that job who understand little, care less and frankly just want to get through their year of whatever of complete poisoned chalice and then move on to something, anything, better than this. And boy have we had them in Lashkar Gah in times past.

But again, the old human system will out. If you are getting nothing from the stuffed shirt in Lash – simply go find the tent of the commander of the people you want to be with in Camp Bastion, make your pitch and it will either happen or not.

That old excuse about lack of helicopter transport…

So it was on one occasion that we had been asking to get up to Kajaki Dam with the Royal Marines for a long, long time. The old excuse about lack of helicopter transport was trotted out. They are in short supply. But they are also a very easy excuse too.

Off I went one night to the requisite tent, tipped off by a sympathetic officer in Camp Bastion. Minutes later the deal was done and we were on one of two

Chinooks leaving for Kajaki the next day. All of this a filming opportunity which the entire machine from Whitehall to Lashkar Gah had been telling us, could not and would not be done.

The reason – simple. He knew and I knew that the Commandos were going to have a major engagement 48 hours hence and we both wanted it on television. It happened. It happened yet again with little reference up to Lashkar Gah I strongly suspect, let alone to MoD in London, until it was simply too late to veto the whole thing.

So what does all this produce? Impartial coverage? Of course not. You are covering what British soldiers are doing, with them, featuring them, from their perspective. Of course it is biased. And so are filming trips with the Taliban for that matter. It is in the nature of the beast.

Do soldiers behave differently in front of camera? Of course they do. Does anyone doubt that? They get the brief before we arrive. They know. They are on watch. Their tongues are being monitored.

Does that mean the exercise is invalid? Well, I don't think so. I've just finished a long film which – over 16 minutes it must be said – painted a pretty unambiguous picture of a bunch of highly-trained, professional soldiers acting with great restraint. But it also showed starkly that they understand little or nothing of the people whose land they occupy. Thus, the job they are tasked to do is, pretty much, impossible.

Importance of human intelligence in counter-insurgent strategy
Worse, their Afghan Army "partners" – Nato's only exit strategy – fared scarcely any better. And you don't need to visit Sandhurst to suss that you cannot win counter-insurgent warfare without first rate Humint – human intelligence.

And the film showed also, that the other side, the insurgents, have that in abundance. Why? Because they watched our every move for one day. They then spent days two and three ambushing, sniping and rocketing our group of soldiers at will, with some accuracy, resilience and flexibility. They are good fighters. You need to see close up how they have held down the greatest arsenal this planet's ever seen, for years now, with few RPGs and Kalashnikov with lots of IEDs into the bargain. Of course, you saw all this from the perspective of the British and Afghan soldiers. But the point is – you saw it.

Note on the author

Alex Thomson is Chief Correspondent and Presenter of ITN's Channel Four News. So he is in the highly unusual position of being both studio anchor and roving correspondent. In more than 20 years with ITN, he's covered over 20 wars and conflicts and won more than 10 domestic and international awards.

The case for the honest embed

Sky News' Stuart Ramsay, at 45, is already a veteran reporter of 16 wars including Chechnya, Sierra Leone, Israel, Gaza, Lebanon, Sudan, Bosnia, Kosovo, Somalia and Afghanistan. Here he argues that embeds are here to stay. But they owe it to themselves and their viewers, readers and listeners never to let their guard down and always ask this basic question: are they lying?

The concept of embedded journalism has raised important questions about impartiality and the cynical "spinning" of information by the British and American governments and military machines.

Some will argue that reporters believe they are reporting the truth or at least as much as they can see of it while, in fact, they are being so restricted they are unable to see the bigger picture. But that opinion, I would argue, is flawed – by ignorance of the reality on the ground and by its assumption that reporters either cannot see beyond the narrow view they are being given or cannot rely on other sources of information to help them gain the bigger picture.

It also assumes that the military at every level is hell-bent on telling lies or at the very least manipulating the truth. Be under no doubt it does happen. Some recent events in Afghanistan have been horrendously dealt with. For instance, wedding parties have been wiped out by bombs allegedly attacking identified Taliban targets while on another occasion innocent people who were helping themselves to looted petrol were killed in air strikes – though a press release, issued immediately afterwards, identified them as Taliban.

But is that representative of the whole military machine in Afghanistan? I would argue from a personal level that it is not the case. Times have changed. The military certainly wish to show themselves in a good light but they are also aware that the best way to do that *is* to do a good job: to allow access to journalists, to stop carrying out deadly pointless raids on innocent targets, to engage with local people and, ultimately, to clean up their act.

The military has started putting some good people in key positions – and that is a sea change in just a few years. Before this the PR effort was hopeless. The worst officers were put in charge of overseeing the "enemy", the journalists. The net effect was distrust and disagreement. Now improvements are being made. But you will only know this if you have done it or seen it first hand. Many commentators have not.

Embedded with the Taliban in Kandahar: "independent, unbiased journalism"

I was first embedded in Afghanistan in 2001. It might come as a surprise as the accepted date for the start of embedding with military units is slightly before the start of the second Gulf War in 2003. But I was embedded with the Taliban in Kandahar. It did not last long; but we agreed ground rules for reporting. We could talk to their foot-soldiers and to local people; filming was obviously a bit of an issue as their leaders did not want their pictures taken, but I was an embed in everything but name.

I filed stories and even back then people said I was being controlled by the Taliban; that I was unable to report freely *because* I was living with just one of the protagonists in the conflict. But we also had reporters with the Northern Alliance and they were no less embedded. We *all* filed our stories and we broadcast as clear a picture as possible of what was going on from *both* sides.

The embed is still going on today. I spend a lot of time with the military while my colleague, Alex Crawford, spends a considerable amount of time with the Taliban and Afghanistan's assorted militant groups. We both file our stories and get equal weighting when it is aired from our headquarters. We both focus on the effects of the war on the non combatant members of society. If you are a Sky News viewer you will know this. It is called "independent, unbiased journalism" and we take it very seriously.

There are those who are, understandably, extremely uncomfortable with the development of embedded reporting. But it has undoubtedly transformed the work of war correspondents. At the start of the Iraq War in 2003, Sky Correspondent David Bowden commentated over live pictures throughout the American assault on the town of Umm Qasr, almost as if it were a football match.

His coverage was broadcast live around the world, complete with "pitch-side" interviews with the Marine commander on the latest developments. Outside the city of Najaf, my cameraman Garwen McLuckie and I jacked up our satellite and video phone near the top of a news bulletin and filmed the Americans as they attacked and cleared the last trenches of the Iraqi army – all live.

There are many instances of "embedded" reporting with non-traditional military. In Lebanon we broadcast Hezbollah rockets being fired from their positions in Tyre and, moments later, showed live pictures of the same rockets landing in Israel. Sky presenter Martin Stanford described the attack in detail noting that the rockets dropped short of a target. Soon afterwards, another volley of rockets hit their apparent target.

We know all sides use television but this was a dreadful first. Hezbollah recalibrated their weapons after watching our output on the television. This was an embedded war. Responsibility to viewers takes on an altogether greater significance in those circumstances.

When impartiality was our protective shield

Over the past two decades the conflicts covered by Sky News have been diverse and geographically separate. After 9/11 and the so-called war on terror, the conflicts in Afghanistan and Iraq added a new dimension to conflict reporting. Before this we covered wars from whichever side we could get to. Generally speaking we were not identified as the enemy; impartiality was our protective shield. It was and remains dangerous of course, but the protagonists are often quite relaxed about our presence. All sides take the opportunity to put their point across and we report it. In my experience their lies soon become manifestly obvious to all.

In Liberia, the West African nation founded by former American slaves, but by 2003 under the control of Charles Taylor, a charismatic lunatic with a hand in all the blood-diamond wars that wreaked havoc in Sierra Leone, Guinea and his own country, I remember walking through the lines of his fighters defending the bridges into the capital Monrovia.

The city was besieged by rebel forces. Our job was to meet the rebels by crossing one of the bridges. The boy soldiers were high on drugs and booze, their average age 16. They lived on dog meat and fought while high as kites. Many had murdered and raped with impunity. The fighting at the front was intense and chaotic, the boys charging too and fro firing from the hip and from over their heads across the bridge.

I stopped and filmed a piece to camera summarising the scene. It really wasn't very good and I stumbled through my words. The firing was deafening with the "soldiers" charging around me; I felt rounds whoosh between me and my cameraman Garwen. It was a one take situation. The point is: nobody was actually firing at us, just in our direction, which of course we had put ourselves in.

During an apparent gap in the battle we slowly drove across the bridge, Sky producer Ben Depear assuring us we would be OK. We were, he insisted, like aliens from outer space, all but invisible. We passed boys pushing dead bodies into the river and amid the carnage found the rebel commander – General Chaos. His No. 2 was Major Madness, I had already met Major Mayhem on the other side, I kid you not.

Exposing the plight of the victims of conflict – that's our job

We filmed the terrible destruction and found thousands of terrified women and children in the midst of the rubble. These people are why we crossed over the bridge and it is why we do this. They suffer the most, and exposing their plight for the world to see and hopefully for the international community to react – that's our job.

That principle of bearing witness is no less significant nor less achievable while working as an embed. But you *do* have to know what you are doing. I think that is a point missed by academic commentators. The reporting of war is and has always been a complicated high-wire act where all the contenders are trying to push you on to their side.

I have been covering wars since I was 22 years old; I am now 45. In the intervening years I have covered 16 wars. But remember this vital point: I have only been officially embedded on just *two* of them. Chechnya, Sierra Leone, Israel, Gaza, Lebanon, Sudan, Bosnia, Kosovo, Somalia and Afghanistan in 2001 are just some of the horrendous wars where millions have died and where journalists have fallen as well. But essentially we were civilians covering a conflict, trying to explain it and put it in context for our viewers.

Since the "war on terror" was launched in 2001, war reporting has developed a new dimension that puts a further strain on the job – when the reporter is as much the enemy as the attacking army. In essence, the embed exists to get reporters to the front line with military units working in Afghanistan and Iraq. It isn't that simple and there are a million hoops, created by the military and the Ministry of Defence and the seemingly thousands of Whitehall civil servants, to jump through on the way, but that is what we basically use the embed for.

Without question you are seen by the Taliban or by insurgent groups in Iraq as the enemy; without question you become close to the soldiers you are living with and without question you have to check continuously that you are not self censoring as a result. But not once have I been stopped from filming nor have commanders or press officers tried to overtly influence or change what I have said, even when they are furious.

The embed comes with a great responsibility because you have to evaluate what you see and what you are told all the time. You have to ignore the propaganda and pour cold water on the "message" of the day to file the truth as you see it.

Embedded with the Parachute Regiment's elite Pathfinder unit

In 2008 I was embedded with the Parachute Regiment's elite Pathfinder reconnaissance unit. A sort of Special Forces Platoon that works unassisted deep in enemy territory. They had never been filmed before. I joined them on a mission in Afghanistan's deadly Helmand province where daily the Pathfinders were in battle with Taliban fighters, and there were lots of them.

About two weeks into the mission problems with some of their brand new "Jackal" vehicles meant we had to tow a broken truck back to base passing within 100 meters of an aggressive Taliban town, through a narrow strip with sheer rock on one side and their dug-in positions on the other. As we approached a complex of houses and mud walled compounds the first salvo of rocket propelled grenades and mortars thumped into the sand around us. This was to be a sophisticated attack. The Pathfinder Jackal call signs ahead of the main body were not initially fired upon leaving them blind to their attack.

Initially the Taliban focused on the rear vehicles which stopped to engage. My vehicle and the tow vehicle pulled to a halt – AK 47 rounds crackled over my head as I tried to film. The column moved off but the Taliban had clearly identified the weakness of two trucks together. The firing intensified and Sky cameraman Jim Foster, an experienced former SAS soldier as well, gunned our vehicle and headed for the "dead ground" protection of a small hillock.

By now the trucks in front were taking fire – they rallied around our trucks as another RPG exploded into a bank 50 feet behind me. Capt Simon Chalmers raced from the disabled truck. He had a problem with his weapons and he was concerned about the tow rope. "Watch out for the mortars and RPG," he screamed above the shooting and the revving of trucks. "My gun's fucked," he added.

As we left the protection of the hill I could see movement near a wall about 200 meters to our left. I heard a bang and the sickening fizzle of an RPG fly above my head. The Talib fighter had the shot but blew it. I looked at Jim and he smiled. Our gunner had seen the firing position and began firing but the Talib had gone. Radio chatter told us that we were now the target – all RPGs to fire at us.

As we moved off three things happened that will stay with me forever. The tow rope broke, the guns on the second vehicle stopped working and we were now taking incoming rounds from our left and right – I was speechless with fear. Jim jumped from the driver's seat and helped replace the tow rope while one of the Pathfinders pushed me to the floor of the vehicle and removed the gun – all the time AK rounds pinged off the rocks and sand around us. Ready to go we pulled away – a dash to the open desert – Pathfinders urging us between them as they returned fire from final compounds of the village.

Surviving "Death Valley"

As the sun began to set I finally realised the three mile contact was over. We had survived "Death Valley". Jim grinned and gripped my knee. "That was a bit close," he said laughing.

Now this was pretty much a disaster that didn't quite happen. Nobody was covered in glory and that was how I filed it. That incident and other reports that I sent showed the resistance from the Taliban and the resistance to the British forces by disgruntled locals who just wanted to be left alone. This is not what the Ministry of Defence wanted to be shown as their mantra was that the Afghan people are embracing the West's efforts to rebuild the country.

A few years earlier with the Royal Marines, Sky cameramen Martin Smith and Richie Mockler stood with me as British soldiers trashed a compound where it was thought they had been fired upon. I filed that it was the ugly face of war and the pictures were graphic and upsetting. The Ministry of Defence were angry and contacted the commanding officer to find out what on earth was going on and why I had been allowed to show the footage. "I just said 'piss off," he told me. "It is war and it is like that, you should show what it is like."

There have been many similar incidents but nobody has, as far as I am aware, been able to stop Sky News reporting what it sees. The truth is, you can embed but you must remain honest and impartial. To do that you must draw on your knowledge and deal with the rules of the embed. This inevitably leads us to this question. Can you really be objective if the military is controlling your every move and actually looking after you?

The agreements we sign with the military – the operating rules in the so called *Green Book* – on the face of it look pretty draconian. Restrictions on reporting casualties until the families have been informed; restrictions on showing the latest equipment and techniques (trust me that can be daft. I met a dog handler who nearly passed out when he saw us filming his dog. I asked him why as everyone including the Taliban knew they used dogs. "No, no this is a top secret dog, it's a Belgian Alsatian, and they don't know we have one!") and an insistence on viewing our material before it goes to air sound awful, except when you look at the rules in a wider context.

Why operational security must not be compromised

For example the military can look at the material but cannot make you change it as long as it is factually correct and there is no danger of operational security ("OpSec") being compromised. "OpSec" is probably the single most important rule and at the root of the biggest arguments between the military and the media.

A simple example of "OpSec" being broken is to report where the soldiers are going to go next. Geraldo Rivera, from Fox News, reporting in Afghanistan is a prime example of "OpSec" being broken. In his full "Hunt Osama" kit of cowboy hat, boots and two handguns at his side, he decided to illustrate to his viewers the planned operation of his embedded unit by drawing a map in the sand and then stamping all over it as they would engage the enemy over the next 24 hours.

The map wasn't accurate but he did identify the mountain range they were crossing. Within two hours he was booted out of the embed and the mission was scrapped. The military take it very very seriously. "OpSec" can be a problem if the military attempt to deem something secret. For example, mine sweeping has been described as secret; the fact that they can listen to the Taliban talking using a system called I-CON, is a secret. But both these facts have been reported many times.

I have found that working with the military over a long period and explaining that something is neither a secret nor going to threaten their safety usually results in their relenting. Innocuous things can, however, threaten their safety. A *Telegraph* reporter in Musa Qala recently wrote a piece that started something like this: "...If the Taliban had buried their IED, their road side bomb, 18 inches nearer the surface we would all have died..." They will now!

Above everything one must also take into account the operational incompetence of the military and not always view it as a poor effort to misinform or worse, a conspiracy to stop the truth being told. The recent Operation Moshtarak offensive by the British and American troops to take areas around the towns of Nad-i-Ali and Marjah is a classic case of incompetence out of control. The military themselves broadcast that they were going to attack yet they tried to prevent the embedded journalists reporting the very details they had distributed!

Often journalists are disappointed when they are unable to get a helicopter for days on end and often resort to slanging matches with their military liaison officers. The fact is that half the time the military can't even get their own soldiers to the front let alone a bunch of civilians.

A question that must be addressed is the relationship that develops between the journalist and the soldier. Does it get too close? It is for certain an issue. During the Gulf War of 2003, I spent three months with the United States 101st airborne division. In 2008 I spent three months on and off with the Parachute Regiment's Pathfinder Reconnaissance unit. You get to know the soldiers, you get shot at together and you do become friends. But I made many friends in Liberia and Gaza and Lebanon and I witnessed their wars and their often atrocious behaviour – and I filed the story just the same – warts and all.

Indeed, the embed is here to stay and we should not be fearful of it. But those who get involved owe it to themselves and their viewers, readers and listeners never to let their guard down and always ask this basic question: are they lying?

Note on the author

Stuart Ramsay is Sky News Chief Correspondent and reports on all the major domestic and foreign stories. Ramsay has received many awards including the London Press Club's Broadcast Journalist of the Year 2009, the Royal Television Society's prestigious Foreign Affairs Award for work in Pakistan's Swat Valley, the Monte Carlo Golden Nymph in 2006 for his coverage of the Pakistan earthquake and, in 2005, Gold from New York Festival for his coverage of the Sudan crisis. In 2004, he was an Emmy Finalist for his coverage of the Liberia war and was nominated for a BAFTA this year. Ramsay has covered wars from Chechnya, through Africa and the Middle East to Afghanistan and Iraq. Since 2003, he has covered Iran and Afghanistan, both as an embedded and independent reporter.

Embedded – with the Taliban

Sky News' Alex Crawford tells how she manages to combine embedded reporting from both sides of the Afghan conflict. And while a general picture of the conflict may be possible based on time spent with either of the fighting forces, she says, much of the truth about how the war is going will be filled in by the civilians at the centre of it all

Parwan Province, Afghanistan, August 2009

They filed past me carrying a range of weapons: one held a land mine, another had an RPG on his shoulder, others had grenades strapped to their waists and AK-47s slung over their shoulders. There was a large home-made bomb which had been built into what looked like a milk urn. "They're easy to make. They take just a couple of hours," the young man tells me. "And we can kill hundreds."

Camp Alpha X-ray, Helmand Province, Afghanistan, June 2007

In the dark, they spotted the enemy. They were moving among the trees not even a hundred metres away. They looked to be taking up positions, planning an attack. Within twenty minutes, bombs had been unleashed on the targets. The bombs lit up the sky and the trees for several seconds as they exploded. A half a dozen men next to me opened fire with machine guns, rifles, mortar shells: everything they had. The movement in the trees had stopped. "They can't match us for firepower," the young man tells me earnestly. "We're killing them in their hundreds. We've got them on the run."

Sound familiar? Sound similar? The first men are the foot soldiers of the Hekmatyar group, one of the two most powerful militant fighting forces in Afghanistan; the second, soldiers from Her Majesty's Armed Forces. Which one is telling the truth? Which one is using me, the reporter, for propaganda purposes? And am I a willing participant by dint of being there and recording what they are doing?

I have sat in on numerous un-attributable briefings while senior policy-makers tell me with no hint of embarrassment or a flicker of conscience just how well the "war" is going. They tell me how much the Afghan people welcome them and how much progress the Western forces are making. And this has gone on for the best part of eight years.

And I have sat cross-legged on a floor and broken bread with militants who tell me the West never hears about the many attacks they launch against US and British forces; that we Western reporters don't tell the truth; that the militants are having numerous battlefield successes, downing Western helicopters and killing many soldiers. They tell me as long as the foreign forces are in Afghanistan, they will never be accepted and there will continue to be fighting and deaths. And that's gone on for pretty much most of the eight years too.

Of course, those on both sides of a conflict want and in many cases *need* to get their message out and, of course, reporters and camera crews are the channels used to do just this. But this does not mean the journalist is any less questioning or that experience and knowledge fall by the wayside.

Importance of reporting from both sides

I am of the firm belief you cannot possibly get a rounded view of any conflict if you only ever get reports from one side. But the very nature of war means it is fantastically difficult, if not impossible, for a single journalist to cover both sides and certainly not possible at the same time. Sky News attempts to cover all the bases by sending multiple reporters to the war zone. Since the Afghan invasion in 2001, my colleague and Sky's chief correspondent Stuart Ramsay has been on multiple military embeds while I have spent considerably more time with the "other side" – the militants.

But the two of us have also done both sides and swapped roles. It is not just important for the viewer to see both sides of the war. It is essential the journalist too sees the conflict from both ends. There may be anecdotal evidence of past reporting of wars being compromised by the actual bias of the journalists involved (the Spanish civil war is a case in point) but in the modern, multi-media age where from our own experience even in the most remote areas we have good communications, it is impossible to imagine you could actually get away with it – or pervert the truth and ignore the facts – unless, of course, you were utterly determined to do so.

The mood, tempo, morale of any conflict is constantly changing – and it is important to get an accurate and informed view of how the conflict is going from both sides at roughly the same period of time to get any handle on how it is going for both sides. So when I entered Basra three weeks after the troops did during the invasion of Iraq in late March 2003, morale amongst the British there appeared high. They had every reason to be optimistic at this point. Their arrival in Iraq had gone fairly well, they had achieved it apparently with little resistance of any note and they were well on the way to achieving their objectives.

My cameraman Martin Smith and I were travelling as "independents" and after staying with the troops at the Presidential Palace and filing a number of reports about the situation in Basra, we then moved up to Baghdad. There, just a few weeks after the American troops had triumphantly swept through the capital declaring victory and drawing no defensive attacks at all it seemed, there was a very different picture.

The Americans may have moved into the city with ease but already the cracks were beginning to show. As we drove round the city there were several fires in buildings which had been started by looters. We spotted some teenage Iraqi boys being marched down an alleyway by three American soldiers. One of them looked no more than ten. The soldiers were handling them rather roughly and Martin bounded out of our vehicle, camera in hand to capture the scene. I was a few minutes behind him (not as quick or as agile as Smithie) and was still on the other side of the street when the soldiers began firing – at Martin.

Policing the peace was not on the agenda
There was a fair amount of shouting and more firing but what seemed to be the gist of it was this: the soldiers had taken great exception to Martin filming them bundling three young men, hands bound behind, them into the back of a truck.

The soldiers looked extremely hot, dressed in full combat gear in mid-April and they were tired: by this stage they believed or hoped the war was all but over. Policing the peace had not been on the agenda and it was apparent they did not much care for it.

We went on to report about a young Iraqi boy who had been kidnapped by a criminal gang which was demanding a ransom from his parents. They spoke over and over again about how rare this was in Iraq, how crime itself had always been so low under Saddam Hussein, how kidnapping was such an unknown phenomenon they had no idea what to do or how to handle it. They were already beginning to articulate the unwelcome changes in their country with the fall of a dictator. Sky News balanced its coverage of the successful military invasion with these reports. Any euphoria the politicians might have felt about how well the military campaign was going must have surely begun to dissipate. Or it should have.

Whenever I meet any militants, the conversation always turns to whether I am a spy either for Britain or more often America. They want to know what I am going to do with my footage, am I garnering their secrets about bomb-making, about weapons stores, about camps, simply to pass on to the intelligence agencies in my own country. I spend a large part of any approach to them reassuring them this is *not* the case, that much the same way the British and American military do not expect you to give away locations or show footage which would give the people they are fighting an unfair advantage, that I will adhere to certain rules of conduct with the militants too. So, describing or identifying locations are a no-no. Generalised filming which gives a loose impression of how they put together a roadside bomb is acceptable but a detailed examination of materials and construction is not. Apart from giving away "secrets", the broadcaster has a responsibility not to unwittingly educate a whole host of others in the art of bomb-building.

Gaining access to the Hekmatyar group

In late August 2009, I was given extraordinary access to the Gulbaddin Hekmatyar group. I travelled to a number of different fighting cells in four different provinces of Afghanistan – Parwan, Logar, Kabul and Wardak. Not only did this give me an insight into how confident they were about moving around the country, I was also able to assess how well trained or armed they were, how well developed their battle plans were/are, how informed their leaders were, how sophisticated their outfit is. During this period I was able to also talk to and interview the main presidential contender, Abdullah Abdullah, British government officials and the Afghan President Hamid Karzai (albeit at a news conference) – and during every encounter with officialdom they poo-pooed the strength of the Hekmatyar group.

There was the diplomatic equivalent of scoffing at whether this former Afghan Prime Minister-turned-renegade had the numbers, the weaponry, the funding or the back-up. Their attitude seemed at odds with the situation I was finding on the ground. Compared to the Taliban groups I had encountered, this outfit was exceedingly well funded. Their weapons appeared new, well looked after and varied and they had plenty of them. The weaponry was a mixture of Russian and Chinese-made as well as equipment and weapons they had snatched from the Afghan army and police during attacks. At one meeting I had, each of the militants had a satellite phone plus walkie-talkies to communicate with each other as well as mobile phones. The arrangements for meeting them were complex and multi-layered involving a number of messengers and different levels of "support staff" – some who clearly knew more than others.

In Wardak province, I found they were extremely comfortable about meeting me outside in the open countryside – and were so confident they would not be discovered that they even fired a couple of shots while showing me their guns. An American aircraft flew over us as we all sat in a gully of a mountain and they barely registered it – glancing upwards but seeing it as no danger or threat. My point is without actively spending time with the "other side", there can be no Big Picture – but the "other side" is pretty much an embed too – just less official but all the usual, standard checks apply.

I had gone to meet the militant group in a vehicle, dressed in a burqa with a trusted driver and an Afghan friend who was acting as my interpreter. We were just given an area to head towards which we did. Once we arrived we were told to ring our "contact". He was clearly watching us via binoculars although we could not see where he was. He directed us by phone off the main road and down a rough track leading through a small community of farmhouses. Here we were met by an older man who was wearing traditional shalwar kameez and was on a motorbike. He beckoned through the car window for us to hand over all our telephones and communication equipment.

We then followed him on his bike until the vehicle could go no further. We continued on foot and made our way up a mountain path until we turned a corner and saw our first Hekmatyar "soldier". He was wearing a green shalwar kameez and had a belt with grenade pockets and a chain of bullets on him and held an A47. He nodded to the farmer who had taken us this far and he returned down the hill. We were searched and then allowed to continue, following our new chaperone deeper into the mountain countryside. After about half an hour of walking, he motioned to us to stop and wait.

"You are a brave woman. What do you want from us"

Four men on the neighbouring hill came over the brow and fanned out, taking up positions behind rocks. I saw one of them kneel down and peer through binoculars looking down at the route we had just taken. He was checking to see whether we had been followed. These men were not taking any chances. Once they were satisfied I had not drawn unwanted attention nor, indeed, led anyone to them, we were allowed to carry on trekking up the mountain. When I finally reached the meeting place (which was a gully with a small stream and surrounding rockfaces on three sides) they were there, waiting for me. A group of fighting men, all carrying weapons and wearing a mixture of black balaclavas or scarves wrapped round their faces. High up on the surrounding rocks several men were taking up positions as look-outs. One of them was filming me as I filmed them. The commander's first words to me were: "You are a brave woman. What do you want from us?"

When I had completed my filming and all my interviews, the commander insisted on sending me back down the mountainside with an escort of four of his men "for my safety". Once back in our vehicle, where I found my confiscated telephones, he rang to check I had made it OK.

Whether you've arrived at a British military base in Helmand after filling out countless MoD application forms or whether you find yourself on a mountainside in Wardak province with militants, you are "embedding" with a fighting force with a particular point of view – and this should and *is* reflected in our coverage/reporting. Each side will naturally attempt to put the best spin on their endeavours and are unlikely to enjoy spelling out their mistakes or short-comings. But more often than not, they will not be able to shield questioning reporters entirely from them.

But by being with them, living alongside them, talking to them, the reporter will be able to get an insight into how they're doing, how well equipped they are, how they feel the conflict is going. Is a reporter more likely to morph into a British soldier if embedded with them than transform into an Afghan militant if time is spent with the rebels? Embeds have always been in existence in various forms although perhaps not officially acknowledged. And reporters since time began, have had to sift the wheat from the chaff, the truth from the lies.

The key difference between the two types of embeds is that the military embed is driven by politics and policy from 10 Downing Street – and the fighters of militant groups are there through ideology and fanaticism. They don't need diktats from Whitehall to know what they are fighting for or the direction they are going – and they are much more likely to go off message as a result.

A general picture may be possible based on time spent with either of the fighting forces, but much of the truth and an accurate perception of how the war is going will be filled in by the civilians at the centre of it all.

Reporters in the business of piecing together the patchwork
I have met poppy farmers and filmed drug traffickers operating in the Tora Bora mountains. My crew and I have trekked into northern Afghanistan and reached remote villages and communities in Badakshan where the maternal mortality rate

is the second highest in the world. I have interviewed families who have sold their children to raise money to eat and sat weeping while a young girl told me how she had been sold at 10 and had set herself alight to escape her cruel "husband". Reporting is a patchwork and we as journalists are in the business of piecing together the patchwork and coming up with a quilt of sorts.

I have seen the gradual change in public opinion in Afghanistan since the toppling of the Taliban in 2001 to the present day. Hindsight is a fantastic weapon but more than two years ago my crew and I detected a strong distrust growing of the British and American troops in Afghanistan. We were embedded in Helmand and travelled from Camp Bastion then on to Lashkar Gar before travelling to FOB Sandford and then to Camp Alpha X-ray which took us to within fewer than a hundred metres of the Taliban attackers.

The idea was to show us not only how much progress the British military was making but also how they were involved in construction, re-building and making strides in reaching out to the Afghan population.

We had only just begun the day's filming at a small community near Camp Alpha X-ray in Helmand when an elderly farmer, clearly unhappy, beckoned the British soldiers and us to come around the back of his house. We followed both the farmer and the British soldier and as we turned the corner we saw the back of his house had been flattened. It was rubble. You didn't need to speak Pashto to work out the farmer was furious and distraught to boot. "He says it was your bomb which did this," the interpreter told the hapless soldier who was acutely aware his mission to show the Sky crew just how welcomed his men were in this community, was now falling apart – quite spectacularly.

Now if we had based our whole report on this one incident that may well have given the impression the British troops were not making any progress at all whereas the situation to us appeared to be mixed – and that is how I wrote my report. No-one stopped me, nor was there any attempt to curtail my reporting. But those are the rules, they actually can't. Like wars, the embeds change too. When the public mood is changing, and that change is negative, then the military hierarchy get edgy, jumpy and defensive.

The militants get edgy, too, when things go wrong. Sound familiar? My reports aim to reflect the ground reality and not just the "message" either side wants to portray. It is a basic journalists' rule. Why should it be any different if you are embedded?

Note on the author

Alex Crawford is Asia correspondent for Sky News and has been based in New Delhi, India, for almost five years. She is about to move to Dubai where she will take up the post of Special Correspondent in the autumn 2010. She is the current holder of the Royal Television Society's Journalist of the Year, an award she also won two years ago. This year she was nominated for a BAFTA for her coverage in Pakistan and has been recognised at the Foreign Press Association awards for the past three years running for her work in India, Afghanistan and Pakistan. She won a Golden Nymph at the Monte Carlo Film Festival for her coverage of the Mumbai terror attacks in 2008. She has been also been recognised at the Bayeaux War Correspondents awards for the past two years. She has covered wars, conflicts and hostile environments in Iraq, Afghanistan, India, Pakistan and Sri Lanka, Thailand and Burma as well as Africa and Europe including Northern Ireland. She has been embedded with the British, American, Sri Lankan and Pakistani militaries but usually operates in a small team independently.

The "brittle" compact between the military and the media

Vaughan Smith argues that news management by the military is a risky business. Though it might maintain a certain level of support for the war that backing becomes more brittle for the deception

So-called "embedding", the term for the practice by which journalists have been allowed to accompany allied troops in the Iraq and Afghan wars, is not just a way for the military to manage information but is an unspoken compact with the media that helps sustain the conflicts themselves.

It is easy to find British journalists like myself who criticise the practice of embedding but jump at every opportunity to accompany British troops at war. Space with the British army is at a premium and so if you can get there you won't face too much competition. Compared with other foreign trips it is relatively easy to acquire strong stories supported by exceptional pictures. One can win awards.

Embedding costs very little money. The military provide food and tents. The press can often use military communications and the British army will fly you out and back for free. As an independent video journalist I should make a profit on an embed. The army will also lend you a flak jacket and helmet. Even better, the soldiers will protect you from danger and deliver excellent first aid if they don't. The risks are less than they appear. Easy pickings really.

It's not just me being careful with the pennies. News budgets are at an all time low and foreign news acquisition is increasingly priced out of reach. Reporting foreign stories is much more expensive than covering domestic ones. As news organisations have tried to realise their duty of care the cost of covering foreign conflicts has further increased. Reducing risk is very expensive, often requiring extra insurance, equipment and the retention of bodyguards or other safety personnel.

Most now rely on cheaper wholesale agency material and whatever they can source from locals or other non-media sources. This includes material filmed or reported by army combat camera teams and blogs by military press officers. There are too few sources of information and even fewer reliable ones. But agency material, being shared with competitors, doesn't promote the news brand nearly as well as the correspondent or television network reporter, so the opportunity for a newspaper or broadcaster to get people out on an action-packed foreign story on the cheap can be irresistible.

Army management of news output

While it is true that journalists have been accompanying armies and navies in wars for at least 150 years, in the past the military has been better at denying access rather than using the press to get their message out. Allied forces are now very sophisticated in managing news output. The effort is well funded and employs many ex-journalists. Lots of reporters have no difficulty crossing over from journalism to PR, leaving a trade that seems to lose its calling as quickly as it loses its funding.

The sign on top of the British media office tent in Camp Bastion in Helmand, Afghanistan, says "Media Operations'. As soon as you walk through the door as a journalist you understand that you are a sort of target, albeit treated much more gently than the Taliban. It is not about public accountability. News management has become an integrated part of the war effort, aiming to maintain public support for the conflict nationally, while winning the information war abroad.

Embedded journalists are normally accompanied by press officers during their visits. Servicemen or women trained in press management. The stakes are high for the press officer as getting it wrong can ruin their military career. With the British army, both sides are guided by a publication called the *Green Book* that lays out the rules of the press embed. It was put together by the Ministry of Defense, but in consultation with media organisations.

It delivers editorial independence for embedded journalists subject to the needs of operational security. It also includes the reasonable provision in my view that the names of casualties should not be revealed until their next of kin have been informed. The conditions set out in the *Green Book* are progressive when compared with the restrictions that the press experienced; say in Northern Ireland in the 1970s and 1980s or the Gulf War of 1991.

When soldiers and journalists bond

Press officers normally work hard to help journalists get stories on their embeds, organising transport and interviews. It would be hard for most of the media to find their way around these battlefields without them and a good working relationship normally develops. Journalists often develop strong relationships with their subjects. Those bonds can be strongest during a tough assignment when discomfort is shared and embedding often puts reporters with frontline troops under stress.

Certainly the military benefit from friendlier reporting for having journalists embedded into units where they have a chance to get to know soldiers and share their experiences. But the primary control exerted by the military is through determining who actually gets embedded and unfavourable reporting is not often rewarded with further opportunity.

The military cannot reasonably be expected to take all the journalists that might want to accompany them. Thousands of journalists descended on Kosovo in 1999 and Afghanistan in 2001. The numbers are far too great. There have been instances when more journalists have applied to go to outposts in Afghanistan than there are soldiers stationed there. But numbers are kept very low, particularly when the military are feeling sensitive about what is happening. Whole operations can go unreported by independent journalists on the ground.

During the recent Operation Moshtarak, in Helmand in February 2010, there were only about 10 members of the press with the whole British force in Afghanistan. The Ministry of Defence will often favour popular commentators, like Ross Kemp, over critical journalists or try to develop a relationship with tabloid newspapers when it thinks that favourable coverage can be widely achieved.

Valuable pool places to regional newspapers

Valuable places are given to regional newspaper reporters who are less likely to be critical, often there to do soft stories on a military unit local to the paper. Even regional newspapers can afford to send correspondents on embeds. Journalists are not allowed to bring their own vehicles. Being compelled to rely on the military for logistics makes it impossible to access the local population independently and if the military don't want you somewhere you are unlikely to get there.

Unfortunately, even if American and European journalists could have all the access they wanted to the military, these days they would deliver less than we need from them. The news industry does not look like it did in the 1960s during the Vietnam war. Most war reporters these days don't really know much about war, in the way that say, sports journalists know about sport. War reporters are rarely students of conflict nor are they normally "defence" correspondents who might need to develop a broader knowledge of military affairs.

Over the last two decades the news industry, particularly television news, has developed a culture that rewards the more self-obsessed operators, pushing them to lead their reporting from a personal perspective to make it more accessible to the audience. Reporting becomes as much about promoting the correspondent, the brand representative, as telling the story. As the industry gets starved of funds the reports get weaker and the branding stronger.

The military and their political masters believe that images of dead or wounded allied soldiers, particularly, have the potential to sap public support for the war at home. The lesson from the conflict in Somalia in 1993, when pictures of dead US soldiers being paraded around Mogadishu were shown around the world, was that such images also risk delivering a propaganda victory to the insurgents abroad.

Casualties – the most sensitive issue

This makes allied casualties the most sensitive issue after operational security to the military. With the British army you are prevented from filming dead soldiers and will only be allowed to film or broadcast pictures of wounded soldiers if you have their permission. There are obvious practical difficulties getting this sort of permission from soldiers who suddenly find themselves in agony and struggling to stay alive. Most soldiers say no if they are fit enough to address the question, which is not easy to ask in the circumstances. Doing so invites a negative answer, which of course is why the requirement is there in the first place.

In theory a cameraman or photographer is allowed to film first and ask questions later. But attempting it will seriously raise the pulse of your military minder and soldiers you hadn't noticed before suddenly become remarkably poor at keeping out of the way of your shot. As a consequence, embeds rarely show the suffering of war but instead offer up a dramatic but sanitised version of it. One that most journalists sex-up to present themselves as well as possible and in doing so normally treat the domestic audience to comforting messages of heroism and military strength.

Limiting the public's real understanding of the cost in human suffering of the war actually betrays those unfortunate young men who become its casualties. Many are teenagers and some lose multiple limbs. A public that is poorly informed is unlikely to show these men the compassion and respect that they deserve. For all the proximity of the journalists and the cameras the reporting has been contained, serving to distance the audience from the reality of war and any great feeling of ownership of it. The wars merge into the background and go on and on.

The current Afghan war has lasted for longer than the US military engagement in Vietnam in the 1960s and appears to a significant number of clued-up observers to have no greater prospect of success. But the US and the British public remain firm. British reporting is heavily informed by the tragedy of dead servicemen coming through Wootton Bassett. But it is not an image the soldiers who come home unscathed identify with. They are mystified when those they meet feel sorry for them. They do not see themselves as victims in the way that the press portrays them. They want public empathy; they get – to their dismay – public sympathy.

Presenting war to fit the grand, Hollywood-esque narrative

Not only does this reporting fail to do real justice to those it professes to honour. It is easier to ignore a war if it is soldiered by hero-victims. But the soldiers are us. They are our professional killers who sometimes enjoy it. But we want more distance from it than that. So we manufacture something else that doesn't seem to require us to take any responsibility. An eroded and underfunded news industry compresses, simplifies and pasteurises, presenting war to conveniently fit into a grand narrative that owes more to Hollywood than the real experience.

Perhaps all parties – politicians and the military, the media, campaigners for forces support groups like Help for Heroes and even the public themselves – have an interest in sustaining this comforting way of seeing it. But news management is a risky business. Though it might maintain a level of support for the war that support becomes more brittle for the deception.

Every now and then a particularly disturbing story breaks through that becomes more shocking for being unexpected and is amplified for running contrary to the narrative the nation is being fed. Faith in our armed forces is imperiled. On the whole generals, admirals and air marshals have enjoyed considerable public respect in Britain since the 1930s. There are signs that this is eroding.

News management, or spin, creates cumulative damage to us all by undermining our trust in the institutions that engage in it and subverting the quality of our conduct more widely in society. We are paying for these wars with more than blood and treasure.

Note on the author

Vaughan Smith founded the Frontline Club in London in 2003 as an institution to champion independent journalism. He is video-journalist, businessman and restaurateur. During the 1990s, he ran Frontline Television News, an agency set up to represent the interests of young journalists who wanted to push the envelope of their profession. The history of the agency has been detailed in, *Frontline: The True Story of the British Mavericks who Changed the Face of War Reporting*, by David Loyn, of the BBC. Smith filmed the only uncontrolled footage of the Gulf War in 1991 after he bluffed his way into an active-duty unit while disguised as a British army officer.

Why embedded reporting is a necessary evil

David Hayward draws on the first-hand experiences of frontline journalists to argue that coverage of the Afghan conflict needs to incorporate the views of the Taliban and the views of the local people and politicians – as well as the perspectives of the US-led forces

> All war reporting is embedded, you can't just stand in the middle.
> It would be an elaborate suicide note.
> *Alex Thomson, Chief Correspondent,*
> *Channel Four News*

> It's always been best to cover a war from one side or the other, rather than being
> stuck in the middle of no man's land trying to jot down a few notes, while the
> bullets hail down from both sides ... the pen may be mightier than the sword,
> but it doesn't look too clever
> against a rocket-propelled grenade.
> *Daniel Bennett, blogger and Phd student, researching*
> *the impact of new media on BBC war reporting*

The two quotations above were taken from the conference at Coventry University titled "Afghanistan: are we embedding the truth?" on 18 March 2010. This chapter compares the views of some of those (including frontline journalists) who took part in the event.

All stressed that wars were dangerous and thus the first rule of war reporting was not to get killed. It's a rule that has, in reality, always been the case, from *The Times'* William Howard Russell during the Crimean War (1854-1856), where he is widely recognised as the first Western war correspondent, coining phrases such as this at the about the siege of Sevastopol: "[The Russians] dash on towards that thin red streak topped with a line of steel…"

Brave war reporting continued with young Winston Churchill, a correspondent for the *Morning Post*, during the second Boer War (1899-1902); Frank Gillard and Richard Dimbleby on the beaches of Normandy, accompanying the allied forces as they landed on D-Day (6 June 1945); Richard Dimbleby again, when he arrived in April 1945 at the gates of Belsen, with the British troops who liberated the Nazi concentration camp; Brian Hanrahan, reporting on the British Harriers for the BBC during the Falklands/Malvinas War of 1982: "I'm not allowed to say how many planes joined the raid, but I counted them all out and I counted them all back" and Max Hastings marching into Port Stanley at the end of that conflict.

Even Martin Bell's powerful description of the slaughter of a Muslim family at their home in the Bosnian village of Ahmici in April 1993, was done while on patrol with UNPROFOR troops, under the command of Col. Bob Stewart:

> They came upon a house in the centre of the village where a family of seven had died. Two in the stairway, another five in the cellar…it's hard to look at some of the pictures, harder to tell the story of Ahmici without them…what happened here can frankly not be shown in any detail, but the room is full of the charred remains of bodies and they died in the greatest of agony. It's hard to imagine in our continent and in our time, what kind of people could do this.

Embedding is nothing new, a point all the journalists highlighted at the conference in a number of different and forceful ways. So what is the point of the question in the conference's title? The accusation seems to be that by embedding with one side or the other, journalists are unable to give a fair, clear and impartial view of what is happening in the war. By embedding with a unit of the Grenadier Guards in Lashkar Gah, a reporter is cheerleading, reporting purely what the military and the Ministry of Defence wants them to, they become a voice-piece of the government.

On the other hand, the argument for embedding puts the reporter at the heart in the frontline, covering the story of, for instance, Operation Moshtarak (launched by the US-led forces in Afghanistan in February 2010), as it happens, seeing it unfold with their own eyes, being at the centre of the story. The reporter has immediate access to the action and a first-hand experience of what the soldiers are going through, an important element of the coverage of any war.

But embedding on either side is and can only be a small part of the coverage of a war and the issues surrounding it. It may be the most dramatic, the best images, the "bang bang", as many contributors put it during the debate, but it is only one element of the coverage by any media organisation.

Jonathan Marcus: embedding just part of the wider picture

Jonathan Marcus. the BBC World Service's diplomatic correspondent and a former defence correspondent, has never been officially embedded on the frontline, but he has covered extensively the conflicts in Bosnia and Kosovo, where, to all intents and purpose, he was embedded. His job was, essentially, to set the context for a conflict. But as he reported for the World Service, as an international broadcaster for an international audience, his role was quite different from that of some of the other reporters for the UK media. He could not, and nor could the World Service, report as though the British Army were "our boys" – a subtle, but significant difference. He began:

> In many ways it's a spurious and pointless question, of course, to ask whether we are embedding a truth. It is the truth of what the people there are seeing. You see the image, you see the films and reports of the correspondents and journalists concerned....I think the problem with it all is that it's a very small part of the truth, the truth is very complex, it's about high politics, it's about what how things affect people on the ground in individual villages. Whatever you are seeing is a particularly small section of the truth, as presented by the journalists embedded with the military.

Jonathan Marcus spent much of the Second Gulf War of 2003 reporting from Centcom, or Central Command, in Qatar, experiences on which he drew to illustrate this point:

If you knew and you very quickly got to know, where individual journalists were and you put this together, you very quickly got quite a good understanding of how the war was unfolding…This was very much the role of the specialist defence correspondent. It was their job to make sense of what was happening on the ground. You had all of the reporters in field, on the frontline, reporting from embedded positions. It was then up to you to give the context and the understanding, to pull everything together.

Marcus was doing just that in Qatar: getting the information, collating and editing it, to give the big picture and produce a narrative of how the war was unfolding. On the supposed glamour and "bang bang" of war reporting, he commented:

While it's exciting, in many ways it's also the least important part of what's actually happening in the countries, riven by the sorts of conflict which we are reporting on. So embedding is important, but only in the sense that it is part of the wider picture. It's a way of safely telling one side of the story, but you need as many vantage points as possible.

Marcus went on to suggest that wars had changed dramatically over recent years: they were taking place within societies in which journalists were seen as part of the enemy. There simply was not the opportunity for journalists to roam freely around Afghanistan or Iraq; it just was not safe enough. So embedding was vital to give the full context. He also pointed out the changing relationship between government and the media:

The government is far more adept at massaging the message, making it so important to recognise that context is crucial, time devoted is crucial and being honest about what you don't know is as important as saying what you do know…We should be far more honest, devote far more time and spend more effort seeing ordinary people on the ground. We should know what the armed forces are doing, but be honest that it isn't all-important, it's only a partial side of the truth.

So the initial conclusions from the reporters are clear: use embedding, but use it in context. Of course, journalists embed the truth if they only cover the war from a military compound in Helmand.

Shoaib Sharifi: role of local Afghan journalists needs to be acknowledged more

Shoaib Sharifi is an Afghan producer who works with the BBC and other British media. He was kidnapped and held for eight days by bandits in the Kunar province while on assignment for the *Guardian*. He was freed along with another Afghan journalist and an Iraqi photographer when they were able to convince their captors they were not US spies. He became one of the few Afghan journalists to survive being taken hostage; many others have been shot or beheaded. His experiences bring into clear focus the dangers of reporting in Afghanistan, both for local and international journalists.

Firstly, he was critical of embed-heavy reporting, in particular, the coverage of the Moshtarak offensive. Too much attention was being given to the military offensive and not enough to the civilians and views of the insurgents and Taliban forces. He accepted that it was costly and often dangerous, but it was absolutely essential to cover the war in a fair and balanced way.

> We had ten days' notice of the current Moshtarak offensive. The BBC should have spoken to the Taliban then and said, on day one, two and three we'll come live to you, with an interpreter. The military are saying it's a success, what do you say?

The second is the relationship between the Western media and the Afghan journalists. He said it was wrong to refer to local journalists as "fixers" – a term he regarded as an insult. "It's the local journalists who are often taking the biggest risks, but getting the least reward."

Splitting the media in Kabul into three groups; the Afghan media, Afghans working for the West and Western correspondents, was divisive. Treating everyone the same would make a huge difference to the coverage of the

Afghanistan war. He would like a far greater appreciation of his colleagues in Afghanistan, who were so often the people on the frontline.

Daniel Bennett: new media taking over the role of the mainstream

Daniel Bennett, a blogger Phd student, researching the impact of new media on the BBC's coverage of war, has a slightly different point of view. Images were increasingly being provided by the military and the NGOs working in the region. He questioned whether the time would come when wars would be covered largely through these sources, along with local camera teams and local journalists. The role of the mainstream media and embedded journalists would then be marginalised because the information would be put online by the new media, bypassing the traditional routes of journalism. He commented:

> We do have access to far more voices if we are willing to look further afield than the traditional media. Just on Afghanistan why not check out things like Captain Cat's blog, Nasim Fekrat and the Afghan Women's writing project…I think a possible challenge for independent embedded journalism is the fact that militaries have started doing this sort of journalism themselves. The soldier is committing acts of journalism....If frontline blogs combat camera teams and uploads to YouTube become the norm, the military might well wonder why they need these embedded journalists to get their message across, especially if the military does believe that "our people" are the best advocates.

At the moment, media organisations still had huge sway, in terms of viewers, listeners and readers but "the times were a'changing".

Conclusions

All of the reporters, journalists and correspondents here are clear about the issues surrounding embedding. In a utopian world the reporter would be free to cover a war from all angles, to give an independent, balanced unbiased view, to have access to all sides and reflect what is truly going on. But we live in a world where journalists are kidnapped and beheaded and so becoming embedded has become a necessary evil. It needs to be seen in context (as the reporters quoted here stress): embedded reporting is only part of the coverage of the war. To cover Afghanistan, reporters also need to be speaking to the Taliban, civilians and the politicians.

But the message from all is clear: if you rely on reporters to tell a fair, balanced and impartial report when not embedded, why suddenly do you think it's impossible to trust them when they are?

Note on the author

David Hayward is the head of the journalism programme for the BBC College of Journalism. It is a series of events, masterclasses, debates, discussions and conferences on journalism issues. He has worked for the BBC for 15 years. He began his career as a reporter, producer and presenter at BBC Radio Leicester before moving to Eastern Europe in the 1990s to work with the World Service Trust; in Sarajevo, Bucharest and Tirana. He returned to the UK as a reporter at BBC East Midlands Today, in Nottingham, before moving to the BBC Radio Newsroom in London. He then took up a role producing *Midlands Today* in Birmingham and worked on the BBC Local TV pilot and as TV Editor in Oxford before joining the College of Journalism. He lives in Leicestershire with his wife, Jo, and two boys, Max and Alexander.

Challenges facing media coverage: an Afghan perspective

Hanan Habibzai, a freelance Afghan journalist, highlights the complexities of the conflict which, he says, the Western media largely fail to understand

Journalists who cover Afghan issues face the anger of many: warlords, drug lords, war criminals, corrupt officials, insurgents and killers – the people who hate truth tellers. Afghanistan is a dangerous country (particularly for journalists who want to tell the truth) quite simply because the people who are in the business of killing and the drug traders are the real power in the land.

The Afghan government has promoted the work of criminals by handing over the power to those who killed and tortured civilians. Everyone sees innocents being targeted but the voices of the victims are rarely heard. That's why telling the truth is a big challenge for media workers. Some British journalists working in Afghanistan understand the Afghan psychology very well but in the military and political fields the international allies of Afghanistan have made many mistakes. When international troops mistakenly or intentionally kill Afghan civilians, that creates anger against foreign nationals and puts the security of foreign journalists at risk.

Local and international media: Facing both ways

Afghanistan has a complicated social and political system. People who consider themselves as democrats are acting as traditional Muslims too. Afghan tribal society has been dominated in the past three decades by the local warlords and criminals. The Afghan community suspect that foreign broadcasters are going to follow only Nato's activities and thus truth will become a casualty of war.

International media in Afghanistan such as the BBC sometimes reveal the truth which lies hidden behind closed doors – and which local journalists are unable to uncover. The Afghan authorities think foreign journalists have the strong support of the international security assistance force and hence they offer them excellent access. However, local journalists do not enjoy such access: there is no security assurance for them to cover big issues such as corruption.

On that issue, local journalists can only report from press conferences. But foreign journalists can investigate it deeper because they enjoy the support of their organisation and the Western countries' military and political presence. Afghan officials note where the journalist is from. If he/she is from America then they cancel their programmes to meet them quickly. A leading politician in Kabul once told me that if the Afghans ignored the requests of an American journalist then the US military in Afghanistan would show their displeasure...

That's why the international media in Afghanistan are playing a double role in the war-torn country. They cover the country's current situation and promote peace through highlighting the facts and giving ideas to the policy makers. Even Afghans watch, listen to and read the international media to find out the about the news of their own country (such as about the fate of Ahmad Wali, brother of President Karzai; about the warlords and corruption; about the killings of civilians by the Taliban and Nato, the massacres in northern Afghanistan). They search for reports of their own everyday experiences – of suffering and insecurity – through the foreign media. But there are many things which are missed by foreign journalists.

Afghanistan is a country of villages and mountains. Most of the people are based in remote areas where they suffering and experiencing the oppression of corrupt and cruel officials who still force local people to give them illegal taxes and leave them without any salary. Where in the Western media are the pictures of daily life in the villages and valleys of Afghanistan? Foreign journalists should travel more to remote villages where people are dominated by local warlords, the Taliban or criminals. In these places, the local government has no control. Admittedly, it is not easy for foreign journalists to travel outside Kabul. But as a result, the current security situation makes them unable to look at the story through Afghan eyes.

In 2001, Afghan people expected advances in the fields of human rights and democracy but when people saw that the politicians ousted by the Taliban were simply rehabilitated after the invasion they were very disappointed. Since then, the international community has clearly failed to install a viable, credible alternative to the Taliban regime. For example, after the defeat of the Taliban by the US-led coalition forces in late 2001, some of the Taliban members who survived entered into a dialogue with new Afghan government led by Hamid Karzai. Why did they later become Taliban once again? There is a clear reason. They had to meet the politicians who were in the power during the 1990s.

On the frontline: death always present

Local journalists are the main victims of the conflict. They don't have life insurance and so they do not dare to go on dangerous assignments. If they are brave and say the truth they immediately face death threats. The BBC's Abdul Samad Rohani was even killed in the heart of Helmand where Karzai's government was supposedly in control, on 8 June 2008. Famously, Rohani once said: "I wish I could see waves of happiness instead of disappointment on the lips and eyes of Helmand people." But for Rohani this hope was not fulfilled and like many hundreds of thousands of Afghans, he became a victim of war in Afghanistan. After the reports of his murder were published, the Afghanistan Independent Journalists' Association condemned the murder as politically motivated and blamed Afghan security officials for the incident.

A British journalist Rupert Hamer, defence correspondent of the *Sunday Mirror*, died when the armoured vehicle in which he was travelling was hit by a roadside bomb in Helmand province in the south of the country in early January 2010. Hamer was the first British journalist killed in Afghanistan. Philip Coburn, a photographer with the same newspaper, suffered severe injuries and was treated at the British military hospital at Camp Bastion in Helmand for two weeks before his death. On 30 December 2009, a Canadian journalist Michelle Lang, a reporter for the *Calgary Herald*, was killed when travelling with Canadian soldiers in the southern province of Kandahar. In August 2009, a US journalist working for CBS, Cami McCormick, was injured when the armoured vehicle she was travelling in hit an IED. Earlier that same month, Andi Jatmiko, a videographer working for AP, lost his foot after the military vehicle he was travelling in hit a roadside bomb. His colleague, photographer Emilio Morenatti, was also seriously injured.

We also have seen a number of kidnappings involving foreign journalists over the last year. Two French television journalists working for the state-owned France 3 channel are still in the hands of Taliban having being kidnapped in 2009 in Kapisa province. A journalist from the *Guardian*, the award-winning Ghaith Abdul-Ahad, was also kidnapped early in 2010 but released safely. In all, Reporters Without Borders announced in December 2009 that 19 journalists (11 of them foreign) had been killed in Afghanistan since 9/11. Five of the victims, including Afghan journalist Zakia Zaki and French journalist Johanne Sutton, were women (see http://en.rsf.org/afghanistan-embedded-canadian-reporter-becomes-31-12-2009,35532.html).

So have the Taliban gone away?
In 2002, a man in Kandahar went to attack a foreign national with a knife in the town. A local shopkeeper arrested him and handed him over to the Afghan government. That was a time when Afghanis were ready to help their government and foreign forces. Now, these shop keepers are no longer prepared to help. International troops and their Afghan friends celebrated the fall of the Taliban by bombing and searching Afghan villages to arrest the rest of the Taliban fighters but the villagers all across Afghanistan were the supporters of President Karzai. There were no Taliban fighters in the villages. People hoped desperately for improvements.

The first ever Afghan presidential election in 2004 even showed Afghan men allowing their women to sit in front of cameras and register for voting! Locals in Kandahar, Helmand , Farah , Zabul, Ningrahar, Kunar, Badkhshan and in the most remote corners of Afghanistan took part in the election. They rejected the Taliban fighters who called for a boycott. A few days before the election a

Taliban commander Mullah Dadullah came to a village in Urozagn province to encourage the people to boycott the election; but a local elder made it very clear to him they wanted to vote – and peace. The international observers declared the poll a success and yet foreign forces in Afghanistan still arrested people who voted in the election.

Losing hearts and minds?

In 2006 in the Shinwari district of Ningrahar province, a Taliban commander came with his armed group to a village to get the sympathy of the local population and to inflame them against the Afghan government. But local elders refused the demands. A local elder spoke loudly to the Taliban armed group, angrily begging them to behead him instead. They told the Taliban militants that they would rise against them if they tried to make their base in the village.

In June 2008, American-led foreign troops attacked a wedding convoy in Shinwari district killing more then 55 civilians including the bride. Most of the victims were children and women. Why did this atrocity happen? Well, the foreign military strategists are using too often the intelligence provided by local personnel. And this information is mostly faulty. The occupying forces are repeatedly committing the same mistakes by bombing villages and entering houses without the permission of the locals. But these activities face little sustained criticism from the international media.

In the middle of 2003, Wali Mohammed Ibrahimkhel, a local commander in the Chamtal district of Balkh province in the north of the country, lay down his arms. He was invited to Japan to learn the skills of civilian life so that he could play a crucial role in the future of the country. As a local commander he had 12 armed bodyguards but he appeared as ordinary civilian when he left the military for his new life. In March 2007, he was at his home with some local friends when American Special Forces blockaded the house and entered his home. As soon as they saw Wali Mohammad they immediately shot him. They picked up his body and left it along the Sheberghan and Mazar e-Sharif highway. A witness later told me that there were a few Afghan intelligence personnel accompanying American special forces.

His killing was for political reasons. Wali Mohammad Ibrahimkhel was very popular among local Pashtuns. But he had some disagreements with the governor of Balkh province, Atta Mohammad Noor. They had fought against each other in the past and Wali Mohammad was not ready to work under Noor's authority. Wali Mohammad Ibrahimkhel had kept close relations with the Afghan defence minister General Rahim Wardak. The rationale for his killing was based on wrong information passed to American Special Forces in Mazar e-Sharif city.

On 12 February 2010, during a night attack American forces entered a house in Paktya province killing five members of the family. Three of them were women and at least two of the women were pregnant, the two men were working for the Karzai government. Later, a family member told me one of the men had pleaded with the Americans not to fire on them because they were friends and working for Karzai government. But the US troops didn't listen to him and shot him in the yard of his house. They also refused the family immediate access to medical assistance. This incident left eighteen family members desolate and without health care. In Afghanistan, one person works and ten others eat what he brings in. If one key member of the family is killed, all the family are killed in a way (and this the international media fail to acknowledge). That's precisely what happened to that family in Paktya. In April 2010, an American general admitted the US troops had mistakenly killed those women in Paktya.

Afghanistan: a special case?

The foreign media are also failing to contextualise the current war in Afghanistan properly. For instance, they too often focus on the post 9/11 period and ignore the pains Afghans went through following the Soviet interventions in the 1980s. Afghanistan suffered a regime worse than the Taliban during the 1980s. The communists abused not only Afghan people but their traditions, religion and honours. They buried Afghans alive in the mass graves. They hanged Afghans without any trial. Some they arrested never returned home. But the Western powers learned nothing from the failures of the communists.

Yet during the Russian occupation of Afghanistan, the country had a strong central government with strong security forces backing them. The Mujahideen who were fighting against the Russians/Afghan puppet government of the time were unable to travel safely across the country. Security was too tight. But since the 2001 invasion, despite the presence of 43 countries in the international force, the occupation army is still unable to control the country.

Money flooded into Afghanistan following 9/11. Yet ordinary Afghans are yet to see any improvements in their lifestyles. Indeed, it was even better for them during the rule of the Taliban! And the international media are reluctant to admit this. Afghanistan then faced international sanctions – but poverty has grown since 2001.

No one was able to enter to the house of another without any permission. No traders were killed during the time of the Taliban regime in the heart of Kabul.

Note on the author

Hanan Habibzai was born in northern Afghan province of Baghlan. He was a less than a year old when the Soviets invaded his country. His family entered Pakistan as refugees and he grew up in a refugee camp near Peshawar. After completing his secondary education in Peshawar, he studied at Kabul University. Following the fall of the Taliban regime in 2001, Habibzai began working with the BBC World Service Pashto section as a correspondent and as a freelance reporter for Reuters News Agency in the north of Afghanistan. In the middle of 2006, he moved to BBC London office as presenter and reporter for BBC Pashto section. In May 2007, he joined the BBC Kabul office as a broadcast and online producer and senior reporter. At the end of 2008, he moved to London working as a freelance journalist covering Afghan-related issues. His work has been published by key international media agencies including Radio Free Europe.

Section 2. Putting it in perspective: journalism and history

Applying the microscope to the Afghan coverage

John Mair

Long before Evelyn Waugh wrote his classic novel *Scoop* (1938) and George Orwell his account of the Spanish civil war in *Homage to Catalonia* (also 1938), the craft of war reporting has been at the top of the food chain of journalism. The roll call of the great war reporters reads like a Journalism Hall of Fame – from Martha Gellhorn, Richard Dimbleby, James Cameron, John Pilger, Charles Wheeler, Nicholas Tomalin, Norman Mailer, Simon Winchester, Christiane Amanpour, Martin Bell, Kate Adie, Maggie O'Kane right up to some of the contributors to the previous section of this book. They all made their names on foreign fields, sometimes embedded with the military, sometimes not.

The Afghan conflict itself goes back nearly two centuries to the First Afghan War (1838-1842). War reporting is at least as old. In this section, some of the sharper minds in the analysis of modern journalism apply their microscopes to the reporting of the current conflict in Afghanistan.

Kevin Marsh, who was editing flagship BBC radio news programmes, *Today*, the *World at One* and *PM* during the early part of the current Afghan conflict, says *mea culpa*: don't blame the reporters on the frontline: blame editors like me back in London for not asking the right questions from the start.

Professor Tim Luckhurst, another broadcaster turned hackademic, argues that embedded journalists can be kosher so long as their work is complemented by that of un-embedded, "free"(or unilateral) reporters. He draws lessons from history.

Phillip Knightley, author of the seminal history of war correspondents, *The First Casualty*, argues that when Britain and the United States finally declare victory and leave Afghanistan, their tails between their legs, there will be a major laying-of-blame exercise. He concludes: "The media either ignored the truth, twisted it, distorted it or found ways of presenting it as a simple story of soldierly valour in the face of evil. It made no attempt to analyse and explain the war and its background to readers and viewers nor to challenge the premises on which the war was based. As a result, the gulf between the people and the politicians over the fighting could scarcely be wider."

Will Barton, of Coventry University, also brings history to bear on the subject. But he finds there is nothing new under the Afghan sun nor in the reporting of it. The platforms may change but the medium and messages are much the same. He concludes:

> The cliché (variously attributed) has it that the first casualty of war is the truth. Today it may better to say that the first casualty is history. The age of continuous news is also the age of the continuous present. Journalism no longer has any function to explain, merely to report. Every new injured or slain hero has her or his allotted five minutes of news space but there is no time to ask why their heroism was necessary in the first place.

Afghanistan, truth and the unexamined war

Kevin Marsh argues that the failure of journalism to give a full account of the Afghan conflict has almost nothing to do with access to the frontline and almost everything to do with the initial special circumstances of that war and the failings of editors in London

Truth!

It was the isolationist senator from California, Hiram Johnson, who coined the epigram, "The first casualty when war comes is truth."

It is an elusive value in the best of circumstances. In war it is a hostage to chaos and to uncontrollable passions and prejudices.[1]

That was how the former *Sunday Times* editor, Harold Evans, captured journalism's "truth problem" (in both peace and war) and corralled, perhaps, the most misquoted quotation on truth and war.

Evans' 2003 work, *War Stories: Reporting in the Time of Conflict*, is an essential read for anyone aspiring to become a war reporter or, indeed, anyone aspiring to write about war in any context – if for no other reason than that he articulates many of the compelling aspirations of war reporters and war reporting. And the paradoxes, too, if one of those aspirations is to tell the "truth".

War reporting and war reporters have a unique place in journalism's halls. They trail "clouds of glory". The only species of mankind that we journalists allow ourselves to revere uncritically. If there is a journalistic Valhalla, war reporters are its Einherjar (in the Norse myth, the heroes who have died in battle): its elite, its select. It is almost as if that small handful of our number who choose to risk their lives in the service of journalism validates the career choices of those of us who, in my case at least, have neither the skill nor courage to follow them.

And it's perhaps because war reporting is, in some sense, the "real thing" that we worry so much about it. In particular when, as in Afghanistan, it is difficult to the point of impossible to bear witness to the war's frontline without the aid, security and, therefore, limitations of one or other of those engaged in conflict. Embedding, in other words.

It is a given that we journalists want – require – to be able to exercise our craft as freely as possible, with as few restrictions as possible and with the right to annoy and offend power, if that's what our freely expressed witness entails. And that, for many of us, the idea of "embedded journalism" is a contradiction in terms. Embedding, a restriction that power places on our witness that is simply intolerable and contrary to any notion of keeping watch on that power.

But the reality of the conflict in Afghanistan is that embedding is virtually the only means Western journalists have of getting anywhere near the frontlines of Helmand and Sangin. Independent operation is at best impractical, at worst suicidal. Does that matter? In theory, of course...but in fact?

Does the fact that our witness at the frontline is almost certainly an embedded journalist deprive us of the "truth"? Are those embedded journalists actually unable to report as truthfully or honestly or accurately as they could as independents? Do the restrictions of embedding mean the public has a lesser understanding of that conflict? Indeed, where there are gaps in the public's understanding, is that because of the limitations of embedding and the deficiencies of embedded reporters? Or is it something else?

Heroism, folly...and idiots in blue flak jackets
There is, in war, Harold Evans writes:

> So much heroism; so much folly; so many brilliant moves; so many blunders; so many might-have-beens. In a current conflict, we fret about loved ones; but in all war reports we share vicariously in the terrible excitement of combat. We exult in victories; but we want to know whether the cause is just, the means proportionate to the end, and the execution honourable.[2]

Much has been written and said about the history of war reporting: we learn how some of the first war reporters – Thucydides, Xenophon and Julius Caesar – cut out the middleman by reporting themselves on the campaigns they led or were involved in. We learn that Alexander took "embeds" with him from Macedonia to the banks of the Indus. And in those days, made painless by the passage of centuries, frontline reporting focused on the heroism and the folly and the might-have-beens; the movement of troops and descriptions of battle; accounts of the habits of the vanquished and, in some cases – most notably Thucydides – the debates the arguments and a taste of its relentless pity.

Necessarily, these accounts seem to us now neatly self-contained – a much more finished account of history than the first draft that journalism ascribes to itself. Ditto the Annales of the Roman empire, ditto the chronicles of Anglo-Saxon England. Somewhen in the 17th and 18th centuries, depending where you were, journalism in something like its current form arrived. But it was not until a little over a century and a half ago, in the 1850s (with the UK in the Crimean War) and the 1860s (the American Civil War) that a distinct craft of war reporting emerged, a craft that set the journalist's interest in revealing truth against the combatants' interests in hiding or shaping it.

A war reporter differs from a war historian in many ways. Two matter more than any others. First: whether accurate and comprehensive or not, a war reporter's work deals in the here and now and those contemporaneous accounts of conflict inevitably feed the political debate about the rightness or conduct of that conflict. Second: the war reporter's accounts are part of the combatants' own real-time understanding of the conflict. For these two reasons if no others, journalists should be concerned when power wants to limit or constrain reporting – for whatever reason.

"It changes everything we do"

The world, the media, the nature of conflict and of power's accountability to people has changed since Archibald Forbes witnessed the "heroism ... and brilliant moves" that constituted the impossible British victory at Ulundi, during the Zulu War in the late 1870s – and rode 120 miles to break the news[3]; or since Mathieu Corman, Christopher Holme, Noel Monks and George Steer attested to (as near victims of) the aerial bombardment and massacre at Guernica in April 1937 during the Spanish Civil War (Southwood 1977); or even since Morley Safer gave his eye witness account of the burning of Cam Ne[4] in Vietnam in 1965.

Few have described those changes more elegantly or eloquently than the BBC's Special Correspondent, Allan Little. In March 2003, in the early days of the Iraq invasion, Little was in Kuwait, describing the familiar foggy chaos of war and the unfamiliar new media order:[5]

> It is just after dark. A US army major is talking urgently into a mobile phone to a journalist who has got lost in southern Iraq. "These voices you can hear," the major is saying. "Are they English or Arabic?" Arabic. "Then lie flat on the ground. Do not move. Switch off your mobile phone because if it rings it will give away your position. Stay there all night. When you hear American forces arrive, wave something white and put your hands up." "Now," he adds ominously, "is there any message you would like me to pass on to your next of kin while you still can?"

This would have had a certain humour about it – had it not been written 48 hours after ITN reporter Terry Lloyd and his crew – cameraman Frédéric Nérac and interpreter Hussein Osman – became lost in southern Iraq and, it was established later, killed by American fire.

Lloyd and his crew were "independents" in a time and place where it was becoming less and less feasible to report independently. But such was the pull of "independence" – something close to a fetish – that even those who, unlike Lloyd, were war virgins were kicking the Kuwaiti stable doors to stampede in suicidal ignorance into southern Iraq to bear independent journalistic witness. While Allan Little was in Kuwait, a veteran cameraman called him to share his fear that:

> None of the team I'm working with here has ever been to a war before and they want to cross the border and go wandering into the battlefield. You should hear them talking about this war. They think it's a reality TV show.

The game had changed – and while holding his nose, Little clerked that change:

There are too many of us here. There are 2,000 reporters accredited with the US military. Of those 500 are embedded with the coalition forces and they are telling the story of this war – graphically, dramatically, instantly and sometimes live, commentating on battles as they unfold, and before the outcome is known. It is astonishing and unprecedented. It changes everything about what we do…Some of my good friends are embedded with the US and UK military. They are doing what seems to me to be a brilliant job. They are keeping cool, distanced, serious. It is not – emphatically not – a reality TV show to them.

"A brilliant job". There are few journalists – let alone war correspondents – I admire more than Allan Little. And when he says embedded correspondents are doing "a brilliant job", I listen. To his qualifications too: "But this feeling that so far we are all inescapably part of someone's war effort is unsettling."

This is the calculus for Western journalists covering the war in Afghanistan. On the one hand, the risks and, frankly, near inaccessibility of the frontline without the protection and assistance of the military. On the other hand, that "unsettling" knowledge that as an embed, our reporting is "part of someone's war effort" – a calculus articulated by veteran war correspondent Patrick Cockburn. Television, he wrote, in particular, finds it impossible to cover modern conflict "properly": "The dangers to correspondent and crew are too great, and the limitations of being embedded with the US or British armies subvert balanced coverage." [6]

And there is a long, long list of journalists and writers to whom the idea of embedding is more than "unsettling". It's intolerable. According to former BBC war correspondent Martin Bell, for example: "News is run by the government…the news organisations have to be in with the government." [7] And, it follows, the last thing a self-respecting reporter should do is collude in that control, conspiring in your own censorship. It's a form of control that has a soft as well as a hard edge – and the soft is probably more effective than the hard. The BBC's World News Editor, John Simpson has commented:

I don't want to spend my whole time with people to whom I owe my safety, my protection, my food, my transport, and then be expected to be completely honest about them, because there's always that sense that you're betraying a trust (Moss 2010).

This is a concern reflected by the Committee to Protect Journalists which, in 2004, said: "The close quarters shared by (embedded) journalists and troops inevitably blunted reporters' critical edge".[8] But it's perhaps *Times* reporter Chris Ayres who articulates battlefield cases of the Stockholm syndrome most forcefully in his book *War Reporting for Cowards,* in particular his realisation of: "…the true genius of the embedding scheme. It had turned me into a marine. I was thinking like a fighter, not a reporter. And yet I wasn't a fighter. I was an idiot in a blue flak jacket" (Ayres 2006).

An "idiot" on two fronts; first, constrained by his own self-image that runs counter to his true role as a reporter and flaws his witness; second, because the constraints of embedding create, according to rights campaigner Alison Banville: "missing pieces of the picture we need if we are to make up our own minds about whether any war fought in our name is just."[9] Banville goes on:

…we are not encouraged to seek motivations, to see complexity or cause and effect, we are only seen fit for the most simplistic propaganda – and we lap it up, because we want so desperately to believe our sons and daughters are fighting and dying for something worthwhile…we never need truth more than in time of war.

In the background of these arguments against embedded reporting is not just the – justified – suspicion that power always seeks to control the story. There is also an unqualified faith placed in eyewitness – a faith that all journalists should share while also being aware to its limitations.

Robert Fox is one of our most experienced war reporters who has also written and lectured widely on frontline reporting's relationship to "truth" and to history. In a 2003 lecture[10], Fox questioned the unqualified faith in eyewitness –

his own, in particular. He weighed the advantages and disadvantages of being close to the action and close to the combatants. On the plus side, he listed being alive to the chaos, frustrations and dangers of war; being close to commanders and understanding what they had in mind; understanding how war is not the simple, coherent, choreographed series of events that reporting can make it seem.

On the minus side, he stressed the interference of point of view; the dangers of interpretation and interpolation; the risks of identifying with "victims"; and, crucially, as Allan Little noted, the inevitability that "reporters become actors in their own drama", assisted and enabled by the demands of live and continuous television or deadline-free writing for the web.

But it's the manufacture of myth, "the transmission from witness to journalism, to false memory and history" that Fox identifies as the greatest danger of eyewitness – or, more accurately, the exaggerated faith that we can be tempted to place in eyewitness reporting by reason of its proximity to events. Fox cites an example from the Balkans in the summer of 1992:

> ... the persistent tales of systematic rape by the Serbian military and paramilitary forces. One of the first references I have found is in the *Guardian* of 17 December 1992, where the correspondent mentions "14,000 rapes" being committed against Bosnian Muslim women ... there are some dreadful first hand reports.

By March 1993, the number had risen to 20,000 in a report of the prosecution of a Serb militiaman:

> Borislav Herak, self-confessed Serbian rapist, killer and ethnic cleanser...is the first Serb to stand trial for war crimes in Bosnia – where, according to international bodies, half the population have been driven from their homes, 120,000 people have been killed and 20,000 women had been systematically raped.

In 2000, an ICRC representative at a Reuters Conference held in Oxford, Urs Boegli, put the true figure at 237. Fox concludes:

> Eyewitness is key to reporting…(it) lays down its own narrative. But this idea of the story can often be distorted by fashion and the dictates of the media. A from of collective false memory can be created…With this comes what Martin Bell calls the journalism of attachment – you take sides and stick to it. Journalists begin to say what they think ought to have happened, rather than what did. Judgment takes over from the forensic investigation of interesting and very often unpleasant facts: I know, and I am right, because I care.

In other words, we should be as sceptical of eyewitness as we are of any other source. We may respect and admire those journalists who take risks in war on our behalf and we may cling to the ideal that independence is best but that it is no guarantee of "truth".

In August 2006, BBC correspondent Orla Guerin was one of a huge number of Western journalists covering Israel's war in Lebanon against Hezbollah. Guerin and other Western correspondents were effectively "independents" in that they were not attached to military units and were responsible for their own safety and movements. On 14 August, Guerin reported from a Lebanese town called Bint Jbeil – it had been the object of a fierce Israeli bombardment and had, according to Guerin, "been wiped out".

By contrast, other Western reporters, including Channel Four's Alex Thomson arrived in Bint Jbeil by another route and reported that the town centre had been "destroyed on a really wholesale scale" and "pancaked". But the outer parts of the town were "pretty much untouched". Guerin was accused of, at the very least, allowing herself to stray from the strict requirements of impartiality; at worst, she was accused of "lying".[11] Clearly, she was guilty of neither – her only "crime" was that she had reported those things she had witnessed as she had witnessed them. As Thomson pointed out in her defence: "What Orla said about the town centre is absolutely 100 per cent true. Orla is an extremely experienced and professional correspondent".[12]

Thomson went on to say that journalists had "to genuinely say what they were seeing". And that is, indeed, all we should require and expect of witness – that it is an account which corresponds to what a reporter has seen. But that eyewitness is no guarantor of "truth" itself – not even when, as in Guerin's case, the reporter is acting independently.

Which should lead us to doubt the essential proposition of those who unequivocally oppose embedded reporting. While it is clear that the conclusions of Banville and others – that there are "missing pieces" in the journalistic account of the Afghan war – it is almost certainly not the case that embedding is *the* cause or even *a* cause of those pieces going missing? The Afghan war is, indeed, insufficiently examined – arguably, has been under or even unexamined from the very start. Complexity, cause and effect are, indeed, missing, but for reasons that have little to do with the constraints of embedding.

An unexamined war

It is easy to forget how rapidly the bombardment and invasion of Afghanistan followed the attacks on New York and Washington on 11 September 2001 – and how unexamined, by politicians and media, was the case for and road to war. From the moment the BBC's Frank Gardner attributed the September 11 attacks to al Qaeda and Osama bin Laden, war in Afghanistan seemed inevitable. An inevitability that effectively silenced proper examination of the case for that war.

The bewilderment on the faces of Western leaders as they heard the news – President Bush, you recall, was reading to schoolchildren when the news came through, and Prime Minister Blair was about to address the TUC in Brighton – was more than just an expression of shock at the unspeakable atrocity. It reflected, also, their certainty that "something must be done", but that, initially, they had very little idea what. There had to be retaliation, a strike back – but against whom? When, why and to what end? They were far from clear.

Three days after the attacks, on 14 September, British MPs were recalled to Westminster to meet in emergency session. There were many words but little debate. The then-leader of the Liberal Democrats, Charles Kennedy, captured the prevailing sentiment when he said: "It seems almost inevitable that there will be some sort of military response at some point – although at the moment we do not know where, when, or against whom." [13] That echoed Prime Minister Blair's declaration that:

> ...these were attacks on the basic democratic values in which we all believe so passionately and on the civilised world...NATO has already...determined that this attack in America will be considered as an attack against the alliance as a whole. The UN Security Council on Wednesday passed a resolution which set out its readiness to take all necessary steps to combat terrorism. From Russia, China, the EU, from Arab states, Asia and the Americas, from every continent of the world, has come united condemnation. This solidarity must be maintained and translated into support for action. [14]

The contribution to this debate from newly elected, Leader of Her Majesty's Opposition, Iain Duncan Smith, could almost be described as fawning: "... the Prime Minister ... is to be congratulated on responding to this crisis quickly and resolutely, and on giving a lead to other nations that value freedom and democracy."[15]

Within three weeks, the government had produced a dossier, setting out the culpability of al Qaeda and Osama bin Laden as well as that of the Taleban regime in Afghanistan.[16] The was the dossier on which Prime Minister Blair was able to lean when he told parliament, recalled for a second time on 4 October, that the Taleban "...allows them (al Qaeda and Osama bin Laden) to operate with impunity in pursuing their terrorist activity."[17]

How many of us remember that dossier? How many of us read it? How many of us gave it the scrutiny we gave to the Iraq dossiers – both the "sexed-up" September 2002 dossier and the dodgy dossier of February 2003? How many of us questioned, in the name of seeking "truth", the simple choices Prime Minister Blair set out – as simple and unavoidable for the UK as they were for the Taleban?

They either surrender the terrorists and close down the terrorist network or they become our enemies. If that happens, and the regime were to change, we are already working in close co-operation with people in and outside Afghanistan to build an alternative and successor regime that is as broad based as possible, unites ethnic groupings and gives people the chance of a stable Government there.

The lack of parliamentary and media scrutiny created a silence in the discourse, filled only by the sound of John Stuart Mill (1859) turning in his grave: "Truth can only emerge from the clash of contrary opinions."

Yet there was much we journalists could and should have scrutinised. The extent to which Britain's haste "to take down the Taleban regime" – the phrase that became common currency at the time – aligned itself with what we knew about Tony Blair's declared principles of foreign intervention, for example. Since 1997, Prime Minister Tony Blair had been straining both to define – and exercise – what had become known as "post-modern"/"humanitarian" foreign policy – broadly, the criteria on which the UK might choose to project its power into another state to right those things which, according to British values, were wrongs.

The key text was delivered in Chicago during the Kosovo War of 1999 (and so became known as "the Chicago speech")[18] and contained five defining tests for military intervention by the West:

First, are we sure of our case? War is an imperfect instrument for righting humanitarian distress; but armed force is sometimes the only means of dealing with dictators.

Second, have we exhausted all diplomatic options? We should always give peace every chance, as we have in the case of Kosovo.

Third, on the basis of a practical assessment of the situation, are there military operations we can sensibly and prudently undertake?

Fourth, are we prepared for the long term? In the past we talked too much of exit strategies. But having made a commitment we cannot simply walk away once the fight is over; better to stay with moderate numbers of troops than return for repeat performances with large numbers.

And finally, do we have national interests involved?

It was a clever speech that appeared to establish Britain as a kind of global "values policeman" – the five criteria were calculated to justify interventions in Sierra Leone (1998) and Kosovo/Serbia (1999), for example. In fact, of course, it was a delimitation of intervention abroad, turning a blind eye towards Saudi Arabia or China, for example, where, by any rational assessment, British values were affronted daily. The unexamined rush to war in Afghanistan blew those limitations away, arguably shaping the paradigm by which Britain became entangled in President Bush's crusade in Iraq. And in telling that 'truth" about Afghanistan, journalism failed.

In his Chicago speech, Tony Blair said nothing about regime change; nothing about de-failing failed states; nothing about assuring the safety of British streets by fighting in foreign fields. In an April 2010 article for the Royal Institute of International Affairs – Chatham House – Patrick Porter, of King's College, London, summarised where Britain's foreign policy stood after Afghanistan. Porter's article is as potent a condemnation of journalism's failure as it is of Britain's loss of focus in Afghanistan and after. The Blair/Brown administration, Porter (2010) argues, had become hyperactive on the world stage because:

> ... it claims the country's security depends on a liberal, "rules based" world order that upholds its values ... Britain is endangered by globe-girdling, chaotic processes such as state failure. Broken countries are incubators of extremism, disease and crime.

Britain had found itself committed to de-failing failed states and doing so in a way that was consistent with Britain's liberal values:

> It cannot tolerate the illiberal. Therefore, London must scan the far horizons and take a forward leaning posture, watching, engaging and intervening on the periphery to protect its core.

This is most true of Afghanistan. There we see for real what an open-ended, bottomless, interminable – choose your term of infinity as you will – policy of intervention leads to. After almost nine years in which British men and women have been fighting and dying in Afghanistan– twice the length of World War Two – the average British newspaper reader or the average British TV news bulletin viewer might well ask whether we journalists have helped locate the "missing pieces".

Can we journalists hold our hands on our hearts and say that we have done all that we could to hold our government properly to account for its expenditure of our "blood and treasure" on a policy in Afghanistan that is maximally interventionist (overturning one regime and putting another in its place), values driven (towards a multi-ethnic, plural democracy) and, in its logic (the safety of British streets is secured on the battlefields of Afghanistan) capable of application anywhere on the globe where states fail? And if we have not done so – and this is crucial – has that failure been the result of constraints on reporting from the front line? Or has it been the result of something else?

"The most simplistic propaganda"?[19]

Without doubt, there has been a shortage of Western journalistic witness to the Afghan war. As Robert Fox argues, whatever its limitations, it is essential to all reporting. Of course, such is the media landscape now that non-Western and unconventional witness is an important component in our understanding of the war. Yet we keep having to ask the question; while accepting that embedded reporting is not the ideal, is it embedding and our inability to operate independently in Afghanistan that has limited the public's access to "truth" or its understanding of the war?

In February and March of 2010, Channel Four's Alex Thomson[20] and BBC *Newsnight's* Mark Urban[21] were both – separately – embedded with British forces in Helmand. It is, of course, impossible to know how different their reporting might have been had they been "independents". However, it is also impossible to accuse them of failing to supply the "motivations…complexity or cause and effect" that opponents of embedding claim is lacking from embedded reporting.

Their reports were insightful, intelligent, critical, textured and nuanced. They were also very long, in television news terms. And seen in their entirety, probably, by fewer than a million viewers: some 2 per cent of the adult population, a large proportion of which were already pretty well informed about the war already. The other 98 per cent have a very different experience of "news from Afghanistan".

Try this, very unscientific, very un-academic, very un-rigorous experiment. Type "Afghanistan war" into Google news (or the search engine of your choice) and take a look at the results for each of the national UK newspapers. On the day I tried it, the *Sun, Mirror* and *Mail* – who together account for over 50 per cent of daily newspaper sales – had not a single eyewitness report from the front line in Afghanistan. And though this was during the election period, when embedding with UK forces was suspended, front line reporting was still available, carried out by Western and non-western journalists. And in any event, the search returns predated the beginning of the election purdah.

By far the biggest single category of stories was short reports of British casualties – for the most part, very little more than casualty notices. There were London based reports on British offensives, royal visits, a soldiers' remake of the latest Lady Gaga video and the return of British troops either to a heroes' welcome or to heartfelt, respectful tribute in Wootton Bassett.

Conclusion

"Truth" is the journalist's most elusive aspiration. In war it is especially elusive and especially important. We journalists have many reasons not to trust power when it seeks to limit or control our access to anything, let alone the frontline of a war in which our fellow citizens are fighting as dying, as well as being responsible for the deaths of others – military and citizens alike.

We have many reasons – particularly if the focus of our attention is how power is being exercised on our behalf, how the values we claim to be defending are being upheld – to distrust limitations on our witness.

But we have to beware of war reporting as journalistic fetish. It has a noble heritage and it is right to admire those who risk their lives in journalism's service. But we have to be hard headed about it too. Reporting from the front line – whether embedded or independent – is now more than ever just one source amongst many. And a source which, history and experience tell us, is at best partially true, at worst the first draft of dangerous myths that can distort forever our understanding of events.

The failure of journalism to give a full account – to tell as far as it can, the "truth" – of the war in Afghanistan is almost nothing to do with access to the front line and almost everything to do with the initial special circumstances of that war and the failings of editors in London. Journalism – even that from non-jingoistic, xenophobic quarters – was hugely influenced by the political consensus in the face of the 9/11 attacks. Both that consensus and the speed at which events careered towards war.

And those failings are the usual ones; daily journalism's aversion to complexity; its centripetal tendency, dragging the apparent plurality of multiple outlets towards common framings; its inevitable preference for the striking event over the telling trend; and its eternal excuse – we're just telling stories.

The result? The war in Afghanistan, while the source of great public anxiety, figured hardly at all in a public discourse as important as the 2010 general election campaign – in part because the only question that now matters (how to bring the war to some kind of conclusion) is itself embedded in a confused understanding of how we got there in the first place and of a policy on foreign intervention, developed in the heat of strike-back, that sprawls far, far beyond any reasoned and considered intentions.

If "truth" is war's first casualty, journalism as a means of understanding war is its second. Something the Greek historian and proto-war reporter Thucydides understood well. He wrote:

The absence of romance in my history will, I fear, detract somewhat from its interest…I have written my work, not…to win the applause of the moment, but as a possession for all time.

Or, to put it another way, in war you can have "truth" or you can have journalism. You can't have both.

Notes

[1] Harold Evans: *Reporting in the Time of Conflict* – shorter essay with same title available online at http://www.newseum.org/warstories/essay/index.htm, accessed 1 April 2010

[2] ibid

[3] Archibald Forbes' death notice, in the *Sydney Mail*, of 7 April 1900, while an account of his reporting is available online at http://news.google.com/newspapers?nid=1302&dat=19000407&id=NH0QAAAA IBAJ&sjid=25QDAAAAIBAJ&pg=7225,4109564, accessed on 1 April 2010

[4] See Morley Safer's despatch in *Reporting America at War*. Available online at http://www.pbs.org/weta/reportingamericaatwar/reporters/safer/camne.html, accessed on 1 April 2010

[5] See BBC News website http://news.bbc.co.uk/1/hi/uk/2880949.stm, accessed on 2 April 2010

[6] Patrick Cockburn: War Reporting in Iraq: Only Locals Need Apply. Available online at http://www.counterpunch.org/patrick03032007.html, accessed on 2 April 2010

[7] Speaking at 2008 conference organised by the International Communications Forum. Jameela Oberman's account available online at http://interjunction.org/news/war-reporting-is-dead/, accessed on 2 April 2010

[8] See Alison Banville: http://www.guardian.co.uk/commentisfree/2010/apr/18/embedded-war-reporting-iraq-afghanistan, accessed on 19 April 2010

[9] ibid

[10] History and War Reporting: Bagehot lecture at Queen Mary, University of London, 23 January 2003. Available online at http://www.history.qmul.ac.uk/events/annual/bagehot/index.html, accessed on 1 April 2004

[11] See Honest Reporting: BBC's Orla exposed. Available online at http://www.honestreporting.co.uk/articles/critiques/BBCs_Orla_Exposed.asp, accessed on 1 April 2010

[12] See http://myrightword.blogspot.com/2006/08/channel-4s-thomson-supports-bbcs.html, accessed on 1 May 2007

[13] See House of Commons *Hansard*: 14 September 2001. Available online at http://www.publications.parliament.uk/pa/cm200102/cmhansrd/vo010914/debtext/10914-01.htm , accessed on 15 September 2001

[14] See House of Commons *Hansard*: 14 September 2001. Available online at http://www.publications.parliament.uk/pa/cm200102/cmhansrd/vo010914/debtext/10914-01.htm, accessed on 15 September 2001

[15] ibid

[16] Full text at http://news.bbc.co.uk/1/hi/uk_politics/1579043.stm

[16] House of Commons *Hansard*, 4 October 2001. Available online at http://www.publications.parliament.uk/pa/cm200102/cmhansrd/vo011004/debtext/11004-01.htm, accessed on 5 October 2001

[17] ibid

[18] See Doctrine of the International Community, 24 April 1999. http://www.number10.gov.uk/archive/1999/04/doctrine-of-the-international-community-2441999-1297

[19] See Banville (op cit)

[20] See http://www.channel4.com/news/articles/politics/international_politics/afghanistan+ambush+behind+taliban+lines/3549942, accessed on 1 April 2010

[21] Mark Urban's reports are available online at http://news.bbc.co.uk/1/hi/programmes/newsnight/8555922.stm, accessed on 1 April 2010

References

Ayres, Chris (2006) *War Reporting for Cowards*, London, John Murray

Mill, John Stuart (1859) *On Liberty*. Available online at http://books.google.co.uk/books?id=ScTePJKjiTMC&printsec=frontcover&dq=J ohn+Stuart+Mill+On+Liberty&source=bl&ots=n5iBqctrnx&sig=u43mGuptW8rq biUY3_oQiz60hxA&hl=en&ei=y1bpS5PSAZCe_gb6he3sCg&sa=X&oi=book_res ult&ct=result&resnum=2&ved=0CCUQ6AEwAQ#v=onepage&q&f=false

Moss, Stephen (2010) John Simpson: "I'm very pessimistic about the future of the BBC", *Guardian*, 15 March. Available online at http://www.guardian.co.uk/media/2010/mar/15/john-simpson-bbc-murdoch-journalism, accessed on 16 March 2010

Porter, Patrick (2010) *The Maps are Too Small*, RIIA, April

Southwood, Herbert, R. (1977) *Guernica!: A Study of Journalism, Diplomacy, Propaganda and History*, Berkeley, University of California Press

Note on the author

Kevin Marsh is Executive Editor at the BBC College of Journalism. He is a former Editor of the *Today* programme and also edited *The World at One*, *PM* and *Broadcasting House* on BBC Radio 4. He writes a regular column in *Press Gazette* and blogs at http://storycurve.blogspot.com/.

Compromising the first draft?

Tim Luckhurst traces the chequered history of the reporting of conflicts by embedded reporters. And, focusing on the current Afghan conflict, he concludes that war coverage has been most effectively performed when the work of embedded reporters is informed by journalism produced by unembedded colleagues operating apart from the military

Michelle Lang, a Canadian journalist working for the *Calgary Herald*, died on her first trip to Afghanistan. Keen to highlight what she considered to be positive achievements by Nato forces in that country (D'Alieso and Wilton 2010) she set out to witness the work of a Canadian reconstruction team. She was killed on 30 December 2009, when a roadside bomb blew up the vehicle in which she was traveling south of Kandahar.

Rupert Hamer, of Britain's *Sunday Mirror*, died when another roadside bomb exploded northwest of Nawa in Helmand province in January 2010 (see Mirror.co.uk). He was a veteran on his fifth visit to Afghanistan. Lang and Hamer were embedded correspondents, Lang with the Canadian Army and Hamer with a US Marine unit.

Reporting Afghanistan poses immense challenges to journalists. Issues including violence, humanitarianism, corruption and development offer a cornucopia of public interest stories. Threats including improvised bombs, crossfire and kidnappings make them dangerous to obtain.

The Committee to Protect Journalists records that 17 news personnel have been killed in Afghanistan since 11 September 2001 (Committee to Protect Journalists 2010). Five of them were, like Lang and Hamer, accidental victims of combat between the Taliban and the Nato-led International Security Assistance Force. More were targeted for murder because they were journalists.

Hamer and Lang decided that embedding, whereby journalists join military forces as their guests and are protected by them was the best way to avoid threats including kidnapping and assassination. Their deaths while working alongside Nato soldiers demonstrate that embedding cannot guarantee a reporter's safety, but many other reporters and news organisations have reached the same conclusion. They believe embedding gets them close to a story they could not otherwise cover. The purpose of this chapter is to explore whether it enhances journalism's capacity to perform its public purposes in reporting Afghanistan to the outside world.

Journalism's core purposes

For the purpose of this analysis journalism's purposes are defined as four of those identified by (Schudson 2008: 11-17); informing the public, investigation, analysis and social empathy and a broader purpose, familiar to diligent journalists, that encapsulates all of them: recording a reliable first draft of history. The question is: does embedding help reporters to inform, investigate and analyse the conflict in Afghanistan is such a way as to help them record a reliable first draft? Or, does it promote collusion, censorship and suppression in ways calculated to serve the interests of the military and Nato governments?

The terms upon which reporters are permitted to work alongside ISAF forces as embedded correspondents in Afghanistan are governed by agreements such as that set out in the latest revision of the UK Ministry of Defence's *Green Book* (Ministry of Defence 2008). This document is the product of dialogue between the Ministry of Defence and news organisations that began after the Falklands Conflict. It has been updated frequently. The MoD with the participation of news organisations including; the Newspaper Publishers Association, the National Union of Journalists, the British Broadcasting Corporation, Independent Television News, Sky News and the Society of Editors produced the current version.

The *Green Book* rules (Section 43) that "Correspondents must accept that in the conditions under which they will be operating the appropriate operational commander has the right to restrict what operational information can be reported and when." It lists as "subjects that correspondents may not be allowed to include in [their reports]" topics including composition of forces, details of military movements, operational orders, casualties, place names, tactics names or numbers of ships, units or aircraft and names of individual servicemen.

It requires (Section 44) that "…correspondents must accept that they may be required to submit all written material, voice items intended for radio or television, films or video recordings produced for television, associated scripts or voice accompaniments, and still photographs for security checking clearance before transmission".

The *Green Book* also sets out (Annex A) the process whereby correspondents must outline the detail of their request to embed before consent will be granted for them to accompany UK Armed Forces in operational theatres. This includes guidance to "decide on subject matter to be covered in as much detail as possible (including issues/locations/interviewees that will facilitate the required coverage if known)".

Journalists who have covered the conflict in Afghanistan as embedded correspondents, and editors who have published their work, have conflicting opinions about the value of these practices and comparable rules set out by the Pentagon and defence ministries in other Nato countries.

National security and secrecy

Unprecedented access for journalists to battlefields is clearly offered on terms that accord higher value to the operational requirements of the military than to free speech. Every democracy acknowledges that national security requires secrecy about the operational aspects of military activity.

It is equally plain that embedded reporters witness only a fraction of what is happening in a conflict zone. Speaking about embedded reporters on *Newshour with Jim Lehrer* during the invasion of Iraq in 2003, US Secretary of Defense Donald Rumsfeld acknowledged that their journalism offered a partial picture. "What we are seeing is not the war in Iraq," he observed, "what we're seeing are slices of the war in Iraq" (*Online Newshour* 2003).

Do the slices proffered by embedded correspondents in Afghanistan convey the true flavour of the cake? Among journalists (Conference, Afghanistan; are we embedding the truth, University of Coventry 18 March 2010), there is consensus that embedded reporters retain a duty to interrogate power. Agreement also exists that embedding is a compromise: reporters get eyewitness experience of Nato forces in action but their access is restricted to a solitary repository of power.

Kevin Marsh, editor of the BBC College of Journalism, asks at the conference where the voice of the Taliban is to be found in journalism reporting Afghanistan to Britain. Does asymmetrical reporting blight this militarily asymmetrical conflict? Other concerns include prior restraint (material censored or blocked before it can be published), the MoD/Pentagon's power to restrict access to embedded missions to reporters deemed friendly to the military (Shane 2009) and fears that living and working with soldiers encourages reporters to concentrate on action stories to the exclusion of broader analyses.

The compromises involved in embedding

Vaughan Smith is founder of the Frontline News agency and a veteran of conflict both as a soldier (he is a former Captain in the Grenadier Guards) and as a journalist. He visited Afghanistan as an embedded guest of ISAF forces in Helmand Province. Smith says that embedded journalists working in Afghanistan believe taking risks to cover conflict serves the public interest, but he is candid about the compromises involved.

Smith says: "Embedding feeds the machine," (i.e. it supplies stories that appeal to audiences and, therefore, to editors and proprietors). He adds that it makes good economic sense. "The army pays for it, which is very attractive in the modern media economy." But he considers it a tainted compact that generates more public relations value to the military than democratic value to the public. Embedding, he says, serves the military objective of effective "media operations".

Other reporters acknowledge that embedding limits a correspondent's freedom, but justify it as "going with soldiers on one side or the other" (Thomson 2010) and therefore useful, providing reporting from the other side is available to secure balance. This argument mistakes neutrality for truth, and even neutrality is hard to achieve in Afghanistan, where access to the "other side" is least available in those areas where Nato forces are most actively engaged in combat.

A crudely ideological analysis might conclude that the political economics are blatant: embedding is choreographed to tell the military's preferred narrative from the battlefield to the grave. It gets reporters close enough to thrilling action to enable them to dazzle and fascinate the taxpayers back home. But, it only rarely risks blighting their appreciation with troubling narratives about wounded civilians. It is, in short, designed to create a version of the Stockholm Syndrome (Bejerot 1974: 486-487; see also De Fabrique et al 2007) in which the embedded correspondent becomes a willing and sympathetic ally of military/political authority that is exploiting them to create a narrative amenable to its interests.

In fact, the relationship between embedded correspondent and military is nuanced. Embedded reporters understand that they have a duty to see beyond what armies want to show them. Military leaders and their political masters know that sustained support for military intervention, particularly in a long and costly conflict, requires informed consent within representative democracies.

History is more useful than abstract theory to mature understanding of journalism. To appreciate the limitations of embedded reporting, and its consequences for the diligent first draft journalism, which, alone, can properly fulfill the profession's duty to representative democracy, awareness of the practice's past is invaluable.

Russell – and the birth of the embedded journalist

The name is modern, but embedding is not a new invention although the rules governing it are more precisely codified than before. The MoD argues that William Howard Russell (Knightley 2004: 1-18), who covered the Crimean War of 1853-1856 for *The Times*, was an embedded correspondent. If that assertion

(MoD 2007) stretches the definition of formal embedding, a recognisable version certainly came into existence during the First World War.

Before the assassination of Archduke Franz Ferdinand of Austria by a Serbian nationalist provoked Germany to invade France through the territory of neutral Belgium and, thence, Britain's declaration of war on August 4 1914, some British newspapers resisted the jingoism promoted in market leaders such as the *Daily Mail* and *Daily Express*.

The *Manchester Guardian*, forefather of today's *Guardian*, carried a full-page advertisement announcing the formation of a league to stop war. Newspapers of the liberal and socialist left, including the *Labour Leader* and *Daily News*, protested that Britain should not become involved in a European war (Knightley op cit: 84-85). But the intense imperial pride promoted in previous decades, not least by popular journalism, delivered 1 million volunteers to Lord Kitchener's New Army by the end of 1914 (Robinson 2009).

Men were encouraged to enlist by the dominant belief that Britain was great, good and civilised and that their duty was to fight in its defence. That view dominated newspapers, too. In January 1915, Baron Herbert Reuter, one of the owners of the powerful *Reuters* news agency, told a colleague: "Every day I realise more deeply the colossal task before us, and the necessity of sparing no sacrifice to succeed where failure spells ruin to three Empires and will involve the unspeakable blight of German military tyranny over the whole Continent" (Read 1992: 111).

Fleet Street placed at the service of the war effort
Lord Northcliffe, owner of the *Daily Mail*, worked for the British government as Director of Propaganda in Enemy Countries. The editors of the *Guardian, Times, Daily Express, Evening Post* and *Daily Chronicle* placed their titles at the service of the war effort. Their abdication of the liberal principle that a free and independent press should speak truth to power was reinforced by reports filed from the Western Front by the first formally accredited war correspondents.

A few reports conducive to holding power to account emerged from the first months of the conflict, but, these simply encouraged the pro-censorship enthusiasms of ministers such as Winston Churchill who believed journalists should cover war by writing what Admirals, Generals and Secretaries of State told them.

This approach generated turgid copy, so ministers realised that, given newspaper owners' enthusiasm for the great crusade against tyranny, eyewitness reporting, of an acceptably sanitised and eulogistic variety, could promote the war effort and sustain newspaper profits. Missing were only the docile journalists to write it. They were found.

These men were; Philip Gibbs of the *Daily Telegraph* and *Daily Chronicle*, Percival Philips of the *Daily Express* and *Morning Post*, William Beach-Thomas of the *Daily Mail* and *Daily Mirror*, H. Perry Robinson for *The Times* and *Daily News*, Herbert Russell for *Reuters* and Basil Clarke for the *Amalgamated Press*.

Their reporting failed, abjectly, to deliver a reliable first draft of the history of combatants' sacrifice and suffering. In the First World War, embedding contributed to one of the most dismal episodes in professional journalism's history. These prototype embedded correspondents wore officers' uniform, held the honorary rank of Captain and relied upon the army for food, drink, accommodation and transport. They went nowhere unless accompanied by a serving soldier known as a "conducting officer". In return for their accreditation their employers had agreed to restrictions that prevented them from identifying places, people or military units.

Hemingway on the propaganda of the First World War

Ernest Hemingway, the American writer and journalist who served briefly in the war as ambulance driver, later observed that it was "…the most colossal, murderous, mismanaged butchery that has ever taken place on earth. Any writer who said otherwise lied. So the writers either wrote propaganda, shut up or fought". The embedded reporters wrote propaganda.

Philip Gibbs wrote of the bombardment that opened the Battle of Vimy Ridge in April 1917: "It was a beautiful and devilish thing, and the beauty of it, and not the evil of it, put a spell upon one's senses." Describing the infantry's advance against German trenches he reported: "They went in a slow, leisurely way, not hurried, though the enemy's shrapnel was searching for them. 'Grand fellows,' said an officer lying next to me on the wet slope. 'Oh, topping'" (Gibbs 1917: 179).

This "beautiful" and "leisurely" collision between flesh and hot, flying steel cost the main allied force of Canadian troops dear. At Vimy, there were 3,598 killed and 7,004 wounded in three days. Gibbs, writing for a British audience, even avoids clarity about the preponderance of Canadian soldiers in the assault. He writes of "English, Scottish and Canadian troops," though the majority involved in the action he describes were Canadian. It hardly matters, to Gibbs who makes no pretence of objectivity; the soldiers are "we," not "they".

In his post war memoir, *Adventures in Journalism*, Gibbs explained: "We identified ourselves absolutely with the Armies in the field...We wiped out of our minds all thought of personal scoops and all temptation to write one word which would make the task of officers and men more difficult or dangerous. There was no need of censorship of our despatches. We were our own censors" (Gibbs 1923).

Lovelace confirms (1978) that formal censorship has been unfairly blamed for British newspapers' glorification of the First World War. Self-censorship by reporters, editors and proprietors played a more important role. In this respect, the *Guardian*'s editor C. P. Scott, who zealously "enforced the principles of civil and religious Liberty", edited in harmony with his Conservative nationalist peers. Scott dismissed as "too damaging for publication" a letter from a wounded corporal in which the soldier revealed that he had seen conscripts shelled by friendly fire (Wilson 1970: 142).

Journalism's failure to tell the truth about the 1914-1918 carnage

So, editors and proprietors share ultimate responsibility for professional journalism's failure between 1914 and 1918 to tell the public the truth about the brutal, squalid war fought in their name. As a result, a student wishing to understand the reality of the Western Front learns more from the poems of Rupert Brooke and Wilfred Owen, or from paintings such as The Ypres Salient at Night and The Menin Road by Paul Nash than from contemporary newspaper reports.

But journalists have consciences, and the pioneer embedded reporters of the British press failed, abjectly, to exercise theirs. For them, embedding was a Faustian pact from which they emerged diminished along with the titles they wrote for. In the clash of cultures between liberal fourth estate ideals and the drilled, obedient hierarchy of army and state, military and civil power triumphed without having to try very hard. Embedding helped power to defeat truth, just as it was designed to.

Politicians and the military learned the lesson; embedding is a convenient way to encourage journalists to privilege the security and strategy of the state over freedom of speech. It trades access for obedience. Some journalists learned too. The Front Generation was deeply embittered about reporting that sanitised the hell they had endured. The great clash of ideologies that emerged from their suffering nurtured enduring examples of the excellence conflict reporting can produce when journalists are free to witness what they choose, to gather facts unimpeded and to report honestly.

Two fine examples of frontline reporting conducted by non-embedded reporters emerged from a conflict in which both sides deployed ideologically partisan and embedded correspondents to their own advantage: the Spanish Civil War. Preston records that in 1938, Martha Gellhorn wrote to her friend, Eleanor Roosevelt:

> You must read a book by a man named Steer; it is called the *Tree of Gernika*. It is about the fight of the Basques – he's the London *Times* man

– and no better book has come out of the war and he says well all the things I have tried to say to you the times I saw you, after Spain. It is beautifully written and true, and few books are like that, and fewer still that deal with war (Preston 2008: 263).

Steer was George Lowther Steer, a short, slight, redhead born in East London in 1909 and educated at Winchester College and Christ Church College, Oxford, where he obtained a double first in Classical Greats.

Steer's courageous reporting of the Spanish civil war

Before travelling to Spain he had covered the German reoccupation of the Saarland for the *Yorkshire Post* and the second Italo-Ethiopian war of October 1935-May 1936 as a special correspondent for *The Times*. He arrived in Spain, again as a special correspondent for *The Times*, in August 1936, less than a month after General Jose Sanjurjo launched the nationalist military coup against Spain's democratically elected Popular Front government that started the civil war.

Initially working under the supervision of Nationalist press censors, Steer witnessed brutal repression and saw civilians murdered, including women who complained that their husbands had been killed by the Falange and Guardia Civil (ibid: 191-238). He was expelled from Nationalist territory, almost certainly on ideological grounds, and returned to Spain in January 1937, landing in Republican territory at Bilbao.

Steer was immensely impressed by the Basque people, a sentiment that probably reinforced his courage when, on the 26 and 27 April 1937, he spent hours interviewing survivors and collecting evidence in the ruins of Guernica. In *The Tree of Guernica*, he would later write that a journalist is "a historian of every day's events, and he has a duty to his public". In the ruins of the Basque capital he performed superbly the journalist/historian's job as a meticulous recorder of reality.

Armed with the evidence of his own eyes, numerous interviews carefully recorded in his notebook, and the remains of German incendiary bombs that he collected from the ruins, George Steer filed a report describing the Luftwaffe bombardment that destroyed Guernica and inaugurated the style of intense aerial bombardment that would soon torture British conurbations including London, Coventry and Clydebank.

His sober, descriptive prose identified this as a new form of warfare. It was published on 28 April in *The Times* and *The New York Times*. On 29 April it appeared in translation in the French Communist newspaper *L'Humanité* (ibid: 280), where it was read by Pablo Picasso and inspired his famous painting (Chipp 1988: 58-70).

The courage of Jay Allen

Comparable with Steer's report from Guernica in terms of its value as a first draft, and even more impressive as testament to its author's courage, is *Chicago Tribune* correspondent Jay Allen's treatment of the Nationalist massacre of Republican prisoners at Badajoz in August 1936.

Jay Allen was among the best informed correspondents to cover the Spanish civil war. He had lived in the country for several years prior to 1936 and had become intimately acquainted with its politics. He knew senior figures on both sides of the conflict, and had interviewed Franco, but his sympathies undoubtedly lay with the Republic, and specifically with the Socialist Party.

Allen had visited Badajoz four times in the year before August 1936 while conducting research for a book about agrarian reform in Spain (Preston op cit: 296-297). He heard rumours of mass killings by the Nationalist troops who had captured the town while he was reporting from Lisbon on the delivery by a German ship, the *Kamerun*, of eight hundred tons of military equipment destined for General Franco's forces. He set off immediately to cross back from Portugal into Spain.

Allen's report, filed from Elvas in Portugal on 25 August 1936, deserves to be read by every student of journalism. It reveals a crime against humanity, the cold-blooded butchery of thousands of Republican, Socialist and Communist militiamen and militiawomen by Nationalist firing squads.

He obtained his story by interviewing witnesses and by traveling through the town, incognito. He did so with the conscious intention of remaining independent, recording: "I believe I was the first newspaperman to set foot there without a pass and the inevitable shepherding by rebels, certainly the first newspaperman who went knowing what he was looking for."

Reporters who avoided "deliberate shepherding" wrote enduring journalism that revealed truth about the terror perpetrated on both sides of that conflict. Though they were outnumbered by partisan colleagues, many of whom meekly accepted shepherding and censorship, they penned first drafts which have served as secure foundations for future historical research.

Independent reporting of the Second World War

In the Second World War, a conflict during which taking the Allied side required no moral compromise, independent reporting continued to prove its worth and to demonstrate, emphatically, the importance of balancing the perspective offered by embedded correspondents with other, more diverse material.

Among the clearest examples of the usefulness to representative democracy of independent reporting of conflict was compiled during the London Blitz by Peter Ritchie Calder, a *Daily Herald* reporter, who later worked as a propagandist in the Political Warfare Executive.

Calder's achievement is to demonstrate through meticulous eyewitness reporting of the Blitz in the East End of London, the incompetence of government preparations for aerial bombardment, and, crucially, for the care and support of those who survived it. His best work is collected in a slim volume, *The Lesson of London*, published in 1941 as part of the Searchlight Books series edited by T. R. Fyvel and George Orwell (Calder 1941).

In narratives laced with authentic quotes and detail, Calder reveals the absence of planning to deal with homelessness and the dearth of facilities to assist its victims. The government had prepared to bury tens of thousands of dead. It had made no effective arrangements to accommodate, feed and console survivors.

His criticism of "official blundering" is fearless. He describes "Maginot lines of official obstructions" separating the needy from help and condemns the bureaucracy of London boroughs as "a jig-saw of parochialism" and "a cockpit of jealous officials as jealous of their territorial integrity as a Beer Baron of his precinct".

Calder reported that Blitzed Londoners were not fighting for "a democracy of privileges and slums" and that during the intense aerial bombardment of Britain's capital by the Luftwaffe, "an epoch went crashing down in the angry brown dust of crumbling property". He depicts class tension: "In the perspective of history, the Lesson of London may be that 'Black Saturday,' September 7th 1940, was as significant in its own way as Bastille Day, July 14th 1789," in a style that is very different from the "all in it together," message assiduously promoted by the Ministry of Information.

Calder's reporting broke with the docile consensus among journalists that had produced the "myth of Dunkirk". It predicted the bold, reforming mood that would be made policy by the Labour government elected in 1945. It demonstrates the value to the public sphere (Habermas 1991) of bold, independent, fact-based journalism published in mainstream newspapers with substantial readerships and concomitant social and political influence.

Post 1945: influential reporting from conflict zones continues

The period post 1945 saw the production of plentiful cases of influential reporting from conflict zones by non-embedded journalists. Some noteworthy examples include; James Cameron's work for *Picture Post* in the Korean War, John Pilger's coverage of the Vietnam War for the *Daily Mirror*, Robert Fisk's reporting of the September 1982 massacres at the Lebanese refuges camps at Sabra and Chatila for *The Times* (Carey 1987), Allan Little, of the BBC's award winning reports for BBC Radio from former Yugoslavia (Little 1996) and Allan Little and Jeremy Bowen's coverage for BBC Radio and Television of the February 1991 destruction of the al-Amiriyah bunker in Baghdad during the first Gulf War.

Such independent coverage has paid dividends in Afghanistan too. Among the most compelling examples is the work for the *Guardian* of Gaith Abdul-Ahad, an Iraqi journalist and deserter from Saddam Hussein's army, who advertises his own work online at the website www.unembedded.net. Abdul-Ahad's reconstruction through witness interviews of the events following a Nato airstrike on two fuel tankers in the Chardarah district of Kunduz province in northern Afghanistan, conveys a powerful impression of the physical, emotional and economic forces unleashed among Afghan civilians. (Abdul-Ahad 2009a).

His investigation of fraud in Afghanistan's electoral process during the 2009 Presidential election and his intrepid excursions to interview Taliban fighters, arms traders, opium farmers and tribal leaders in rural Afghanistan have supplied priceless and salutary context (Abdul-Ahad 2009b). Such reporting attains the highest standards of depth and accuracy. It is compiled at immense risk to the reporter. In December 2009 Abdul-Ahad and two Afghan journalists with whom he was working were held hostage for six days by an armed gang in the mountainous region of Afghanistan bordering Pakistan's North-West Frontier Province (Taylor 2009).

In September 2009, Stephen Farrell, a *New York Times* reporter who resolved to investigate the Kunduz fuel-tanker bombing, was also abducted together with his interpreter, Sultan Munadi. The men were held by Taliban fighters. Mr. Farrell was rescued when British soldiers assaulted the compound in which he was held. Mr. Munadi died in crossfire. Farrell's release came about approximately three months after another unembedded reporter, David Rohde, also of the *New York Times*, escaped after being held hostage for seven months in Afghanistan and Pakistan (Schmitt 2009).

Other unembedded reporters, including Yvonne Ridley of the *Daily Express* (in 2001) and Kosuke Tsuneoka, a Japanese reporter (in 2010) have been kidnapped and detained while attempting to cover Afghanistan without the formal protection of the military .

Unembedded reporting from Afghanistan today

Despite the risks, unembedded reporters continue to work in Afghanistan. The BBC's Kabul bureau is routinely staffed by a correspondent operating independently of ISAF (author's interview, 8 March 2010). This journalist's security is protected by a private force recruited by the BBC. The arrangement has facilitated coverage of social and economic conditions beyond the conflict zones e.g. Allan Little's exploration of economic prospects in Herat for BBC television (BBC News 2010).

The lesson from journalism's history has not been forgotten entirely. Quality broadsheet editors and their counterparts in radio and television know that embedded reporting can easily turn into cheerleading for "our boys". Embedded correspondents know it too. Among the insights offered to the 18 March 2010 conference at Coventry University by reporters recently embedded in Afghanistan was that embedding is safer, because, in Vaughan Smith's words: "You have a lot of guns protecting you," but it reduces the human interest content of coverage and privileges reports concerning combat and military derring-do.

Vaughan Smith showed the conference images of the nuclear mushroom cloud over Hiroshima and children in Vietnam. He said: "In Afghanistan we are doing the mushroom clouds, but not the babies." Embedding tends to produce that outcome and when the dangers of operating independently are extreme the narrowing of journalism's perspective may become acute.

The diverse, chaotic and unlovable market-based news industry, which liberal theorists and democratically elected politicians believe protects liberty and safeguards truth, has understood the compromises inherent in embedded reporting since 1918. It has acknowledged through editorial decisions that, while embedding may be a necessary compromise, it is not an intrinsically virtuous technique.

Before the multimedia era, the news industry performed its duty to democracy by ensuring, whenever possible, that embedded reporting was partnered and balanced by the work of brave and dissident reporters operating beyond the restrictions embedding imposes. Since the advent of online news it has often deployed user-generated material to convey perspectives not available to professional reporters.

Why the embeds tell only a small fraction of the story

In Afghanistan user-generated content is rare and the difficulties confronting independent journalists are uniquely hard to overcome. Embedding is easier and cheaper. It enables correspondents to witness an important aspect of the conflict. They see ISAF and Afghan soldiers in action. They report on training and reconstruction projects in which ISAF forces are involved. They fill pages, websites and programmes with dramatic reports. They only tell a small fraction of the story.

Embedded reporters do not wholly define their own missions. They are shown things their military sponsors believe they should see. Their liberty to seek out stories and follow leads, already limited by security concerns and, often, by lack of language skills, is further restricted by the terms of their contract with the military.

The bravery and team spirit of military units in conflict zones are intriguing to journalists. The atmosphere they generate is distinct from the atmosphere of a newsroom. But, despite cultural dissonance, many embedded correspondents perceive drama and glamour in military activity. Their response is amplified in newsrooms outside the conflict zone, where the circulation and ratings boosting potential of vivid action stories from the frontline have been familiar to editors for centuries.

The military's interest in ensuring that conflict is depicted in ways that supports their mission is legitimate. Equally important is an accurate first draft of history that can inform electorates in ISAF nations, analyse the consequences of the ISAF mission, investigate allegations of wrongdoing by ISAF forces and their allies and promote social empathy for the victims of war, civilian and military.

Historical precedent offers suggestions that these core journalistic duties have, in the past, been most effectively performed when the work of embedded reporters is partnered and informed by journalism produced by unembedded colleagues operating apart from the military.

Some of the many questions posed by the current Afghan coverage

The news industry's coverage of Afghanistan poses questions that merit empirical research. To what extent does the risk of kidnapping and violence permit non-embedded reporters to gather facts and impressions independently? How many news organisations permit their journalists to work in Afghanistan if they are not embedded and, when this does occur, are they able to work in the zones where conflict is intense?

Does the pulsating glamour and dazzling martial imagery of much embedded reporting squeeze out of news coverage reporting that does not depict combat? Finally, when even embedded correspondents such as Lang and Hamer can lose their lives, is Afghanistan now too dangerous to allow journalism to produce a reliable first draft and so perform effectively its duty to the public sphere?

References

Abdul-Ahad, Gaith (2009a) Victims' families tell their stories following Nato airstrike in Afghanistan. Available online at http://www.guardian.co.uk/world/2009/sep/11/afghanistan-airstrike-victims-stories, accessed on 7 April 2010

Abdul-Ahad, Gaith (2009b) New evidence of widespread fraud in Afghanistan election uncovered. Available online at http://www.guardian.co.uk/world/2009/sep/18/afghanistan-election-fraud-evidence, accessed on 8 April 2010

BBC.co.uk. Available online at http://news.bbc.co.uk/1/hi/events/newstalk/correspondent_biographies/228081. stm, accessed on 7 April 2010

Bejerot, Nils (1974) The six day war in Stockholm, *New Scientist*, Vol. 61, No. 886 pp 486-487

Calder, Ritchie (1941) *The Lesson of London,* London, Secker and Warburg

Carey, John (ed.) (1987) *The Faber Book of Reportage,* London, Faber and Faber

Chipp, Herschel B. (1988). *Picasso's Guernica: History, Transformations, Meanings,* Berkeley California, University of California Press

D'Alieso, Renata and Wilton, Suzanne (2010) Tenacious, eager and skilled, Michelle Lang was a natural reporter, *Vancouver Sun,* 3 January. Available online at http://www.vancouversun.com/news/tenacious+eager+skilled+Michelle+lang+na tural+reporter, accessed on 2 April 2010

De Fabrique, Nathalie, Romano, Stephen J., Vecchi, Gregory M., and Van Hasselt Vincent, B (2007) Understanding Stockholm Syndrome, FBI Law Enforcement Bulletin July, Vol. 76, N,. 7. Available online at http://www.fbi.gov/publications/leb/2007/july2007/july2007leb.htm#page10, accessed on 18 May 2010

Committee to Protect Journalists (2010). Available online at http://www.cpj.org/killed/asia/afghnainstan/murder.php, accessed on 22 March 2010

Gibbs, Philip (1917) *Report on the Battle of Vimy Ridge, 9-10 April 1917.* Available online at http://www.firstworldwar.com/source/vimy_gibbs.htm, accessed on 29 March 2010

Gibbs, Philip (1923) *Adventures in Journalism,* London, Heinemann

Habermas, Jurgen (1991) *The Structural Transformation of the Public Sphere,* Cambridge, Polity Press

Knightley, Phillip (2004) *The First Casualty,* 3rd edition, London, André Deutsch

Little Allan (2010) *Afghans more optimistic for future, survey shows.* Available online at http://news.bbc.co.uk/1/hi/world/south_asia/8452284.stm, accessed on 8 April 2010

Little, Allan and Silber, Laura (1996) *The Death of Yugoslavia,* London, Penguin

Lovelace, Colin (1978) British press censorship during the First World War, George Boyce, James Curran and Pauline Wingate (eds) *Newspaper History from the 17th century to the present day,* London, Constable

Ministry of Defence (2007) *Exclusive: Embedding – the MoD's view.* Available online at http://www.mod.uk/DefenceInternet/DefenceNews/MilitaryOperations/Exclusiv eEmbeddingTheModsView.htm, accessed on 22 March 2010

Ministry of Defence (2008) *Green Book*

Mirror.co.uk (2010) *Sunday Mirror* reporter Rupert Hamer killed in Afghanistan, 1 January. Available online at http://www.mirror.co.uk/news/top-stories/2010/01/10 sunday-mirror-reporter-rupert-hamer-killed-in-afghanistan-115875-21956665, accessed on 2 April 2010

Online Newshour (2003) Embedding reporters with the military. Available online at http://www.pbs.org/newshour/bb/media/jan-june03/warcoverage_3-22.html, accessed on 23 March 2010

Preston, Paul (2008) *We Saw Spain Die: Foreign Correspondents in the Spanish Civil War*, London, Constable

Read, Donald (1992) *The Power of News – The History of Reuters*, Oxford, Oxford University Press

Robinson, Bruce (2009) *The Pals Battalions in World War One*. Available online at *http://www.bbc.co.uk/history/british/britain_wwone/pals_01.shtm*, accessed on 2 April 2010

Schmitt, Eric (2009) *Seized Times reporter is freed in Afghan raid that kills aide*. Available online at http://www.newssafety.org/index.php?option=com_content&view=article&id=15347:seized-times-reporter-is-freed-in-afghan-raid-that-kills-aide&catid=109:afghanistan-media-safety&Itemid=100105, accessed on 7 April 2010

Shane, Leo (2009) Army used profiles to reject reporters, *Stars and Stripes*, Mideast edition, 29 August

Schudson, Michael (2008) *Why democracies need an unlovable press*, Cambridge, Polity Press

Taylor, Matthew (2009) Guardian team released by Afghanistan kidnappers. Available online at http://www.guardian.co.uk/world/2009/dec/16/ghaith-abdul-ahad-guardian-afghanistan, accessed on 7 April 2010

Wilson, Trevor (ed.) (1970) *The Political Diaries of C.P. Scott 1911-1928*, London, Collins

Note on the author

Tim Luckhurst is Professor of Journalism at the University of Kent and the founding head of the university's Centre for Journalism. He is best known as a former editor of the *Scotsman*, Scotland's national newspaper. He began his career in journalism on BBC Radio 4's *Today* programme for which he produced, edited and reported from the UK and abroad. For BBC Radio he covered the Romanian Revolution of 1989, reported from Iraq, Israel, Jordan and Kuwait during the first Gulf War and reported the Waco Siege. He reported conflict in Former Yugoslavia from Kosovo, Macedonia and Serbia for the *Scotsman*. He was co-editor of Today's coverage of the 1992 General Election and worked as the BBC's Washington Producer during the first year of the Clinton presidency. He returned to the UK to become a senior member of the team that designed, launched and edited BBC Radio Five Live. From 1995 to 1997 he was Editor of News Programmes at BBC Scotland. He joined the *Scotsman* in 1997 as Assistant Editor and was appointed Deputy Editor in 2008 and editor in January 2000. He has won two Sony Radio Academy Gold Awards for news broadcasting (*The Romanian Revolution 1989* for Radio 4's *Today* programme and the *IRA ceasefire of 1995* for Radio Five Live). His publications include *This is Today: A Biography of the Today Programme* and contributions to *What a State: Is Devolution for Scotland the End of Britain?* He writes for publications including the *Guardian* and the *Independent* and is a frequent contributor to programmes on BBC Radio and Television, Sky News, LBC and Talksport. He is a member of the jury for the annual UACES/Reuters Reporting Europe Competition.

How the media distorted the truth on Afghanistan, ignored it or focused on soldiery valour in the face of evil

Phillip Knightley, author of the seminal history of war reporting, *The First Casualty*, argues that the mainstream media, by deciding that in time of war its best interests lie in supporting the government of the day, has surrendered its right to report and its duty to provide the first draft of history

In south Mumbai, India, on the road to the military cantonment, the navy hospital, and the English cemetery, lies the Church of St. John the Evangelist. Built by the British to commemorate the dead of the disastrous First Afghan War of 1838, it is known locally as "the Afghan Church". Just inside the entrance is a marble plaque inscribed: "In memory of the officers, non-commissioned officers and private soldiers, too many to be recorded, who fell mindful of their duty, by sickness or by the sword in the campaigns of Sind and Afghanistan 1838-1843." It is unlikely any current American general, Nato general, British general, Western politician or war correspondent has read this plaque. They should have.

The campaigns of Sind and Afghanistan were an unmitigated disaster and ended in a humiliating rout. After five years of optimistic alliances, skirmishes, "final pushes" and full-on battles, 16,000 British soldiers and their Indian allies began a final retreat from the battlefields of Afghanistan. They were wiped out. Only one, a medical officer, Surgeon Dr William Brydon, survived to tell what had happened.

There was no real apportioning of blame. This was the British Empire at its imperial peak. Military setbacks in far corners of the world were part of life. To have questioned why would have been considered unpatriotic and little short of treachery. All that was important, as the Afghan Church memorial makes clear, was that the dead had been "mindful of their duty".

It will be different this time. When Britain and the United States finally declare victory and leave Afghanistan, their tails between their legs, there will be a major laying-of-blame exercise. And one outstanding candidate for this blame will be the role played by the Western media. If it is to have any value in wartime, then surely the duty of the media is to tell the people what is really going on, as distinct from what the government says is going on; to penetrate propaganda and lies; to provoke debate and discussion and reach a first draft of the history of the war.

With few honourable exceptions, in the Afghanistan war the media failed on all these counts. It accepted the military's version of the war. It either ignored the truth, twisted it, distorted it or found ways of presenting it as a simple story of soldierly valour in the face of evil. It made no attempt to analyse and explain the war and its background to readers and viewers nor to challenge the premises on which the war was based. As a result, the gulf between the people and the politicians over the fighting could scarcely be wider.

The British army suffered casualties at a level not seen since the 1950s. The United Nations reported that Afghan civilian deaths doubled in 2009. Two-thirds of the British public believed that the war was unwinnable and that the troops should be brought home as soon as possible. Yet the political class in Britain seemed determined to cling to Nato and the United States rather than represent the will of the voters. And it did so supported by much of the media.

No one even sought to explain how the Taliban grew from a few dozens fighters in the 1990s to become the bane of the West and why an international coalition of 130,000 troops was insufficient to defeat it. Few drew attention to the military's lack of understanding of its enemy, of Western troops' failure to appreciate Afghanistan's culture and traditions or to speak one of the local languages: their only communication with locals was through the barrel of a gun. Instead, ignorance and hubris was rife. For instance, the senior British commander involved in planning deployment of British troops in Helmand province in 2006, Rear Admiral Chris Parry, admitted four years later: "We didn't realise the complexity and character of the context in which we were going to fight. In fact, we didn't realise that we were going to fight."[1]

How the media under-estimated the 9/11 trauma in America

The media's first error occurred early on. It was to under-estimate the trauma that the 9/11 terror attacks inflicted on the American psyche. The nature of the attacks deprived Americans of an essential part of their traditional "coming-to-terms" healing process – that of revenge. This is deeply ingrained in the American narrative and expressed in almost all the legends of the West: the good man grievously wronged confronts the perpetrators and kills them.

This was not possible with 9/11; the perpetrators were already dead. But George W Bush and his advisers realised the need to hold someone to account and chose an awe-inspiring display of American military might against the country that had "harboured" the terrorists, Afghanistan. They justified this by saying that Afghanistan's Taliban government was sheltering the instigator of 9/11, Osama bin Laden. Bush, dubbed by *Time* magazine "the lone Ranger", announced: "We're coming to getcha", and put bounties on the heads of terrorists, payable, as it said, on the old Western wanted posters: "Dead or alive".

The Pentagon already had in place a plan for its media strategy in the war. The principal architect of the American plan was Bryan G. Whitman, deputy assistant Secretary of Defense. Its essence can be summed up in four points:
1. emphasise the dangers posed by the Afghan regime;
2. dismiss and discredit those who cast doubt on these dangers;
3. do not get involved in appeals to logic but instead appeal to the public's hearts and minds, especially hearts;
4. drive home the message to the public: "Trust us. We know more than we can tell you."

Whitman convinced his Pentagon bosses that this plan could not only shape opinion in the United States but all over the Western world. He was proved right.

Obviously, Afghanistan was in no position to invade the United States or Britain so both governments had to claim that they needed to fight the war in Afghanistan to keep the streets of their home cities free from terrorists. Surprisingly, remarkably few commentators in the media highlighted how ludicrous this claim was. Among the exceptions were the veteran White House correspondent, Helen Thomas, and Simon Jenkins, of the *Guardian*. Thomas asked President Obama: "Mr. President, when are you going to get out of Afghanistan? Why are you continuing to kill and die there? What is the real excuse? And don't give us this Bushism: 'If we don't go there, they'll all come here'."[2]

Simon Jenkins wrote in the *Guardian* that there had never been a shred of evidence that the Taliban wanted to conquer Britain. He quoted the then-Prime Minister Gordon Brown as claiming: "Three quarters of terrorist plots until now that we have had to deal with...emanate from the Afghanistan-Pakistan border." And then Jenkins commented, "But what does emanate mean? 9/11 emanated from Germany but we did not bomb the Rhine."[3]

The media allowed the government to get away with "keeping the streets safe" justification and labelled anyone querying it as "disloyal to our troops". The media then colluded in keeping any dissent quiet throughout the general election. Afghanistan was simply not on the agenda. What little reporting there was from the front emphasised how well the campaign was going. Every "final push" was followed by a claim of victory, which may have boosted military morale but was no help to public comprehension.

How to explain the media silence on Afghanistan?
Can we explain this media silence on Afghanistan? There were indications in the first days of the fighting of how it came about. This pre-emptive, punitive war began at night. That was appropriate because the governments of Britain and the

United States seemed determined to keep their citizens in the dark about what was really happening in Afghanistan.

No Western war correspondents were on the ground where the air strikes took place. Hundreds had gathered across the borders in nearby countries but many were confined to their hotels by local authorities. All they could do for the television cameras was to point to plumes of smoke from local riots in the distance.

Journalists in London interviewed fellow journalists in Pakistan, each as ignorant as the other. Television cameras showed crowds of journalists outside 10 Downing Street. In the TV studios expert after expert paraded their expertise. Rumours and speculation were rife. The truth was that nobody outside government knew anything. The public was forced to rely on statements by Defence Secretary Geoff Hoon, the Chief of Defence Staff Admiral Sir Michael Boyce, President Bush, Prime Minister Blair, a US Air Force spokesman, the Taliban ambassador to Pakistan, Abdul Salam Zaeef, and Arab TV stations. But all of these were parties to the war and had cases to make. History showed us that we had no reason to trust any of them. Where oh where was the voice of the informed, objective war correspondent?

No doubt the coalition was delighted that war correspondents had no real access to the war because the bombing of Afghanistan was always going to be difficult to "sell" to the public. No matter how you "spin" it, the spectacle of two of the most powerful, industrialised nations on earth bombing a Third World agricultural country in the middle of a famine could only cause humanitarian concern.

Bombing: not so pinpoint after all

This was why President Bush and Prime Minister Blair stressed that they had no quarrel with the people of Afghanistan and no quarrel with Islam. They insisted that allied strikes had specifically targeted Taliban military installations, air fields and air defence sites and added that civilian populations had been deliberately avoided. The British government said: "Neither the Afghan civilian population nor their homes or property have been targeted." They may not have been targeted, but were any hit? We were told during the Gulf War of 1991 and the Nato bombing in the Kosovo conflict in 1999 that the "pinpoint" accuracy of modern bombing and missile strikes ensured minimum civilian casualties – only to learn when the wars were over that this was not so.

Civilians died in large numbers. The Taliban ambassador in Pakistan said that this was also the case in Afghanistan. But he refused to give figures, or say where they died and how he knew. The other tactic of the Alliance to win and keep public support for strikes on Afghanistan was to mix food and medical supplies with the bombs, surely the first time in history something so bizarre has occurred. But both Bush and Blair realised that all it would take to shatter this support would be one image– television or photograph – of an Afghani woman cradling in her arms a the body of baby killed by an air strike.

For this reason the greater the secrecy surrounding the air war the better as far as the British and American governments are concerned. They were not too happy to allow even something as innocuous as interviews with the bomber pilots, much less invite war correspondents to fly with them as they did in the Second World War.

The one interview with a pilot who took part in the first strike was so tightly controlled that he was given a code name – "Woodstock" – and revealed only that his mission had "come together like a finely-oiled machine". This reluctance to say anything was no doubt the result of criticism an interview with a young American pilot in northern Italy before he went off to bomb Kosovo: "It's a lot of fun. I love my job. It's like playing a video game and riding a roller coaster at the same time."[4]

So the coalition had an easy ride from the media because the balance had swung even further in favour of the military because of the coalition's reliance on air power and special operations (off limits for the media). Even the few pools for correspondents that were arranged were abandoned. In one instance, when US forces were hit by "friendly fire", journalists stationed in a nearby Marine base were locked in a warehouse so that they could not report it. Later public affairs officers distributed to these journalists a press release giving an account of what had occurred. The release had been compiled back in the United States at Central Command in Tampa, Florida.

When American special forces raided the headquarters of Taliban leader Mullah Omar in the middle of the night, the only coverage they allowed was their own. The raid was a disaster, the official account a whitewash, and the whole charade exposed by Seymour Hersh in a devastating account in the *New Yorker* magazine on 12 November 2002. Mulling this over, Whitman wondered if the Pentagon's whole approach to the media needed reappraisal.

The Kosovo campaign – unprecented in the history of warfare

Since the end of the Cold War, the United States had developed methods of warfare that reduced the number of American military casualties. Then in 1999, Nato's first war, the 78-day bombing campaign against Yugoslavia, was won by air power alone, employing the highest proportion of precision weaponry ever used in an air operation and without any loss of life in combat operations on Nato's side – an event unprecedented in the history of warfare.[5] This success had an unexpected side effect – with few or no British and American casualties to report, the Western media began to concentrate on enemy casualties, especially civilian. The military regarded this as a dangerous development because it could erode public support for a war

This was true. Slowly and then with a rush, reports began to appear of civilian casualties from American bombing in Afghanistan. "More than 300 people killed in one night," wrote Richard Lloyd Parry of the *Independent*. "In a family of 40 only a small boy and his grandmother survived." John Pilger wrote in the *Daily Mirror*:

> Out of sight of television cameras, at least 3,767 civilians were killed by US bombs between 7 October and 10 December, 2002 an average of 62 innocent deaths a day, according to a study carried out at the University of New Hampshire in the US. This is now estimated to have passed 5,000 civilians deaths: almost double the number killed on September 11.[6]

So the Pentagon polished up media strategy that would turn attention back to the military's role in the war, especially the part played by ordinary American service men and women. This would require getting war correspondents "on side". But every system that the Pentagon had tried for managing the media in wartime had aroused the media's ire precisely because it felt it was being managed. What if, instead of *managing* the media, the Pentagon *incorporated* the media into the national war effort and enlisted its vast resources in the service of the country as it had done in the Second World War.

Whitman had formulated a system of "embedding", transmitting "products" from the Pentagon, from foreign capitals, and from "in theatre", via correspondents attached to military units, and via mobile press pools, combined information press centres (CPICs) and sub-CPICs. Public Affairs Officers (PAOs) from the Pentagon would scan all the media print – electronic, domestic and international – all the while calculating markets and circulations, and blending 24-hour news channels, nightly news shows and news-magazine formats with entertainment companies. This would provide saturation coverage of the war focusing public attention on the troops in the field "as the best representatives to convey America's intentions and capabilities".[7] It was a comprehensive and cleverly-devised plan but one in which although not many realised it until too late – the traditional war correspondent had been by-passed.

Propaganda to encourage support for war

But Whitman wanted more from the system than just that. He envisaged it as generating the sort of propaganda that would encourage the American public to support the war. The way to produce this propaganda, Whitman had decided, was to make real war more like a Hollywood movie. He had reached this conclusion after the amazing success of "Profiles from the Front Line", a primetime television documentary series which followed the US forces in Afghanistan. The idea for the series had come from Jerry Bruckheimer, the producer who had made *Black Hawk Down* (2001), the feature film which transformed an American military disaster in Somalia into a movie triumph.

Back in 2001, Bruckheimer and fellow producer Bertram van Munster, the man behind the reality television show *Cops*, pitched to the Pentagon the idea of *Soldiers*, a reality television series that would show war through the eyes of American servicemen and women. Van Munster argued: "What these guys are doing out there, these men and women, is just extraordinary. If you're a cheerleader of our point of view that we deserve peace and that we deal with human dignity – then these guys are really going out on a limb and risking their own lives."

Then – and this is the key concept behind "embedding" – Van Munster said: "You can only get accepted by these people [soldiers] through chemistry. You have to have a bond with somebody. Only then will they let you in."[8] Defense Secretary Donald Rumsfeld himself gave the project a green light, Hollywood and the Pentagon working in perfect symmetry. The series went to air just before the invasion of Iraq and its success was influential in deciding the American media strategy for the war.

The media should have noted public reaction to the attack on Afghanistan. All five major US television networks acceded to a request from National Security Adviser Condoleezza Rice to censor statements from Osama bin Laden and al-Jazeera TV, bookseller Barnes and Noble began cancelled readings of books critical of President Bush, and *The New York Times* ran a report on an anti-war rally under the headline: "Peace protesters in Washington urge peace with terrorists". Website columnist Joel Lee described the reporting from Afghanistan as "parochialism of fantastic proportions, ten-second soundbites at the expense of context and substance, all-terror-all-the-time (as one friend of mine put it)…a shameful and uncritical acceptance of Pentagon handouts instead of substantial critical coverage of the ground situation in Afghanistan".[9]

Why Al-Jazeera became target of US missiles

And to make certain that the media had got the message, the Pentagon bombed it home. In 2002, the BBC sent one of its top reporters, Nik Gowing, to Washington to try to find out how it was that its correspondent, William Reeve, who had just re-opened the corporation's studio in Kabul and was giving a live, down-the-line television interview for BBC World, was suddenly blown out of his seat by an American smart missile. Coincidentally, four hours later, a few blocks away, the office and residential compound of al-Jazeera was hit by two more American missiles.

The BBC, al-Jazeeera, and the US Committee to Protect Journalists thought it prudent to find out from the Pentagon what had gone wrong. The Pentagon, in the figure of Rear Admiral Craig Quigley, deputy assistant defense secretary for public affairs, was frank. Nothing had gone wrong. Quigley said that the Pentagon was indifferent to media activity in territory controlled by the enemy, and that the al-Jazeera compound in Kabul was considered a legitimate target because it had "repeatedly been the location of significant al-Qaeda activity".[10] Al-Jazeera said that this activity consisted of interviews with Taliban officials, something that it had hitherto thought to be normal journalism, and that it believed that its office was bombed in revenge for acting as a broadcast conduit for tapes from Osama bin Laden.

All three organisations concluded that the Pentagon was determined to deter Western correspondents from reporting any war from the "enemy" side, would view such journalism as activity of "military significance", and might well bomb the area. Former BBC war correspondent Kate Adie, who had been making her own enquiries at the Pentagon, reached the same conclusion. The officer who briefed her went even further than Quigley. When Adie queried the consequences for correspondents of such a potentially fatal policy, the officer replied: "Who cares…They've been warned."[11]

In the history of war reporting, Afghanistan will, I believe, be regarded as a turning point, the moment marking the military's final triumph over the media. By introducing embedding, media strategy, Hollywood techniques and crude appeals to patriotism, by labelling all dissent "a betrayal of our boys at the front", and by encouraging apathy about civilian casualties, the military/political class in the United States and Britain has removed the reason for the war correspondents' existence. The media, for its part, by failing to provoke debate about policy, by allowing discussion about the issues to wither, and by a conscious decision that in time of war its best interests lie in supporting the government of the day, has surrendered its right to report and its duty to provide the first draft of history.

Notes

----

[1] BBC Radio 4, *Today* programme, 12 June 2010

[2] Associated Press, 8 June 2010

[3] Jenkins, Simon (2010) Let Cameron hasten the end of our absurd Afghan war, *Guardian*, 1 June

[4] BBC, 16 October 1999

[5] Thussu, Daya Kishan (2002) **Managing the media in an era of round-the-clock news**: Notes from India's first tele-war. *Journalism Studies*, Vol. 3, No. 2 pp. 203-212

[6] Pilger, John (2002) The rogue state: America's bid to control the world, *Daily Mirror*, 2 July 2002

[7] Brightman, Carol (2003) Pentagon's recipe for propaganda, Alternet, 20 February. Available online at http://warincontext.org/2003_02_23_archive.html, accessed on 2 January 2010

[8] BBC 2, 18 May 2003, *War Spin*

[9] Zena.Secureforum.com

[10] Gowing, Nick (2002) Don't get in our way, *Guardian*, 8 April 2002. Available online at http://www.guardian.co.uk/media/2002/apr/08/mondaymediasection8, accessed on 10 April 2002

[11] RTE *The Sunday Show*, 9 March 2003

Note on the author

An Australian by birth, Phillip Knightley became part of the celebrated *Sunday Times* Insight team from the 1950s to the 1970s, breaking such famous stories as the Kim Philby spy scandal, the Profumo sex scandal and exposing the effects of thalidomide on new-born babies. Now an acknowledged expert in the dark arts of warfare, having written the seminal text of wartime propaganda *First Casualty*, he lives in London and works as a freelance journalist for publications all over the world. He is the author of some 10 books, covering in depth some of the biggest stories of recent times. Most recently he has written his autobiography *A Hack's Progress* and the critically acclaimed history *Australia: A Biography of a Nation.*

"You have been in Afghanistan, I perceive": SherlockHolmes and the Wootton Bassett jihad.

**Will Barton places the current Afghan conflict in its historical context –
which is so often missed by reporters embedded with the British military.
As a British activity, he says, war in Afghanistan predates fish and chips,
the football league and seaside holidays**

Introduction

Embedded reporting is one of the ways in which war journalism has become
more concerned with stories of immediate individual human interest and less
with the wider coverage of the issues surrounding them. The popular culture of
the 19th century shows that people then knew more of the context of the
campaigns of the British army than we do today. This chapter looks at the
reporting of the current Afghanistan campaign in relation to embedded
reporting, the focus on stories of individual heroism and the need for a wider
perspective that takes into account the sensibilities of more people than just
military personnel, their families and their supporters.

The cliché (variously attributed) has it that the first casualty of war is the truth.
Today it may better to say that the first casualty is history. The age of continuous
news is also the age of the continuous present. Journalism no longer has any
function to explain, merely to report. Every new injured or slain hero has her or
his allotted five minutes of news space but there is no time to ask why their
heroism was necessary in the first place.

Yet Britain's fingerprints are all over Afghanistan and have been for centuries.
Far from being the remote and strange place from which untold and unknown
enemies strike at our way of life and the flower of our youth, it is a country
where we have been interfering and causing trouble since before the days of
Empire. As a British activity, war in Afghanistan predates fish and chips, the

football league and seaside holidays. For that reason it is scattered throughout the popular culture of two centuries.

We do not know exactly when Dr John H. Watson met Sherlock Holmes but we can date it to the early to middle 1880s and we know from Watson's account that the great detective impressed him immediately by deducing, purely from his appearance, where he had recently come from:

> The train of reasoning ran: "Here is a gentleman of a medical type but with the air of a military man. Clearly an army doctor then. He has just come from the tropics, for his face is dark and that is not the natural tint of his skin, for his wrists are fair. He has undergone hardship and sickness as his haggard face says clearly. His left arm has been injured. He holds it in a stiff and unnatural manner. Where in the tropics could an English army doctor have seen so much hardship and got his arm wounded? Clearly in Afghanistan" (Conan Doyle 1887/1986).

It was clear to Holmes as it might be clear to us today if we met a young man with a military haircut, a suntan and a new artificial limb, but Holmes would have known that the occasion for Watson's injury was not the first time the British army had been sending its young soldiers to pointless slaughter and injury in that unhappy land. Watson's campaign was in the Second Afghan War (1878-1880). The first had been fought between 1839 and 1842 and had resulted in one of the worst debâcles in British military history. The second war could be said to have resulted in some advantage to Britain but it was largely redressed by the third Afghan War fought from May to August of 1919.

Britain, Russia and "The Great Game"

Holmes would also have known that these wars were merely phases in the power struggle between European powers, principally Russia and Great Britain, for strategic control of this part of the world known by those white men who happily played chess with the lives and land of the Afghan people, as "The Great Game". His newspapers, secure in their certainty of the moral and racial superiority of the white man to the Afghan, could report these wars in the context of Britain's imperial role.

Such a context is largely absent from today's contemporary coverage of the war. The strategic importance of Afghanistan to the old imperial powers of Europe and Russia, as well as to the USA and the emerging powers of China and India, is hardly ever mentioned. The only context for the war is that given by politicians who claim that it is being fought to deter terrorist attacks on Britain, the US and Europe. This justification is, of course, based on secret intelligence reports that cannot be released into the public sphere for operational reasons. We have no way of confirming whether these reports are as reliable as, say, those of the Iraqi weapons of mass destruction. Nor is much mention made of the fact that the very forces ranged against British troops now are those supported, armed, trained and to some extent even created by the US with the full support of Britain in the proxy war against the Soviet Union in Afghanistan in the 1980s.

This profound "ahistoricalisation" of Britain's present Afghan adventurism is typical of much contemporary news reporting practice. It has become a commonplace to note that the demands of 24-hour broadcast news militate against considered and contextualised reporting and create pressure for immediate sensation. This works alongside the practice of embedding journalists with the armed forces to produce a form of coverage that focuses on the effects of the war on British troops and their families, at the expense of coverage of the actions and operations of the enemy, enemy casualties or collateral damage, or the overall aims and purpose of the war.

Prioritising stories of individual heroics
The news values predominating in coverage of Afghanistan prioritise individual stories of heroism or tragedy among the British forces. There are two recurring motifs: returning heroes (dead or alive) and equipment shortages – the "scandal" of under-equipment.

We are so used now to the ongoing complaint that troops are not being given the up-to-date tools of their trade and that lives are being needlessly lost through this callous negligence, that it takes some effort of imagination to consider how this may look from any other perspective. But let us try.

The British army is a professional force and is one of the most highly trained and best equipped military machines the world has ever seen. British troops are armed with sophisticated modern weapons and have extensive recourse to helicopters, armoured vehicles and advanced systems of electronic surveillance and observation. The are able to call on support, particularly air support, from the US forces, who are, at least in terms of training, equipment and firepower, unquestionably the most awesome fighting force the world has ever seen.

Ranged against them are groups of irregulars, some more trained and disciplined than others, but in no sense a professional or modern army. They appear to have no central command structure or even coherent loyalties. They have no surveillance systems, no air support and are armed mainly with hand-held weapons – assault rifles and rocket launchers. Their most effective means of inflicting casualties is the improvised explosive device – the IED – which stripped of this military nomenculature means a home-made bomb. This is the context in which we need to consider news coverage that reflects unquestioningly the assertion that our troops are being denied the means of basic self protection – mainly helicopters and body armour – that they need to carry out their task.

Of course, it is a legitimate area of concern that troops acting on our behalf and instructions should be properly equipped, but to concentrate arguments on this at the expense of questioning the purpose, legitimacy and value of the action itself is to prioritise a secondary ethical consideration over a primary one. The electorate of a democracy can be said to have ultimate responsibility for a war fought by its armed forces.

Soldiers' professional role will entail hardship and danger

British forces are professional soldiers and must expect that their role will entail hardship and danger, but they are not mere mercenaries, they have a right to expect that they will be sent into action in the national interest. If the actions they take and the casualties they incur and inflict are plainly justified, then it is time to ask whether they are being adequately prepared and equipped for the task. If they are not, they should not be there and the question of equipment doesn't arise. Bluntly, if they should not be there, they should leave and then they will not need any more helicopters or body armour.

However well armed and armoured, any military force engaged in counter insurgency will experience casualties. The main ethical question is whether any of these are necessary, or productive. If the war prevents terrorist atrocities on a large scale, then we can establish a calculus of how much sacrifice is justified to balance how much terrorism. But if the war itself is a cause of terrorism, then such actions are counterproductive and endanger, rather than protect the lives of British citizens.

Embedding, by making it inevitable that reporters will concentrate on the lives and actions of the British troops, is bound to lead the news agenda away from this primary ethical question. Unlike the invasion of Iraq, there has been comparatively little discussion of the reasons for going into Afghanistan. The rhetoric of the Wild West, as George W Bush called for bin Laden to be found "dead or alive" and the extravagant speculations about al-Qaida's state-of-the-art command centre under the Tora Bora mountains (in eastern Afghanistan near the border with Pakistan) modelled less, it seems, on any reliable intelligence than on the models provided by Dr No, Fu Manchu and Ernst Stavro Bloefeldt, are forgotten now. After the US-led forces in December 2001 deployed weapons of astonishing destructive power, only to find that the caves in Tora Bora were just caves, with no computer installations, communications nerve centres or missile launchers, indeed with no terrorists and no Osama bin Laden, the direction of the "war on terror" shifted to Iraq.

The mission to "Get bin Laden" morphed (or "crept" in US military jargon) into regime change and the story was told of the establishment of a modern democracy, under the new father of the nation, Hamid Karzai. Eight years on the regime stands accused of blatant corruption and electoral malpractice, but is still propped up by the USA and Britain, a puppet government, whose writ runs hardly beyond the outskirts of Kabul. The pretence of a police action to apprehend the criminal masterminds Osama bin Laden and Mullah Omar is forgotten.

For more than two hundred years, Afghanis have been fighting to rid their country of foreign occupiers. They have invariably been irregular forces, poorly equipped against massively superior fire power and they have never been crushed. Given the apparent futility of such imperialist adventures, we need to ask whether we shouldn't look at the conflict another way and see beyond the stories of heroics in the face of equipment shortage. It is interesting to look at one of the few attempts made to commend such a change of perspective – the challenge to the Wootton Bassett death cult.

Wootton Bassett and "grief tourism"

Throughout the 21st century, the practice of the British armed forces was to repatriate the bodies of fallen servicemen and women via RAF Lyneham, and from there they are taken to the John Radcliffe Hospital in Oxford for the attention of the coroner. The cortèges pass through the small town of Wootton Bassett and the tradition grew up among the townspeople of honouring the dead by assembling silently to line the route as they passed by. Perhaps inevitably, this dignified response was highlighted by the media and people started coming from further afield, leading to unpleasant suggestions of "grief tourism" (Pavia 2009) and concerns that the event was open to being manipulated for propaganda purposes.

In January 2010, the media reported that an Islamic group known as Islam4UK were proposing to march through Wootton Bassett to highlight the deaths of Muslims in the Afghan conflict (Henry 2010). The reaction was predictable. Politicians, including the Prime Minister, Gordon Brown, denounced this action as "insensitive and provocative", right-wing groups pledged to stage counter-demonstrations and the popular press were incandescent. After a few days, the "leader" of "Islam4UK", Anjem Choudary, announced that the march had been called off, since the important point had been made.

No application to march had ever been lodged with the police. There is no reason to suppose that any preparations had been made by anyone for such a march, nor is there any reason to think that the membership of Islam4UK is greater than one, namely Mr Choudary himself. A single telephone call from him to a newspaper had been sufficient to generate a front page story in the national press, threats of fascist retaliation, condemnation at all levels including the highest and including a number of Muslims who were as appalled, it seems, as the *Daily Mail*.

The stated intention of the "group" was simply a peaceful march. It is hard to see why this should be in itself considered so incendiary (compared say to the marches of the Orange Order through Catholic districts of Northern Ireland, or the marches of racist and fascist organisations through areas of high immigrant populations in England). No breach of the peace was proposed. No insult was being offered to British troops, alive or dead, nor to their families. The question, it seemed, was one of "obvious" offensiveness. No one supposed that any actual harm could come to anyone as a direct result of the proposed march, but the context of the bereavement of military families made it seem a wildly provocative action.

I suspect most people missed the obvious parallel, as I did myself until it was brought to my attention by a colleague (Meah 2010). The central dilemma of both *The Satanic Verses* affair and the matter of the Danish cartoons, was the conflict between the right of free speech enjoyed by citizens of Western democracies and the anger and offence caused by the exercise of the freedom in attacking the Muslim religion by mockery and insult. At the time of controversy over Salman Rushdie's novel, *The Satanic Verses* (from 1989 onwards) when many prominent Muslims accused it of being blasphemous, Western commentators largely took the line that offence was always regrettable but mere offence could not be grounds for challenging freedom of expression. Simply being offended gave no one the right to demand that a book be withdrawn.

By the time of the controversial publication by a Danish newspaper *Jyllands-Posten* (2005) of cartoons offensive to Islamic sensibilities, people were more circumspect, and no national newspaper in the UK published them, yet there were still many who stated publicly that freedom of speech, however distressing to some sensibilities, was indivisible.

Sensibilities of families of war heroes

The chimera of the Wootton Bassett Islamist march neatly turns the argument. That freedom of expression (and the right of public assembly and demonstration enshrined in law) should take precedence over the sensibilities of the families of war heroes was not to be countenanced. When Choudary maintained that the purpose of the proposed march had been fulfilled by the public debate, was he not rightly highlighting the fact that there is one law for Muslims and another for others when it comes to freedom of expression?

The fact remains, however, that the stated purpose of the march – to draw attention to the deaths of others besides the British service personnel that result from their continued presence in Afghanistan – is a legitimate one and one that is obscured, rather than exposed by most of the reporting of the conflict. Coverage that concentrates on the experience of the British armed forces, to that extent is complicit in obscuring a wider and greater tragedy – one that is being carried out in the name of the British electorate. Embedded reporting is at the heart of this distortion of news values. Reporters can only report what they see and in Afghanistan that largely means what is happening to British troops. That emphasis is increased by the attention paid to the campaigns for better equipment and the stories of heroism tied to the repatriated coffins.

The "First Afghan War" (that is the first British-Afghan war) ended in debâcle:

> On January 13th, 1842, soldiers on guard at the British fort in Jalalabad saw a single horseman riding towards them, with all the speed that his maimed and worn-out horse could muster. It was the surgeon Dr Brydon, the only man, it seemed, to survive the fearful journey from Kabul (Dixon 1976).

It was doubtless the story of this other army doctor, the only European survivor of the 1842 campaign (a few Indian troops made it back in the following days) that was in the mind of Sherlock Holmes when he met Dr Watson. Reporting of the present conflict would do well to seek to leave readers as well informed of the context as the Victorians were of theirs. But that would involve sourcing the stories from beyond the compounds of the British army.

References

Conan Doyle, Sir Arthur (1887/1986) A study in scarlet, *The complete illustrated Sherlock Holmes*, Ware, Hertfordshire; Omega Books

Dixon, Norman (1976) *On the psychology of military incompetence*, London; Cape

Henry, Robin (2010) Extremist Muslim group to march through Wootton Bassett, 2 January. Available online at http://www.timesonline.co.uk/tol/news/uk/article6973792.ece, accessed on 1 April 2010

Jyllands-Posten (2005) Editorial cartoons, *Jyllands-Posten*, 30 September

Meah, Azad (2010) Personal communication, 10 January

Pavia, Will (2009) Wootton Bassett fears being in front line of "grief tourism", *The Times*, 29 July

Note on the author

Will Barton is a Senior Lecturer in Media and Communication, Coventry School of Art and Design. He has published a number of papers on the representation and commodification of war and is co-author, with Andrew Beck, of *Get set for communication studies* (EUP 2005). He is currently working with Shao Hongsong on a book about the New Confucianism in contemporary China.

Section 3. Other battles, other frontiers

Banging the drums of war – and promoting peace

Richard Lance Keeble

Too often, the mainstream media bang the drums of war – backing the military and government of the day in their latest imperial adventures. Yet the media can also work to resolve conflict, promote international understanding and cultural harmony. For instance, between 1999 and 2001 the mainstream media worked alongside other civil society organisations in protests against President Estrada in the Philippines culminating in what became known as the Second People's Power Revolution.

In 2001 all-women teams at the Philippines Center for Investigative Journalism produced a series of television reports exposing government corruption that gained massive publicity and were considered as crucial in helping inspire the mass non-violent protests, in part sparked by Estrada's fuelling of civil discord in his brutal clampdown on the Moro Islamic Liberation Front.

Over recent decades interest has been growing across the globe in the possibilities and achievements of peace journalism (see Shinar and Kempf 2007). This journalistic approach draws its inspiration from a particular critique of society and history both national and global, of the mainstream media and its activities particularly in relation to the coverage of conflict. As a result peace journalism tends to promote the role of media as instruments for conflict resolution rather than as propaganda for war. It also theorises the role of progressive journalists within the mainstream and more importantly within alternative media.

One of the most original contributions to the debate over its practical and theoretical aspects appears in *Peace journalism* by Jake Lynch and Annabel McGoldrick (2005). Drawing particularly on the peace research theories of Prof.

Johan Galtung (1998), they argue that most conflict coverage, thinking itself neutral and "objective", is actually war journalism. It is violence and victory orientated, dehumanising the "enemy", focusing on "our" suffering, prioritising official sources and highlighting only the visible effects of violence (those killed and wounded and the material damage).

In a major critique of peace journalism, Agneta Söderberg Jacobsen (2010) highlights the way in which mainstream coverage of conflict marginalises the voices of women. She found that 85 per cent of the news subjects were men while men appear in 75 of the images (ibid: 107). At the same time, Jacobsen argues that a gender perspective is usually missing also in peace journalism theorising (ibid: 113): "Despite an obvious overlap between peace journalism and feminist perspectives on news media there were no references to any common analysis of power structures or society as a whole."

However, in this text, Jake Lynch and Annabel McGoldrick (with additional research by Indra Adnan) celebrate the work of Channel Four's Lindsey Hilsun and the *Guardian*'s Suzanne Goldenberg and their efforts to "humanise" the enemy. And they argue that a lot more peace journalism and the "feminisation" of the Afghan coverage are long overdue.

Significantly, one of the most distinctive features of the propaganda strategy deployed by the US and its allies in the lead-up to the invasion of Afghanistan in 2001 was the stress on "freeing" the local women from oppression. This appropriation of "feminist" rhetoric to legitimise the military strategy received massive media coverage. And yet, as Corinne Fowler, of Leicester University, points out, despite the rhetoric the plight of Afghan women remains largely untouched and their voices unheard.

Commenting on Lynch and McGoldrick's chapter, Fowler argues that, regardless of whether reporting of Afghanistan requires "feminising", only a small minority of reporters – some men, some women – have so far managed to foreground the limitations of their ability to understand Afghan women. And she concludes: "What has not changed is the pro-feminist justification for 'fighting on' (and on) in Afghanistan. Continuing to exclude Afghan women from media spaces, and retaining key assumptions about their passivity, journalists have yet to adopt a critical stance towards political leaders' advocacy for gender equality in Afghanistan."

Being able to report from the frontlines may be crucial for journalists. But it is also important to recognise that there is, in fact, an important price to be paid for it, according to Alpaslan Zerdem, of the Centre for Peace and Reconciliation Studies at Coventry University, argues that there appears little news in the British media about the intentions and work of Provincial Reconstruction Teams (which include combat forces, military personnel in a wide range of programmes such as relief aid distribution, needs assessment, coordination of aid work, liaison with regional commanders and security).

The priority is usually given to reports about the fighting carried out by the British forces against the Taliban and al-Qaida. "The news of fighting and killing are clearly more suitable for headlines but, as those journalists who have been to Afghanistan would only know too well, the 'story' is, in fact, much bigger than that."

Finally, Professor Oliver Boyd-Barrett, of Bowling Green State University, Ohio, does a massively detailed content analysis of the reportage of highly prestigious *New York Times* – and finds that the interests of US/Nato in Af/Pak (Afghanistan and Pakistan) are also the interests of the *NYT*.

References
Galtung, Johan (1998) High road – low road: Charting the course for peace journalism, *Track Two*, Vol. 7, No. 4, Centre for Conflict Resolution, South Africa. Available online at http://ccrweb.ccr.uct.ac.za/archive/two/7_4/p07_highroad_lowroad.html, accessed on 7 April 2009
Lynch, Jake and McGoldrick, Annabel (2005) *Peace journalism*, Stroud, Hawthorn Press

Shinar, Dov and Kempf, Wilhelm (eds) (2007) *Peace Journalism: The State of the Art*, Berlin, Regener

Jacobsen, Agneta Söderberg (2010) When peace journalism and feminist theory join forces: A Swedish case study, Keeble, Richard Lance, Tulloch, John and Zollmann, Florian (eds) *Peace Journalism, War and Conflict Resolution*, New York, Peter Lang pp 105-119

How to improve reporting of the war in Afghanistan: feminise it!

Jake Lynch and Annabel McGoldrick (with additional research by Indra Adnan) argue that a lot more peace journalism and the "feminisation" of the Afghan coverage are long overdue

A cricketing joke from the 1980s saw Mark Waugh, the Australian batsman, nicknamed "Afghan". Struggling to emerge from the shadows of brother Steve, he was always in danger of being overlooked: "the forgotten Waugh". The war in Afghanistan is a canvas on to which powerful intervening nations project their own preoccupations; one that goes through alternate periods of attracting attention and being forgotten.

International media scrutiny suddenly focused on the Taliban early in 2001, over their plan to blow up a treasure from antiquity: the giant Buddhist statues at Bamiyan, on the old Silk Road in the Hindu Kush mountains. Dating from the sixth century, the images were condemned by Taliban leader Mullah Mohammed Omar, as idols – forbidden under sharia law – and duly dynamited. Notable among the interventions to avert their destruction was an offer from the Metropolitan Museum of Art, in New York, to dismantle the two statues and move them to Manhattan.

Indeed, some attributed the decision to "press the button" to anger among clerical rulers at the comparative indifference of the outside world to the suffering of Afghans in daily life. The then-Taliban ambassador-at-large, Sayed Rahmatullah Hashemi, said the destruction was ordered by the Head Council of Scholars after a Swedish monuments expert proposed to restore the statues' heads. Hashemi said: "When the Afghan head council asked them to provide the money to feed the children instead of fixing the statues, they refused and said: 'No, the money is just for the statues, not for the children.' Herein, they made the decision to destroy the statues" (Kaisaimah 2001).

What children? True to form, this flurry of attention followed a display of indifference. January 2000 saw the latest in a series of major earthquakes in the region, which left tens of thousands living under canvas through the harsh winters. In vain did the UN rattle the collecting tin for relief contributions from donor countries, and according to a rare report on BBC Television News, a year later, children were dying of cold owing to a shortage of blankets. Terence Wright recalls this piece, by reporter Matt Frei: "The refugee Sirijillin, who shows us his son's grave, explains that the lack of blankets was responsible for the death. Secondly, seven-month-old motherless child Marjula. And finally the Mohammed family who have just lost two children and a third is dying. The viewer is reminded that nightfall is looming, temperatures will drop, there is overcrowding in the available shelter and that more refugees are on their way" (Wright 2004: 103).

At Turtle Bay, where UN Headquarters gaze down on New York's East River, there was not enough money to pay for blankets to keep children alive. A Taliban representative spoke to the BBC because, he explained, the situation was so grave as to justify breaking the general ban on creating images by giving television interviews. Meanwhile, a few dozen streets uptown, on the edge of Central Park, the Met art gallery stood ready to raise the millions needed, at short notice, to remove the Buddhas from their niches in the sandstone of Bamiyan and transport them thousands of miles to the West.

The vandalism of the statues served to demonise the Taliban, with even the few countries that recognised the legality of their regime – such as Saudi Arabia and the United Arab Emirates – condemning the act as "savage" (Bearak 2001). It left them as a convenient "fall guy", and, sure enough, a few months later came an intense outburst of propaganda against Afghanistan over its alleged complicity in the 9/11 terrorist attacks in New York and Washington – although, as Robert Entman (2003) pointed out, it required a huge campaign of "cascading activation", through layers of representational networks, to deflect attention from the fact that most of the known hijackers were Saudis.

Heikki Luostarinen (1994) produces a formalist model of war propaganda, a narrative form distinctive, he suggests, for being rich in polarising references to positive and negative identification and socialisation. Terence Wright goes on to contrast the initial BBC report on the refugees with another, by the same journalist, in November of that year, after the US had allied its air power to the Northern Alliance forces to rout the Taliban out of Kabul. Now, "the Taliban are no longer treated as reluctant informants, but more as if a strange tribe… The friendly Talib, who was prepared to break his code of conduct to speak to the camera, is replaced by a shadowy figure carrying a Kalashnikov and adorned with confiscated audiotape" (Wright op cit: 104).

These are elements of a group of representational conventions identified, originally by Johan Galtung, as "war journalism" (see Lynch and McGoldrick 2005: 6):

- war/violence-orientated;
- elite-orientated;
- propaganda-orientated;
- victory-orientated.

These elements are mutually reinforcing. "War or violence-orientation", dominant in mainstream journalism by corporate media, sees conflict represented as a zero-sum game of two parties, contesting the single goal of victory. The present authors describe the picture thus constructed as a "tug-of-war", in which "anything that is not, unequivocally, winning, risks being interpreted – and reported – as losing" (ibid).

Each party, thus, acquires a readymade interest in escalating the conflict – trying harder to win – since the only alternative is defeat. Escalation is justified by recourse to propaganda, demonising and dehumanising the "other". War journalism focuses on "the suffering of 'our' side, [especially] able-bodied white males", Galtung continues, at the expense of hiding the human cost of organised violence, both physical and psychological.

"Humanitarian" warfare

The human cost of war has been a site of particular contestation in the conflicts of this century, in Iraq and Afghanistan. Philip Hammond (2007: 38) identifies "humanitarian spectacle" as the visionary objective of conflict involving the US and its allies, to replace the previous crusade of anti-communism: "American military muscle was thus to be given new meaning in the post-Cold War era, no longer as a guarantor of the West's freedoms against the menace of communism but as the steel fist inside a humanitarian velvet glove."

Thus, media representations foreground an implicit "balance of humanitarian advantage" in debates over any decision to go to war in the first place, and proponents typically seek, in representing such a decision and its consequences, to minimise assessments of its impact, in particular in terms of the cost in human lives and displacement of people. Hence the attempts, in Washington and allied capitals, to rebut and downplay the only professionally conducted epidemiological study of the number of extra deaths in Iraq after the invasion of 2003, by the team from Johns Hopkins University in their articles for the *Lancet*, at more than 600,000 in the first three years alone; let alone the millions displaced from their homes (see Brown 2006).

In late 2009, as Nato members met to discuss deploying more troops to Afghanistan, the British foreign secretary, David Miliband, told reporters: "We all know that in the 1990s, Afghanistan was the incubator of international terrorism, the incubator of choice for global jihad" (Schmidt 2009). Leaving aside the point made by Entman and others, that there is little evidence of any connection between Afghanistan and the 9/11 attacks, it appears, from UN figures, that Afghanistan's population grew in the 1990s far more than in the present decade. Those years were, to be sure, troubled, with the infamous "battle of Kabul" of 1994-96 being settled only when the Taliban drove out the warlords carving out their turf, but it was not marked by the systematic aerial bombardment and massive deployment of foreign troops that followed the US intervention of October 2001.

According to calculations derived from figures published by the Population Division of the UN Department of Economic and Social Affairs, there "should" be millions more Afghans alive today, based on extrapolating the 1990s figure for population growth, than there actually are.

Table 1: Changes in population, Afghanistan by comparison with Least Developed Countries and South Central Asian countries (UN 2008):

Area	1990 population (millions)	2000 population (millions)	Increase % 1990-2000	2010 population (millions, projected)	Increase % 2000-2010
Afghanistan	12,580	20,536	63.2%	29,117	41.8%
Least developed countries	524,764	676,929	29.0%	854,696	26.3%
South Central Asia	1,250,453	1,518,322	21.4%	1,780,473	17.3%

In the two categories of which Afghanistan is a member, the Least Developed Countries and South Central Asia, the rate of population growth edged downward by a few percentage points in the first decade of the 21st century as compared with the 1990s. But it slowed in Afghanistan to a much greater extent. Nine years after the US-led invasion and occupation of the country, several million people appear to have gone "missing". Had the growth rate remained the same, over the two decades, the population projection for 2010 would be over 33 million, compared with the actual 29 million.

Because there has been no professionally conducted epidemiological study of Afghanistan, since the US intervention in 2001, there is no way of knowing what has "happened" to them. The United Nations Assistance Mission in Afghanistan recorded 1,798 civilian casualties between January and the end of October 2008, 695 of which were attributable to the US and allies (AIHRC 2009). An early attempt to chart the number of civilian casualties, by Marc Harold, pieced together solely from media and NGO reports, concluded: "What causes the documented high level of civilian casualties – 3,000 to 3,400 [7 October 2001 to March 2002] civilian deaths – in the US air war upon Afghanistan? The explanation is the apparent willingness of U.S. military strategists to fire missiles into and drop bombs upon, heavily populated areas of Afghanistan" (Herold 2002).

The figures reaching the outside world for deaths caused by air strikes and in crossfire cannot, by themselves, account for the disparity, however. The mystery is deeper still when you consider that, since 2002, the UN High Commission for Refugees has repatriated some five million Afghans who fled the country in earlier wars, so they are included in the 2010 figure, and account for nearly two thirds of the increase since 2000 (AIHRC 2009).

War journalism

For much of the period in question, the war in Afghanistan was obscured, in the media of troop-contributing countries, by news from Iraq, to the extent that it became, once again, "the forgotten war" (Ricchiardi 2006). Those assessments came on the basis of reporting in 2006, but since then Afghanistan has come back into focus. The vast majority of reports, in those same media, still deal almost exclusively with the deeds – and deaths – of the occupying soldiery, and/or statements from senior politicians about why they are determined to "stay the course".

This record testifies to the enduring predominance of war journalism. Robert Hackett and Birgitta Schroeder (2008: 34) analyse the content of 522 articles in the Canadian, Israeli and US press as well as Al Jazeera Online, covering the war in Afghanistan and the simultaneous war in Lebanon, in 2006. Ten specific war journalism criteria, derived from the Galtung model, are found to be present in 51.9 per cent of the articles on average, whereas the equivalent score for peace journalism criteria is just 31.6 per cent. War journalism is more dominant in stories filed from Afghanistan itself than any other one of ten locales, and "elite orientation" is the second most frequently occurring war journalism criterion in the whole study, after "focus on the here-and-now".

It suggests the human cost of the war in Afghanistan is being systematically downplayed, according with impressions, from countless stories in Western corporate media over the years, that the voices of Afghan people themselves are nearly always excluded. In Australia, for instance, every time there is news of a further troop deployment or diplomatic development, the sourcing, in the vast majority of local news coverage, is confined to military and/or political leaders. Opinion polls consistently suggest Australians would rather see their troops called home, but there is little or no political traction to that idea since the front benches of both major parties take the opposite view; and it almost never surfaces in the media. So there is little or no perception of urgency, to promote what William Crano (1995) called the "salience" of the issue.

Because there is no familiar human face to the suffering caused by the war – and perhaps inscribed in the population figures – publics in the belligerent countries may – to lend a metaphor to Crano's concept – feel it as an itch, requiring an occasional scratch, but not such an irritant that a salve has to be applied in the form of a change in policy.

This pattern has allowed political leaders and policy-makers in the age of President Obama – a period preceding his actual inauguration and probably dating from his successful campaign for the Democratic nomination – to portray Afghanistan as the "good war", in contrast with Iraq as the "bad war". From before the first night of "shock and awe" over Baghdad, in March 2003, numerous correspondents in the city were sending reports to influential Western media, in which "humanising the enemy" – telling the stories of ordinary Iraqi citizens – was a keynote. One prominent exponent was Suzanne Goldenberg, a foreign correspondent at Britain's *Guardian* newspaper, whose editor, Alan Rusbridger, told a London conference:

> In every war you try and depersonalise the enemy and dehumanise them but I think having someone like Suzanne Goldenberg's quality inside Baghdad talking to ordinary Iraqis and making them terribly human I think is a new element in war, and you can see why politicians don't like it but it also makes it extremely difficult to go to war on a nation when you

are getting that kind of image and I think the humanity of her reporting and Lindsey's (Hilsum, of Channel Four News) was just of a different calibre and texture from the reporting we'd seen before and I think that will in some way make fundamental changes in how war is seen (L:ynch 2008: 213).

War reporting and gender

Is it coincidental that the two reporters Rusbridger picked out were women? Before 1970, only 6 per cent of US foreign correspondents were women (Gibbons 2002). Today, the Brookings Institution estimates that more than one third of US war correspondents are female and they are, according to Sheila Gibbons, having an increasing influence on the content and tone of the coverage. "As the number of women war correspondents approaches critical mass, they appear to be focusing more clearly on the toll that today's wars take on the civilian population – the women and children – who have little or no say in the decisions that lead to mass killing and wounding" (ibid).

Coverage of the war in Afghanistan has remained largely, up to now, "unfeminised", at least in Western corporate media. The deployment of such reporters as Goldenberg and Hilsum to Baghdad has not been emulated, for a variety of reasons. There is not one identifiable "centre" of direct violence, and for Western-employed correspondents, setting out to talk to "ordinary Afghans" has been fraught with dangers and difficulties. Gibbons' comment about traditional, male-dominated war reporting rings true: "dominated by tactical questions, political infighting and policy disputes, [it] can obscure the trauma experienced by women who live in areas targeted for attacks" (ibid), especially since, according to international estimates, women, along with children under 15 who are generally in their care, between them comprise 70 per cent of Afghanistan's population.

With Operation Moshtarak, a Nato attempt to extend the writ of the Karzai government to the "Taliban stronghold" of Marjah, in early 2010, some reporters did pick up on local voices which took issue with the standard propagandistic narrative of polarising references. One source who spoke to

National Public Radio effectively reversed the positive and negative identification:

> Some of the residents are leery. They complain that the last time the government was in charge in Marjah two years ago, corrupt police officers terrorised residents. A tractor driver named Faqir Mohammad said the Taliban brought peace to Marjah and generally didn't interfere in people's business. He added that residents were happy with them. By comparison, he said, police officers in Marjah stole people's motorcycles and cash, and were involved in kidnapping (Nelson 2010).

This perception, brought to listeners by NPR's female Kabul bureau chief, Soraya Sarhaddi Nelson, seldom reaches Western audiences, however. How widespread is it? An important clue can be detected in a rare opinion poll among Afghans, conducted by the US-based International Republican Institute in May 2009, in the run-up to the country's presidential election. Its leading questions, on voting intentions, along with most media reports of its findings, projected on to Afghanistan the foreign political system imposed on the country, in which power is concentrated in the hands of a single centralised presidency.

Buried on the last page of the IRI's own press release, however, is an interesting snippet: "Sixty-eight per cent of respondents feel that the government should reconcile with the Taliban, 14 percent do not." It's unsurprising, when considered in the context of Afghanistan's home-grown political culture, expressed in structures such as *jirgas* and *shuras*, with their round-table format, emphasising the need to reach decisions by deliberation and consensus (International Republican Institute 2009).

In at least two different ways, the continued presence of foreign troops is the chief impediment to reconciliation. The Marjah offensive recruits Afghans, willy-nilly, into what the US field commander, General Stanley McChrystal called "a war of perceptions… in the minds of the participants" (Shanker 2010). They are, in the words of President George W Bush as he announced the invasion, "either with us, or with the terrorists", and civilians who make insufficiently clear, to

McChrystal's men on the ground, which side they're on, run a grievous risk. And as long as they are on the ground, they offer a readymade target to the myriad of armed groups gathered under the simplifying title, Taliban. Follow through on good reporting such as that supplied by Soraya Sarhaddi Nelson; emphasise backgrounds and contexts, and ventilate initiatives to end the violence, from whatever quarter, and you have peace journalism.

Essentialism?

Observing that peace journalism may be a more "feminised" mode of reporting need not essentialise gender characteristics. A useful perspective can be read across from sociolinguistics, in which the focus is "not on biological sex, nor even on the culturally constructed category of gender, but rather on the diverse realisations of the dynamic dimensions of masculinity and femininity", according to Janet Holmes (1997: 215). She finds that "stylistic variability is often greater in women's speech than men's", and relates that to "the ways in which women are often required to use language to construct a much wider range of social identities and express a wider range of social roles than men" (ibid). A peace journalist will have to give voice to people far outside the narrow circle of "official sources": a task that may therefore come more readily, in general, to women than men.

It echoes debates about gender in the context of political discourses and styles, notably over the notion of "soft power". Indra Adnan, Director of the Soft Power Network, explains: "Hard power is the use of force whereas soft power is the use of attraction – two ways to get results in any field of endeavour". Peace journalism "is both a tool and a vehicle for soft power," she adds, "as it enables and models those more open, reciprocal relationships between countries or actors of any kind" (personal communication).

Joseph Nye, who has popularised the term, sees "female skills" of empathising, mediating and seeing the bigger picture as vital to its effectiveness (Nye 2004). Simon Baron-Cohen (2003) calls these characteristics biological and neurological, whereas Susan Pinker (2008) prefers to see them as cultural, arising from the different roles that women traditionally and still occupy in order to bring up children within a community of support.

The now longstanding "disconnect" from public opinion on the Afghan war – both in the country itself and in those supplying the occupying forces – is attributable to "the brute unresponsiveness of institutional frameworks" (Lynch 2009). Media have often presented the same blandly indifferent face, both to the suffering of the Afghan people and to calls, in belligerent countries, for troops to be pulled out. A bit more peace journalism, and a bit more feminisation, are long overdue.

References

AIHRC (2009) *From hope to fear: An Afghan perspective on operations of pro-government forces in Afghanistan*, Afghanistan Independent Human Rights Commission

Baron-Cohen, Simon (2003) *The essential difference*, London, Basic Books

Bearak, Barry (2001) Over world protests, Taliban are destroying ancient Buddhas, *New York Times*, 4 March

Brown, David (2006) Study claims Iraq's "excess" death toll has reached 655,000, *Washington Post*, 11 October. Available online at http://www.washingtonpost.com/wp-dyn/content/article/2006/10/10/AR2006101001442.html, accessed on 15 December 2009

Crano, William D. (1995) Attitude strength and vested interest, Krosnick, Jon, A. and Petty, Richard, E. (eds) *Attitude strength: Antecedents and consequences*, Mahwah, NJ, Erlbaum pp 131-158

Entman, Robert M. (2003) Cascading activation: Contesting the White House's frame after 9/11, *Political Communication*, Vol. 20, No.4 pp 415-32

Gibbons, Sheila (2002) Female correspondents changing war coverage, Women's ENews, 16 October. Available online at http://www.womensenews.org/story/uncovering-gender/021016/female-correspondents-changing-war-coverage, accessed on 15 December 2009

Hackett, Robert A and Schroeder, Birgitta (2008) Does anybody practice peace journalism?', *Peace and Policy*, Vol .13 pp 26-46

Hammond, Philip (2007) *Media, war and post-modernity*, Oxford, Routledge

Herold, Marc (2002) A dossier on civilian victims of US aerial bombing of Afghanistan – a comprehensive accounting, March. Available online at http://www.cursor.org/stories/civilian_deaths.htm, accessed on 15 December 2009

Holmes: Janet (1997) Women, language and identity, *Journal of Sociolinguistics*, Vol. 2, No. 1 pp 195-223

International Republic Institute (2009) Afghanistan public opinion survey 3-16 May 2009. Available online at http://www.afghanconflictmonitor.org/2009/06/afghanistan-public-opinion-survey-may-316-2009.html, accessed on 14 April 2010

Kassaimah, Sahar, (2001) Afghani Ambassador speaks at USC, Islam Online, 13 March 2001. Available online at http://www.islamonline.net/english/news/2001-03/13/article12.shtml, accessed on 15 December 2009

Luostarinen, Heikki (1994) *Sergeants of the mind: News management and journalistic counter-strategies in military conflicts*, Helsinki, Hanki ja Jaa Oy

Lynch, Jake (2008) *Debates in peace journalism*, Sydney, Sydney University Press

Lynch, Jake (2009) What is the point of peace?', *Uni News*, University of Sydney, March

Lynch, Jake and McGoldrick, Annabel (2005) *Peace Journalism*, Stroud, Hawthorn Press

Nelson, Soraya Sarhaddi (2010) Afghan government enters Marjah to cool reception, National Public Radio, 22 February 22. Available online at http://m.wcbu.npr.org/news/World/123979363?singlePage=true, accessed on 13 April 2010

Nye, Joseph (2004) *Soft Power: the means to success in world politics*, New York, Public Affairs

Pinker, Susan (2008) *The sexual paradox*, London, Scribner

Ricchiardi, Sherry (2006) The forgotten war, *American Journalism Review*, August/September. Available online at http://www.ajr.org/Article.asp?id=4162, accessed on 15 April 2010

Schmidt, Christophe (2009) 7,000 troops pledged as US seeks help in Afghanistan, Sydney Morning Herald, 4 December. Available online at http://news.smh.com.au/breaking-news-world/7000-troops-pledged-as-us-seeks-help-in-afghanistan-20091204-kb5c.html, accessed on 15 April 2010

Shanker, Thom (2010) Afghan push went beyond traditional military goals, *New York Times*, 19 February. Available online at http://www.nytimes.com/2010/02/20/world/20military.html, accessed on 13 April 2010

UN (2008) Population Division of the Department of Economic and Social Affairs of the United Nations Secretariat, *World Population Prospects: The 2008 Revision.* Available online at http://esa.un.org/unpp, accessed on 15 December 2009

Wright, Terence (2004) Collateral coverage: media images of Afghan refugees, 2001, *Visual Studies*, Vol. 19, No. 1 pp 97-111

Note on the authors

Jake Lynch is Director of the Centre for Peace and Conflict Studies at the University of Sydney. Before that he was a professional journalist, having worked as a Political Correspondent for Sky News, Sydney Correspondent for the *Independent* and a presenter on BBC World television news. He is chair of the organising committee of the International Peace Research Association conference in Sydney in July 2010 (see www.iprasydney2010.org)

Annabel McGoldrick is researching audience responses to war journalism and peace journalism, part of a project investigating prospects for a Global Standard for Reporting Conflict, with funding from the Australian Research Council and partnership by the International Federation of Journalists and the aid agency, Act for Peace. She is a practising psychotherapist and a former reporter and producer in television and radio news.

Indra Adnan is Director of the Soft Power Network and The Downing Street Project, and a regular contributor to the *Guardian* and the Huffington Post. She has consulted on public relations, event producing, training, strategic planning and presenting, for clients including the World Economic Forum, the British Council, the Scottish Executive and the Institute of Contemporary Arts.

The three produced the first Peace Journalism Summer School, in 1997, with Johan Galtung, which launched the worldwide movement for peace journalism among journalists, civil society activists and academic researchers.

"Enduring Freedom": reporting on Afghan women from 2001-present

Corinne Fowler compares the media coverage of Afghan women during the 2001 US-led invasion of Afghanistan with current reporting and argues that despite all the rhetoric about "women's rights" their voices are rarely heard in this coverage

In February 2010, US Special Operation Forces shot five family members during a night-time raid near Gardez in south eastern Afghanistan. Among the dead were two Afghan men and three women. Two of the women were pregnant. At first, US forces claimed that the dead men were Taliban supporters who had opened fire. Troops had then stumbled across the bodies of three dead women, which were tied up, gagged and hidden in the house after being murdered by their male relatives.

Local eye-witnesses told a very different story. The men were not Taliban supporters, they insisted, and the women were accidentally shot during the raid by US soldiers who then dug the bullets out of their bodies to cover up their mistake (Oppel and Waheed Wafa 2010). [1] Following Nato's later statement that the women had, indeed, been accidentally shot during the raid rather than murdered by their male relatives, the report was taken up by *The Times*.

Nato officials continued to brief journalists in Kabul yesterday that the women were victims of an "honour" killing. However, they did not explain why the bodies would have been kept in the house overnight, against Islamic custom, nor why the family had invited 25 guests to celebrate the naming of a newborn child the same evening (Starkey 2010).

As Jake Lynch and Annabel McGoldrick point out elsewhere in this volume, Afghanistan has consistently been portrayed as the "good war" by George Bush,

Tony Blair and their political successors. Promoting Afghan women's rights has been central to their depiction of Operation Enduring Freedom. Throughout the past nine years, too, Prime Ministers and Presidents have continued to provide pro-feminist justifications for the ongoing military operations (Berger 2010: 3 and 10; Fowler 2007; Hunt 2002: 119).[2] Yet the image of Nato soldiers digging bullets from the bodies of Afghan women suggests more sordid realities. Moreover, the detail of "honour killings" deserves some scrutiny.

As an indirect allusion to the war's humanitarian dimension, the prominence of "honour killings" in the soldiers' version of events bears out a consistent feminist charge that Operation Enduring Freedom perpetuates an old colonial patriarchal order whereby, as Gwen Berger puts it "brown women must be saved from brown men by white men" (Berger 2010: 2). The "honour killing" explanation evokes precisely this order, indirectly reminding us that liberating Afghan women from the patriarchal practices of their fellow countrymen has been central to the humanitarian aims of Operation Enduring Freedom.

This is not to detract from the adverse situation of Afghan women, one that has been, and remains, "unspeakable", according to Sahar Saba, of the Revolutionary Association of the Women of Afghanistan (RAWA)[3]. Rather, it identifies a connection between journalists' historical tendency to medievalise Afghan scenes and settings (Fowler 2007: 64) with a corresponding inclination to attribute Afghan women's subordination to a form of Afghan cultural pathology. The alternative, of course, would have been to place this subordination in the context of critical factors such as class differences, regime change, migratory genocide, decades of warfare, international political interference and enforced social reform during the Soviet occupation (1979-1989) (Saikal 2006: 23; Khalid 2007: 73; Rostami-Povey 2006: 33). Despite these complexities, journalists have tended to go with the grain of political leaders' justifications for the war, interpreting the military coalition's role largely in the terms expressed by Channel Four's Jonathan Miller (2004), to collectively "drag Afghanistan's brutalised men and invisible, downtrodden women out of the dark ages".

147

In November 2001, there was a rash of celebratory reconstruction stories about the Bonn talks to establish an interim government headed up by Hamid Karzai (Fowler 2007a: 4). Following this brief reporting period, however, women's rights fell off the international news agenda. By 2010, nine years after the conflict began, mainstream news media coverage rarely drew public attention to Afghan women's rights, a topic that had long since become the province of occasional magazine and feature articles. In 2010, British media has concentrated on UK foreign policy towards Afghanistan, the lack of military equipment for British troops, human interest stories about soldiers killed in combat and, to a lesser extent, Afghan government policy towards the Taliban. When this book went to press, the top "Afghan" newspaper stories were: "British troops to stay in Helmand, says Defence Secretary" (*The Times*, 8 June 2010), "Afghanistan: a war we're winning" (*Independent*, 8 June 2010)[4] and "So much for peace: Taliban suicide bomber blows himself up at Afghan 'jirga' peace conference" (*Daily Mail*, 2 June 2010)[5]. No headline coverage of the suicide bombings at the "jirga" dealt with Afghan feminist objections to the conference despite a RAWA statement that condemned it: "inviting criminals like the Taliban [...] and other "*jehadi* leaders [...made it] crystal clear [that US claims to bring] "women's liberation" to Afghanistan was the biggest lie of the century" (2010: June 2).

By 2010, then, news media outlets had shifted their focus from the *burqa* to military strategy and governmental policy on the Taliban. This chapter contends that the protracted media silence about Afghan women since 2002 indicates that this humanitarian aspect of Operation Enduring Freedom has acquired a taken-for-granted status and operates as an underlying value that is periodically evoked to serve various strategic purposes (as with the "honour killings"). Furthermore, the official assertion that women's liberation is a major reason behind the Nato presence in Afghanistan remains largely uninterrogated by journalists.

In order to better understand this dynamic, it is necessary to return to the early days of reporting Operation Enduring Freedom after September 2001. Despite intensive media focus on Afghan women's rights during 2001, journalists consistently failed to promote the agency of Afghan women as commentators on their country's affairs. Given this failure nine years ago, today's silence on the issue was inevitable, founded as it was in what Maliha Chishti and Cheshmak Farhourmand-Sims (2010) describe as the "temporary engagement of women's rights discourse" by politicians and reporters at the start of the conflict.

Returning to earlier contexts of news media coverage, then, this chapter explores in detail how and why Afghan public opinion, especially that of women, has come to be so persistently disregarded by a media that repeatedly and no doubt sincerely expresses concern for the way in which – in the words of David Williams of the *Daily Mail* – "the brutal Taliban regime…made its women non-people" (29 September 2001). Indeed, mainstream British news coverage has consistently "invisiblised" Afghan women by excluding their voices. Moreover, despite calls for more "feminised" modes of reporting linked to women journalists (see Lynch and McGoldrick in this volume), my in-depth survey of reports broadcast at the onset of Operation Enduring Freedom suggests that there has been no qualitative difference between reports from male and female journalists.

The veil as a metonym for oppression

Although the war in Afghanistan was until recently eclipsed – in reporting terms – by the war in Iraq, this was not initially the case. To understand current reporting tendencies, it is necessary to return to the beginning of Operation Enduring Freedom, when the concealment of female bodies under the *burqa* was a major focus of attention for British reporting on Afghan women (2001-2002). It is important to stress here that it was the *burqa* and associated debates about Afghan women's oppression that dominated the news during this period more than any detailed focus on legal and structural gender inequalities.

The enduring currency of the veil as a metonym for oppression has been the subject of many articles and commentaries by women from Asia and the Middle East advising that the garment be situated in its shifting historical, political and social contexts. Nadia Wassef sums up a frequent charge that Euro-American understandings of the veil reveal "a gross essentialisation of a fabric worn by different women in different ways and in different settings to express different things" (2001: 118). Nevertheless, repeated vilification of the Afghan *burqa* during 2001 suggests how under-theorised this garment was in public debates throughout Britain and the United States during the 2001-2002 reporting period.

There is a clear need to complicate British popular understandings of the garment. On 1 October 2001, for example, the *Mirror* carried an article headed by a photograph of a *burqa*-clad woman with a caption reading a "mother in traditional Islamic dress" (15 November 2001). This depiction may be criticised on two fronts. Firstly, it peddles what Nirmal Puwar has called "homogenised, static readings" of the garment (2002: 65) and, secondly, it implies that Islam is, in the words of Nadia Wassef, the ultimate "explanatory force behind women's lives" (ibid: 113). One means of combating "homogenised" readings of the garment is to historicise the *burqa*'s origins and to catalogue its changing significance at different historical junctures. The *burqa* made its first appearance in the Ottoman Empire, where it was used as a curtained sedan-chair by upper-class Christian women to denote status and as protection from thieves and dust (Lederman 2002: 51). The head-to-toe *burqa* thus evolved within a Christian context, making its relationship to Islam by no means as straightforward as the *Mirror* caption implies.

Moreover, it has a more complex relationship to political patriarchy than journalists' coverage of the *burqa* issue generally allows. As Christine Aziz notes, during the twentieth century, Afghan women have "slipped in and out" of the *burqa* "according to the male dictates of the day" (1998: 44). Although Amanullah's rule between 1919 and 1929 was in many ways an emancipatory time for Afghan women, they had to adhere to a strict policy of forcible unveiling (1998: 54). Neither has the *burqa* been a classless garment. For this reason alone, it is important to attend to the considerable variation in social position and status between urban and rural women, Hazara, Tajik and Pashtun women, and between upper-class women and their maids.

Burqa as a visual symbol of women's oppression

The actions and experiences of Afghan women hardly begin and end with their apparel. As Sahar Saba, of RAWA, argues, adopting the *burqa* as a visual symbol of women's oppression proved a counterproductive media strategy by her organisation; it set the parameters of discussion within such narrow confines that some Afghan women actually declared they could even live with the *burqa* if they had the right to pursue their chosen life goals, to receive an education or have access to healthcare. However, despite the complex history of Afghan women's alternate involvement and exclusion from national politics since the early-twentieth century, disproportionate news-media focus on the *burqa* risks defining women as victims and precluding them as agents of change.

Relatively emancipatory times, as Aziz (op cit) argues, have paradoxically involved a degree of coercion – such as enforced mixed-sex education – despite strong local opposition and reprisals during the Soviet invasion. Indeed, many commentators have noted how "the Soviet assault on Islam" (Khalid 2007: 50) in Central Asia had adverse, if unintended, consequences for gender equality and regional development. The conversion of mosques into community centres and the destruction of the region's Islamic educational infrastructure led to highly localised devolved modes of Qur'anic interpretation and dissemination (ibid: 55), necessitating many of the *madrassas* that featured so prominently in journalists' 2001 coverage.

These kinds of interferences came to be regarded as synonymous with the Soviet policy of enforcing girls' education, thereby creating an indelible association between imperialism and calls for gender equality. Despite their overwhelming depiction by journalists as passive victims (Berger 2010; Fowler 2007b), Afghan women have been central to the armed struggle against, and occasionally for, the Soviet occupation, joining the resistance, enlisting in militia and regular army units, participating in the establishment of mujaheddin organisations and sometimes using explosives and teaching young men how to use them (Aziz op cit: 55-56).

More recently, Herati women organised themselves into militias against the Taliban and set up a university (ibid: 59). Rashid's Taliban, Islam, Oil and the New Great Game in Central Asia notes that Afghan women have "had as many roles as there were tribes and nationalities", and points to the significant role played by Hazara women both in defensive operations against the Taliban in the

Bamiyan district and recounting that the eighty member Central Council of the Hazara Hizb-e-Wahadat party had twelve women members (2000: 69 and 110). This sort of information about women was scarce during coverage of Operation Enduring Freedom.

Interaction of international politics and gender politics

The complex interaction of international politics and gender politics is of central importance to this chapter because, back in 2001, it landed journalists in an ethical quagmire. This was because Afghan women and their burqas featured so prominently in coalition rhetoric of political and social liberation. Despite the morally compromising alliance between the United States and the Saudi Arabian royal family, coalition leaders understood the political expediency of adopting the *burqa* as a potent metaphor of liberation (Roy: 2002). Correspondents were thus faced with the problem that feminist discourses of liberation were appropriated for the purpose of promoting secular democracy by means of military intervention.

For commentators such as Krista Hunt, this was nothing less than "violence cloaked" in women's rights (2002: 119). The events of 11 September 2001 saw a sudden surge of interest in women's organisations, especially RAWA, which was the most prominent of these on the worldwide web. As Saba relates, a RAWA film that had been posted on the association's website featuring a woman's execution in Kabul Stadium had been offered to media outlets two years previously, including the BBC and CNN. However, news channels turned the film down on the grounds that it was too shocking to show to news audiences. After 11 September, however, the Pentagon took the film from the website without permission and showed it during a press conference to justify military action against Afghanistan.[6]

The pro-feminist content of coalition rhetoric depended on an astonishing degree of historical amnesia regarding unofficial US support for the Taliban between 1994 and 1996. As Ahmed Rashid points out, during this period the position of Afghan women under the Taliban was "conveniently ignored" until Clinton was forced to reverse his policy when he required the help of the feminist lobby to survive the political fall-out from the Lewinsky affair in 1997 (2000: 176). However, as much as being a quest to save Afghan women from Afghan men (and Muslim women from Muslim men), the *burqa* – or its absence – was co-opted as a sign of Western freedom as much as Afghan unfreedom (Rogers 2003: 206).

The apparent feminist turn in coalition liberation rhetoric, then, was not – as Roy (op cit) points out – because US soldiers were on some "feminist mission" but, instead, related to the flexing of moral and military muscle with the declared aim of restoring order amid the clamour of "medieval" Islamic misogyny. Correspondingly, the burqa's vilification was intimately related to the self-image of British, US and Australian society as providing an emancipatory environment where women are, as Chandra Talpade Mohanty suggests, "secular, liberated, and have control over their own lives" (2001: 481).

Journalists' narrow focus on the veil – irrespective of gender

My investigation into men and women's news media coverage of Afghanistan at the onset of Operation Enduring Freedom revealed that, irrespective of gender, journalists tended to adopt a narrow focus on the veil without taking into account their own role in reducing women's bodies to ideological battlefields for the moral high ground. In wartime, opposing sides readily introduce the subject of women's rights or obligations as a means of discrediting the other (Hunt 2002: 120). Forcible veiling and unveiling, in Afghanistan, Egypt, Iran, Turkey and in a range of countries across Europe have long been used as a means of signalling identification with changing models of progress. As John L. Esposito points out, regimes have used the veil as a means of displaying Westernised identity. To this purpose the veil has been banned by Reza Shah Pahlavi, of Iran, Attaturk, of Turkey, and Bourghiba in Tunisia (2002: 131).

The coercive nature of forcible unveiling has occasionally been touched upon in news reports such as George Arney's for BBC Radio 4's *From Our Own Correspondent*, which notes an historical instance of this phenomenon at work in Afghanistan during the reign of Amanullah: in a "mirror image of Taliban edicts, he forbade women to walk the streets of Kabul unless they were bareheaded"

(*Talking, Afghan-style*, 30 November 2001). The challenge for journalists in 2001 was not only to interrogate the rhetoric of women's "honour" as a pretext for violence but to resist – or, at least, question – the co-option of women's rights for the same purpose (Hunt op cit: 119).

The war in Kosovo had already seen the defence of female "honour" as a strong component in the rhetoric of nations opposing the UN intervention, such as Cuba, Iran and Pakistan (DelZotto 2002: 146). An ongoing responsibility for journalists is the way in which the relentless intrusive and voyeuristic gaze of the United States and its allies has been used by Muslim conservatives as justification for curtailing women's freedoms. Nevertheless, 2001 news reports about Afghan women tended to blame Islamic misogyny or medieval conservatism for women's suffering, and this explanation was generally preferred to more nuanced explanations. Connections were not made, for example, between Taliban repression and the fear of being seen as a puppet government of the United States which, as Rashid contends (2000: 112), had a major bearing on the escalating strictness of Taliban policies on women, a policy that became the last outpost of non-compromise and the sustainer of their political morale.

Journalists' attention to the Afghan women's "plight", therefore, ran the attendant risk not merely of complying with the coalition's moral and ethical justification for military intervention but of indirect complicity with forms of Islamic conservatism more closely related to a history of foreign domination than images of "medieval Afghanistan" allow. Fahima Vorgetts suggests that "fanaticism" be redefined as the forcing of one's views on others, making the point that, during the Soviet occupation, the policy of coercing village women to attend school meant that education became forever associated with "un-Islamic and anti-Islamic' foreign domination, which was in the end counter-productive for women's rights" (2002: 96).

Women as passive victims rather than active agents

Afghan women are commonly depicted in the possessive mode in news reports ("their women"), which underwrites – rather than contests – their depiction as the property of Afghan men. Details such as these suggest that British and US critiques of women's position in Afghanistan are at least partly driven by men and women journalists' shared self-construction as liberators and liberated. This returns me to the theme of unexamined assumptions implicit in the prevalent mode of news media coverage described so far in this chapter.

Among the most common of these entails the construction of Afghan women's liberation as past to Western feminism's present, as illustrated by a rather paternalistic statement by journalist Yvonne Ridley about starting "a bum-[sic]-the-burkha campaign just as women had burned their bras in the sixties" (2001: 105). Aside from the customary reduction of the *burqa* to a symbol of oppression, the statement contains many ironies in the face of unrelenting emphasis in the West on women's social duty to be attractive while commercial markets rapidly expand to target teenage women.

However, back in 2001, more open readings of agency beneath the *burqa* were adopted under two very particular and restricted circumstances. The first was when Afghan women were depicted as would-be Western women hiding make-up or high heels under their *burqas*. There have been many books published since 2001 that celebrate this form of rebellion. Among the most popular – and controversial – of these is Deborah Rodriguez's memoir entitled *Kabul Beauty School: The Art of Friendship and Freedom* (2007).[7] The second circumstance that produced more open readings was when garments were "donned" in a form of cultural transvestism, by British female, and occasionally male, correspondents. When Yvonne Ridley (who was captured – and released – by the Taliban just before the US-led invasion of 2001) first wears the *burqa* she expresses regret at the way she "went from being a Western woman in charge of a project to someone who had no significance at all" (ibid: 91). However, as with Victorian women travellers such as Lady Wortley Montagu in Turkey, she also recognises the power of being "invisible" to give her heightened powers of observation (ibid: 95), a common claim by *burqa*-wearing journalists, one that is rarely extended to *burqa*-wearing Afghan women.

By contrast, focus on the garment's subversive potential for Afghan women tended to be restricted to its ability to conceal make-up or high heels. Once worn by Western journalists, the garment does not automatically efface her or his presence but rather tends to liberate an undercover, trickster spirit capable of fooling Taliban border guards, and Afghans in their own marketplaces. An important consequence of journalists' *burqa*-wearing in 2001 was the tension it set up between empathetic identification on the one hand, and its power to qualify her or him to speak for and on behalf of Afghan women on the other.

This is apparent in Ross Benson's account of wearing the *burqa*:

> I know what it feels like because last time I was [...in Afghanistan], I had to disguise myself as a woman in order to avoid the Soviet border patrols.
> I was forbidden to speak because in Afghanistan women are allowed no voice. For several hours my only sight of the world was through the fretwork of my enshrouding *burqa*.
> It was a terrible view from the inside of how women were subjugated (2001).

Benson's act of transvestism might be classified as a form of empathetic identification. Even so, when it comes to cross-dressing, acts of identification are rarely straightforward, since they accrue power as readily as they relinquish it. The reasons for this are twofold. Wearing the *burqa* in many senses acts as a verifiable marker of an indigenised "view from inside" – an apparent acquisition of "double consciousness"', leading to a powerful knowledge-claim ("I know what it feels like") (Fowler 2004: 213). It is this position of apparent knowledge and insight that permits Benson to speak. This apparent indigenisation (Goldie 1989: 210), of which cross-dressing is a tangible sign, tends to detract from the asymmetrical power relation, in representational terms, between journalists and the *burqa*-clad women who are the subject of their articles.

This is not to deny the existence of empathy. Rather it is to temper over-optimistic readings of cross-dressing by recognising its built-in elements of voyeuristic theatricality, its tangible demonstration of having "boldly gone where no reader has ever gone before" (Fowler 2004: 213). Empathy, therefore, does not necessarily lead to insight. As is so often the case, Benson's manipulation of the clothing register is not accompanied by self-reflection on the part of the journalist on his article's acts of narrative exclusion. Despite the claim that Afghan women "are allowed no voice", Benson's account of his "several hours" as a woman receives absolute primacy, while the implied experiences of his fellow *burqa* wearers are ventriloquised through his commentary.

Caroline Wyatt's report for *From Our Own Correspondent* on BBC Radio 4 points to a common self-image of British journalists as agents of, or advocates for, Afghan women's liberation. This is conveyed by a metaphor of Afghan women as "silent shadows": "Their husbands insist they wear the *burqa*. Not to, they tell me, would bring shame on their family and insults on the streets [...] They give me a last wry smile and then the veil comes down on their faces and the lively women I've spent the day with turn back into silent shadows" (2001) This symbolism clearly pertains not merely to the women's social eclipse but to the power of the correspondent to rescue them from obscurity by bringing their plight to news audiences' attention. In this sense the narrative cannot shake off the connotations of Afghan damnation and Western (possibly feminist) redemption.

Moreover, the voiceless women claim falls in easily with the myth of universal male dominance and female subordination with little regard to important variations in experience from man to man, woman to woman, region to region and historical moment to historical moment. Moreover, coverage of war tends to heighten an already well-established sense of female victimhood. War reporting tends to exacerbate women's portrayal as victims since, as DelZotto found with coverage of Kosovo, women's commentary is sought only within restricted roles denoting passivity: women tend to feature as passive refugees and waiting wives (where   contrary to all statistical evidence – "men die and women mourn") (op cit: 145-146).

Like femininity, masculinity is plural and negotiable

News professionals' sustained focus on the *burqa* tended to be narrowly confined to the oversimplified and restrictive dichotomy of victimhood and liberation. As Amanda Cornwall and Nancy Lindisfarne point out (1994: 10 and 86), however, throughout Central Asia and the Middle East, there is an entire spectrum of male responses to ideals of male honour, a spectrum along which "many nuanced masculinities are created" and to which women respond differently according to personality, class and a range of political and economic circumstances. Like femininity, masculinity is plural and negotiable.

Moreover, it is subject to all sorts of variable social conditions. As Rashid points out, by contrast with even the most conservative of Pashtuns where male and female relatives mixed relatively freely, segregation was the norm for youthful Taliban brought up in *madrassas*. Indeed, so diverse a nation has never had a "universal standard" for women's social role (2000: 33 and 110). However, there was no sustained, internal critique of Afghan women's portrayal as helpless victims. Moreover, Sima Wali calls for journalists to resist demonising Afghan men, pointing out that many have supported Afghan women and advocated their rights. Wali advises that Afghan men also be regarded as part of the solution (2002: 5).

This leads me to another major consequence of the mode of reporting on Afghan women that was prevalent in 2001. It shows a clear correlation between assumptions of Afghan women's universal subordination and the exclusion, or muting, of their voices. The commonly applied descriptor "invisible" is at least as performative as it is descriptive. The danger was then, and remains, that the metaphor of invisibility executes its own form of exclusory agency, providing a pretext for conjuring women off the news scene. This is apparent in Robert Kaplan's claim at the beginning of Operation Enduring Freedom that Pashtun women "simply don't exist". After some time as a journalist near the North West Frontier, he writes that he forgot about Pathan women "altogether" (2001: 50). This is representative of much of the reporting of that year, which portrayed Afghan women as both literally and psychically unreachable by removing them – metaphorically – to another historical period and setting, generally the European Middle Ages (Fowler 2007b: 69-75).

Afghan women denied access to media spaces

While the quest for any single, "authentic" female Afghan voice is by definition doomed to failure, I have found that, despite the prominence of women's liberation in the British news agenda during the 2001 conflict, the prevailing norm of coverage was to deny Afghan women access to media spaces during Operation Enduring Freedom. In the case of reporting on Afghan women, I would also add that, aside from professional careers, what is at stake in reporting on Afghan women is British reporters' self-image as neither oppressors nor oppressed which, I have argued, has a clear bearing on correspondents' approaches.

The overwhelming tendency was to exclude them as commentators on their own "plight"; for example, I found only two television news reports where an Afghan woman was asked directly about the *burqa* while Afghan women's rights were still on the international news agenda (*Channel Four News*, 13 November 2001; *ITV Evening News*, 13 November 2001). Most markedly, however, Afghan women were typically excluded as commentators on the conceptual and ethical premises of Operation Enduring Freedom and the "war on terror". They were commonly portrayed as "non-people" or referred to as possessions by female and male reporters alike. This supports Hannerz's suggestion that, while women journalists have frequently commented on the machismo of male colleagues, a range of professional constraints mean that there is often little real difference in terms of men and women's tone and mode of reporting (2004: 94).

Ultimately, however, since women represent one of the world's highest concentrations of female-headed households, the practice of privileging minority male voices over the explanatory narratives of their female counterparts in newspapers, radio and television news reports alike reveals the profoundly anti-democratic tendencies of British news coverage during Operation Enduring Freedom.

Contradictions and hypocrisies in coverage remain today

The "veil" debate still rages. Muslim women throughout Europe and the US have come under increasing pressure to remove their veils as, once more, the garment has been viewed as synonymous with women's oppression, cultural isolationism or – most recently in Britain – as a threat to national security. The 2001 coverage of Afghanistan was an important precursor to current debates, not least because it highlights the contradictions and hypocrisies that have long been housed within Western public discourses on women's rights.

Despite its temporary prevalence on international news agendas in 2001, the theme of women's liberation has failed to alter the prevailing norm of coverage, which continues to deny Afghan women access to media spaces. Now, as then, Afghan women are invariably the subjects rather than the agents of such debates. Moreover, regardless of their gender, the vast majority of journalists reporting the 2001 conflict failed to recognise and confront the co-option of women's rights for the purpose of justifying military aggression on humanitarian grounds. There was no sustained critical commentary in mainstream news media coverage on the pro-feminist discourse of chief political players.

An item on 3 June 2010 on BBC Radio 4's *From Our Own Correspondent*[8] offers evidence to support the contention that the media's engagement with women's rights in 2001 was neither permanent nor transformative. Retaining the motif of invisibility so prevalent in 2001 ("Afghan women's invisible struggle for rights"), reporter Martin Patience visits a women's refuge, the presence of which he interprets as a sign of positive change.

While conditions remain bad for Afghan women, he argues, "the refuge in itself, opened four years ago, is a symbol of progress in Afghanistan, a place where women can gather, a place where they will be protected" (Patience 2010). Patience takes a specific example of a women's refuge and, ignoring Afghanistan's long history of women's activism, superimposes on it the kind of celebratory reconstruction story that was a marked feature of the 2002 news media coverage: "Before [...the refuge] was established, many of the women now sheltering behind its walls would probably have been killed for bringing shame on their families. But slowly Afghanistan is producing a generation determined to fight for their freedoms" (ibid).

The coverage, then, is representative of two assumptions that have persisted since the onset of Operation Enduring Freedom. First, that Afghan women were overwhelmingly passive before 2001. Indeed, scholars themselves are only now beginning to attend to what Chishti and Faroumand-Sims (op cit) have called "the vast and impressive Afghan women's movement" that has been so persistently overlooked by journalists. Moreover, Patience's implicit solution to this perceived passivity is to provide Afghan women with a form of assertiveness training rather than supporting Afghan efforts to effect major legislative or structural change. Again, this approach to women's rights characterised the 2001-2002 period of news coverage.

This is followed by a second assumption, that Nato's military presence – coupled with the coalition's political interventions – has brought about significant improvements for Afghan women. But in a nation where one Afghan woman dies in childbirth every half hour and 87 per cent of Afghan women remain illiterate,[9] the contrast between this mode of reporting and recent statements released by RAWA could hardly be more striking. While it would be a mistake to view RAWA as speaking for all Afghan women (and which organisation ever could?), its recent press release on International Women's Day 2010 is particularly bleak:

> Afghan women are being auctioned in open market and…their young daughters [are putting…] an end to their miserable lives by self-immolation. But the perpetrators of all these crimes…are still holding their official positions…The world believes that the US and Nato has donated liberation, democracy and human and women rights for Afghanistan; whereas, after eight years of the US and allies' aggression under the banner of "war on terror", they empowered the most brutal terrorists of the Northern Alliance and the former Russian puppets – the *Khalqis* and *Parchamis* – and…instead of uprooting…the Taliban and *Al-Qaeda*…the US and Nato continue to kill …women and children, in their vicious air raids.

Conclusions

Whatever the political affiliations of individual Afghan women, there can be little doubt that, as Chishti and Farhoumand-Sims have argued, transnational feminist efforts to support Afghan women have become increasingly embroiled in "the complex web of politico-military objectives, priorities and criminalising partnerships" whereby the rhetoric of gender equality sits uneasily with governmental support for groups and individuals who have historically been the agents of women's oppression (2010). The almost exclusive focus on the *burqa* that characterised the 2001-2002 coverage did not manage to capture these dimensions of the struggle for women's rights and recent coverage has yet to overcome this shortcoming.

Regardless of whether reporting of Afghanistan requires "feminising", only a small minority of reporters – some men, some women, have so far managed to foreground the limitations of their ability of understand Afghan women (Fowler 2007b: 202-204). Much has changed since 2001. Afghanistan has come back into sharp political focus, this time with the spotlight on military strategy, soldiers' deaths, potential terrorism at "home" and, to a lesser degree, Afghan governmental policy. What has not changed is the pro-feminist justification for "fighting on" (and on) in Afghanistan. Continuing to exclude Afghan women from media spaces, and retaining key assumptions about their passivity, journalists have yet to adopt a critical stance towards political leaders' advocacy for gender equality in Afghanistan.

Notes

[1] On the 5 April, *The New York Times* reported that, in the light of compelling evidence to support the assertions of friends and family in Gardez, Nato had announced a formal investigation into the incident (Nato "covered up" botched night raid in Afghanistan that killed five, Oppel and Waheed Wafa 2010). A few weeks later Nato said that five civilians had indeed been shot by US personnel and that they would be compensated. The relatives of the dead, however, have said that they will refuse the money and instead avenge the deaths

2 Although, at the beginning of 2010, Barack Obama and Prime Minister Gordon Brown emphasised the importance of Operation Enduring Freedom in keeping Euro-American streets free of terrorist incidents. This does not, however, contradict my assertion that the goal of women's liberation remains as a key value that is periodically, and strategically, evoked

3 Communicated by Sahar Saba at the Women Against Fundamentalism and for Equality (WAFE) conference in Paris, 25-26 February 2005. Formed in 1977, the Revolutionary Association of the Women of Afghanistan is the oldest women's humanitarian and political organisation in Afghanistan. Based inside Afghanistan and Pakistan, RAWA is an independent, non-violent organisation staffed by volunteers and calling for multilateral disarmament and a secular democratic government that can promote women's full participation in public life

4 In this article, Lt. Nick Kitson of 3 Rifles, writes of military gains in favour of "the Afghan government we support" and argues that "while the local population might not yet be…throwing flowers at the feet [of the allied forces…] our Afghan partners, military and civilian, bade us farewell with genuine and deep gratitude for the small steps we enabled on the long path to solving their problems"

5 It was reported that "the Taliban said in a statement to news organisations that the *jirga* does not represent the Afghan people and was aimed at 'securing the interest of foreigners'". It does deal briefly with former Prime Minister Hekmartyr's objection to the *jirga*, but does not register Afghan feminist opposition to it

6 Interview with Saha Sabar, 3 March 2002. Saha Sabar is a pseudonym to protect her identity.

7 Afghan co-founders of the Kabul Beauty School have accused Rodriguez of distorting incidents in her book and of exaggerating her own involvement in the school's establishment.

8 This weekly Radio 4 programme is a useful indicator of the extent to which reporters have been able to present relatively nuanced views of Afghan women. In my study of 2001 coverage I found that the opportunity the programme provided for extended coverage of Afghanistan led to some relatively self-reflexive accounts of Afghan women in relation to most mainstream news coverage (Fowler 2007b: 189-204).

[9] Integrated Regional Information Networks (IRIN) is an online UN humanitarian news and information service. Available online at http://www.irinnews.org/, accessed 9 June 2010

References

Aziz, C. (1998) Defiance and oppression: the situation of women, Girardet, E. and. Walter, J. (eds) *Essential Field Guides to Humanitarian and Conflict Zones: Afghanistan*, Geneva, Crosslines Communications Ltd pp 102-106

Arney, G. (2001) *Talking, Afghan style, From Our Own Correspondent*, BBC Radio 4, 30 November

Beaumont, P. (2001) Tyranny of veil is slow to lift, *Observer*, 30 December

Benson, R. (2001) Into the War Zone, *Daily Mail*, 1 October

Berger, G. (forthcoming, 2010) Nationalism, Feminism and the War in Afghanistan: Media (Un)Coverage of Afghan Women, Jalalzai, Z. and Jefferess, D. (eds) *Globalizing Afghanistan: Terrorism, War and Rhetoric of Nation Building*, Durham, USA, Duke University Press

Chishti, M. and Farhoumand-Sims, C. (forthcoming 2010) Transnational Feminism and the Women's Rights Agenda in Afghanistan, Jalalzai, Z. and Jefferess, D. (eds) *Globalizing Afghanistan: Terrorism, War and Rhetoric of Nation Building*, Durham, USA, Duke University Press

Cornwall A. and Lindisfarne N. (1994) *Dislocating Masculinity: Comparative Ethnographies*, London and New York, Routledge

DelZotto A. C. (2002) Weeping Women, Wringing Hands: How the Mainstream Media Stereotyped Women's Experiences in Kosovo, *Journal of Gender Studies* , Vol. 11 pp 91-108

Esposito, J. L. (2002) *Unholy War: Terror in the Name of Islam*, Oxford, Oxford University Press

Fowler, C. (2004) The Problem of Narrative Authority, Karko, K. and Oddie, C., Siegel, K. (eds) *Gender, Genre and Identity in Women's Travel Writing*, New York, Peter Lang Publishing pp 80-98

Fowler, C. (2007) Journalists in feminist clothing. Men and women reporting Afghan women, *Journal of International Women's Studies*, Vol. 8, No. 2 pp 4-19

Fowler, C. (2007) *Chasing Tales: Travel Writing, Journalism and the History of British Ideas about Afghanistan*, Amsterdam and New York, Rodopi

Goldie, T. (1989) *Fear and Temptation: The Image of the Indigene in Canadian, Australian and New Zealand Literatures*, Montreal, McGill-Queen's University Press

Hannerz, U. (2004) *Foreign News: Exploring the Worm of Foreign Correspondents*, Chicago, University of Chicago Press

Hill, F. and Aboitiz, M. (2002) Women Are Opening Doors. Security Council Resolution 1325 in Afghanistan, Mehta, S. (ed.) *Women for Afghan Women: Shattering Myths and Claiming the Future*, New York, Palgrave Macmillan pp 156-165

Hunt, K. (2002) The Strategic Co-optation of Women's Rights: Discourse in the "War on Terrorism", *International Feminist Journal of Politics*, Vol. 4 pp 27-39

Karim, H. K. (2002) Making sense of the "Islamic Peril": Journalism as cultural practice, Allan, S. and Zelizer, B. (eds) *Journalism After September 11*, London and New York, Routledge

Khalid, A. (2007) *Islam After Communism: Religion and Politics in Central Asia*, University of California Press

Lederman, A. (2002) The Zan of Afghanistan: A 35-Year Perspective on Women in Afghanistan, Mehta, S. (ed.) *Women for Afghan Women. Shattering Myths and Claiming the Future*, New York: Palgrave Macmillan pp 46-58

Miller, J. (2004) First Lady. Available online at www.channel4.com/news/2004/week_1/03_afghanistan.html, accessed on 1 December 2004

Oppel, R. and Waheed Wafa, A., (2010) Afghan Investigators Say US Troops Tried to Cover Up Evidence in Botched Raid, *New York Times*, 5 April

Patience, M. (2010) Afghan women's invisible struggle for rights, BBC Radio 4, *From Our Own Foreign Correspondent*, 3 June 2010

Puwar, N. (2002) Multi-cultural fashion...stirrings of another sense of aesthetics and memory, *Feminist Review*, Vol. 71 pp 56-70

Rashid, A. (2000) *Taliban, Islam, Oil and the New Great Game in Central Asia*, London and New York, I.B. Taurus Publishers

RAWA (2010) Peace with Criminals, War With People 1 June. Available online at www.rawa.org, accessed on 9 June 2010

Rodriguez, D. (2007) *Kabul Beauty School: The Art of Friendship and Freedom*, London, Random House

Rogers, J. (2003) Icons and Invisibility: Gender, Myth, 9/11, Thussu, D. T. and Freedman, D. (eds) *War and the Media: Reporting Conflict 24/7*, London, Sage pp 66-75

Rostami-Povey, E. (2007) *Afghan Women. Identity and Invasion*, London, Zed Books

Roy, A. (2002) Not Again, *Guardian*, 27 September

Saikal, A. (2006) *Modern Afghanistan. A History of Struggle and Survival*, London and New York, I.B. Taurus Publishers

Starkey, J. (2010) Nato covered up "botched" night raid in Afghanistan that killed five, *Times*, 15 March

Talpande Mohanty, C. (2001) Under Western Eyes: Feminist Scholarship and Colonial Discourse, Durham, M.G. and Kellner, D. M. (eds) *Media and Cultural Studies: Key Works*, Oxford, Blackwell pp 221-251

Vorgetts, F. (2002) A Vision of Justice, Equality and Peace, Mehta, S. (ed.) *Women for Afghan Women. Shattering Myths and Claiming the Future*, New York, Palgrave MacMillan pp 23-30

Wali, S. (2002) Afghanistan: Truth and Mythology, Mehta, S. (ed.) *Women for Afghan Women. Shattering Myths and Claiming the Future*, New York, Palgrave Macmillan pp 1-14

Wyatt, C. (2001) Afghan Women's Life in the Shadows, *From Our Own Correspondent*, BBC R4, 16 October

Websites

www.wafe.org, accessed on 12 June 2005

www.fao.org/News/2002/020105-e.htm, accessed on 13 June 2005

- An earlier, shorter version of this chapter first appeared in the *Journal of International Women's Studies*, Vol. 8, No. 2, 2007 pp. 4-19

Note on the author

Dr. Corinne Fowler lectures in postcolonial literature at the School of English at Leicester University. She specialises in travel writing and postcolonial feminist theory. Her monograph, *Chasing Tales: Travel Writing, Journalism and the History of British ideas about Afghanistan*, was published in 2007.

Humanitarian cost of the media's military embeddedness in Afghanistan

Being able to report from the frontlines may be crucial for journalists. But it is also important to recognise that there is, in fact, an important price to be paid for it, according to Alpaslan Özerdem, of the Centre for Peace and Reconciliation Studies at Coventry University

Introduction

Since the end of the Cold War, the military has become a key "humanitarian" actor and this phenomenon is particularly the case in the post-9/11 peace-building operations in Afghanistan and Iraq. Such an involvement by the military has had a number of impacts on humanitarianism and it has particularly meant a high level of risk to its key principles of the "obligation to assist", "neutrality" and "impartiality". A second level of risk to humanitarianism has emerged from the way the media has opted for being embedded into military structures in order to have a better access to the frontline operations. In other words, to a large extent the military has become the key "gatekeeper" for information through its close links with both the media and humanitarian actors. Therefore, by focusing on Afghanistan as a case study, this chapter aims to highlight how the media's embeddedness has led to a distorted understanding of the objectives and consequences of the military-led relief and reconstruction programmes.

Humanitarianism in the post-9/11 era

Humanitarianism as a concept is much more than the provision of relief aid. It has its roots in such areas as international law, solidarity and social justice. Its three deontological principles, particularly in the way they are implemented by the International Committee of the Red Cross (ICRS), emphasise the independence of aid from any consideration of interest, opportunity or prodigality; as well as reaffirming that all humans are equal and that all civilians are innocent in a war and have a right to equality of treatment. Moreover, the intervention to assist them should be completely unrelated to the political and military aspect of conflict (Özerdem and Rufini 2005).

In other words, in its purest sense humanitarianism is apolitical but the reality is that it has always been undertaken in a very political world, and hence, the basic principles of humanitarianism come under threat in war-affected environments (Anderson 1996; El Bushra 1999). Humanitarianism during the Cold War years was heavily influenced by solidarity movements for human rights and development aid, and the 1984-85 Ethiopia famine was an important turning point as the response to it marked the involvement of a wide range of non-governmental organisations (NGOs) and public initiatives such as the Band Aid. During this period, although the way that different humanitarian NGOs related to other actors such as governments, international institutions and the mass-media started to have a substantial impact in the way humanitarian aid was provided; the level of politicisation was, nevertheless, relatively low.

However, in the early years after the Cold War, it was evident that many humanitarian operations were not without ulterior political objectives, and as such were selective in their application. However, the military was still subordinate to humanitarian responses in such post-conflict environments as Mozambique, Cambodia and El Salvador in the early 1990s. It was with the military's wider involvement in Bosnia-Herzegovina in 1994-95 and particularly in the aftermath of the Nato intervention in Kosovo in 1999 that the power structures of relationships between civilian and military actors started to change drastically. Under the banner of "new humanitarianism", intertwining political objectives such as democratisation and development with humanitarian ones has become an inevitable step in the moves towards a new vision of international security by the international community (Özerdem and Rufini 2005).

The events of 9/11 have allowed such "politicised" humanitarianism to become increasingly common, thinly veiled under the pretext of a fight against terrorism. Humanitarian principles have been systematically invoked and violated to justify "humanitarian wars" in the name of "human rights". Aid is also now perceived by some to masquerade as a branch of military operations. In other words, although the politicisation of humanitarian aid was clearly the case in many operations until 2001, the military interventions in Afghanistan and Iraq indicated that it has gone further and become, to a large extent, an integral part of political and military objectives. Even some humanitarian NGOs had to face the dilemma of taking a position in relation to the G. W. Bush administration's policy of "you are with us or against us" in such operations, since any refusal to take part in such aid operations could endanger funding for aid operations in the future. The risk faced by humanitarianism was clear when the bombs were being dropped by the same US Air Force planes that were also providing food rations, as was the case in Afghanistan in 2001. Then, the principles of humanitarianism were truly forgotten.

Afghanistan: the demise of humanitarianism

After a devastating armed conflict with a number of distinct phases over the previous 23 years, the US-led international military intervention in coalition with the Northern Alliance forces in Afghanistan took place in 2001, which led to a new opportunity for "peace" with the Bonn Conference in December of 2002. The model of state building process put forward by the international community for Afghanistan has been structured over a "pillar-system" under the name of a Security Sector Reform (SSR) framework. There is a lead country for each pillar of SSR with the US being responsible for the restructuring of the new Afghan National Army, Germany for the National Police Force, Japan for the Disarmament, Demobilisation and Reintegration (DDR) of former combatants, UK for the fight against narcotics and Italy for the reform of justice system.

Moreover, with the widespread and devastating socio-economic, psychological and physical impacts of such a protracted war, one of the main challenges in the post-Bonn context was the establishment of security throughout the country. However, the US military response to the presence of the Taliban and Al-Qaida members in different parts of the country, particularly in the south, has meant the continuation of armed conflict with corresponding high levels of violence. In tandem with the "war against terrorism" waged by the US, there has also been a vicious lawlessness in most parts of Afghanistan.

In the north, the power struggle between the Tajik Jamiat-i-Islami, Uzbek Junbish-i-Milli and Hazara Hezb-Wahadat continued well into the 2002-2003 period, fuelling rivalry and occasionally resulting in fighting in urban centres such as Mazar-i-Sharif, illustrating that even the local allies of the US were not willing to create a secure environment (Sedra 2002). The security in the Pashtun-dominated south, has gradually worsened following the regrouping of the Taliban to such an extent that in 2007, most parts of the south once again, became no-go areas for the international community. Though the international military forces have been waging a war against the Taliban and Al-Qaida in the south on a daily basis, they have found it very difficult to remain in control of the region. Furthermore, the military attacks on the international community's presence, both military and humanitarian; kidnappings; assassinations of local and national politicians; suicide bombings; and looting and extortion of private properties have, unfortunately, become part of day-to-day life in post-conflict Afghanistan.

ISAF – to deal with the security challenge

The deployment of International Security Afghanistan Force (ISAF) was supposed to deal with the security challenge in the country, but its jurisdiction was limited to Kabul and its immediate vicinity, and until Nato's takeover of command in 2003 there was a major security vacuum in the countryside in the early days of the reconstruction process (Suhrke, Harpviken and Strand 2004). This has been used as a justification for the military's extensive dominant role in the relief and reconstruction programmes in the country. The Provincial Reconstruction Teams (PRTs) which include combat forces, military personnel (usually up to 90-95 per cent of 50-300 staff) and civilian expertise have been involved in a wide range of programmes such as relief aid distribution, needs assessment, coordination of aid work, liaison with regional commanders and security.

The first PRT was established by the US in Gardez in December 2002. As a reconstruction model they represent a comprehensive involvement of the military in all aspects of relief and reconstruction programmes. This is a reversal of the structure of relationships between the military and civilian actors of the early 1990s, and the civilian recovery programmes are now undertaken with a clear military objective of "stabilisation" in low security areas where the "war against terrorism" is being waged. In fact, the core argument for the justification of PRTs as an alternative approach to civilian-led recovery was the provision of such activities in areas where humanitarian NGOs cannot operate effectively due to security challenges. However, it should be noted that most PRTs were actually not deployed in low security areas such as southern and south-eastern regions of the country until 2004. Moreover, with 26 PRTs led by 14 different countries such as the US (12 of them), UK, Canada, Germany, Turkey and France (Adams, 2009), the work of PRTs "refers to a variety of different mandates and forms of organization, and is as such difficult to pin down" (Suhrke, Harpviken and Strand 2004: 48).

Therefore, the type, approach and quality of relief and reconstruction work undertaken by different PRTs tend to show a great level of variations. In most cases, there are serious operational problems too, as the staff employed often lack of essential capacities and experience to undertake comprehensive relief and reconstruction programmes. The lack of awareness of the cultural values of traditional rural communities of Afghanistan has been, for example, a serious stumbling block for PRTs, especially in their interaction with women. The lack of coordination among different PRTs, and between PRTs and other international organisations, is another major operational challenge that is yet to be overcome (Adams 2009).

Confusion over role of PRTs

Secondly, there is an overall confusion within the aid community concerning the role of PRTs in general and their mandate for winning "hearts and minds" of Afghans. From the assessment of needs and selection of projects, the work of PRTs raises serious question marks. As for most of them the priority is to be able to create enabling environments for stabilisation and the continuation of military operations, the effectiveness and relevance of undertakings are often questionable. For example, while the UN and humanitarian NGOs would have adequate capacity to undertake such programmes as drilling wells, reconstructing schools and health facilities, most PRTs tend to focus on such quick impact projects too, resulting in duplications.

It is also important to recognise that there are, indeed, variations in the way PRTs operate. For example, the UK PRTs emphasise the separation of military and reconstruction programmes by keeping those projects related to recovery and development under the jurisdiction of the Department for International Development (DFID). The military components, on the other hand, are apparent in such programmes as the collection of weapons, mine clearance and security sector reform activities (Jacobsen 2005). However, the overall ethical question for all PRTs, but particularly those run by the US, is about their real intention of "winning hearts and minds" of Afghans, as it seems that their military and political priorities are the ones that really motivate them. Moreover, if providing assistance in return of the intelligence about the Taliban and Al-Qaida is part of this strategy, then there is a serious problem with the humanitarian credentials of their work.

Thirdly, the separation between the military and humanitarian assistance has been completely blurred, which has in return made the work of humanitarian organisations particularly dangerous. Operating under the same command structure as their coalition forces, the PRTs present a confusing identity for local populations. Since they wear similar uniforms and carry similar weapons to those of the combat forces, they are considered part of the US-led war machine in most parts of the country (Eronen 2008). Clearly, even their impartiality is under question. However, as they undertake recovery programmes throughout the country, there is now hardly any distinction between who is a military and who is a civilian actor for most Afghans. For example, humanitarian organisations can no longer assume the protection of their "humanitarian identity" as they are considered an element of the US-led military intervention in almost the entire country.

Finally, the use of relief and reconstruction assistance in a way to ensure the loyalty of local populations has also meant the creation of a parallel governance structure, as PRTs have much more resources to respond to the needs of

Afghans than their local and national governments. Ironically, the PRTs were originally considered to be a vehicle to extend the Afghan Transitional Administration's presence throughout the country, but today, some of them at least, have become a competitor to the Afghan government's own efforts at reconstruction and development (Eronen 2008). In other words, the PRTs are to some extent, undermining the local ownership of the reconstruction process, and their continuing presence is now doing more harm than good.

"Reporting" Afghanistan

With these concerns in mind, the next question we should ask is why the military embeddedness of the media in Afghanistan actually matters for humanitarianism. However, before that it should be noted that there are already serious question marks about such embeddedness for the well-being of journalists, as the military operations in countries such as Afghanistan and Iraq have been coming under direct attack from a wide range of insurgency groups. In fact, many journalists now realise that their embeddedness in military units results in more risks to their well-being in the long term than the protection they receive from such an affiliation. However, it can be argued that this is a decision that journalists need to make on a case-by-case basis according to the priorities of why and how they consider such embeddedness as essential for their work.

There are three primary consequences of such embeddedness that should be considered carefully. Firstly, as it is the case for humanitarian NGOs, the media's presence as part of military structures poses a serious risk to their neutrality. Considering that the Western's media has audiences all over the world, including in those war-torn environments, seeing journalists reporting as part of foreign military structures encourages local populations to question the neutrality of their reporting. In fact, the military embeddedness might actually limit the media's movement and reporting to some extent in countries such as Afghanistan and Iraq.

Need to build up trust of local communities

Being able to report from the frontlines may be crucial for journalists, but it is also important to recognise that there is, in fact, an important price paid for it.

This is because being able to have the trust of local communities is an essential consideration for the media when they start to move from the frontline reporting to more conventional journalism in war-affected environments. However, having seen the Western media as part of "occupational" military forces for weeks or months on their television screens, the local populations not surprisingly see them as being far from trustworthy, neutral third parties.

Secondly, from an ethical perspective, it is important to consider how "independent" such reporting can be. For example, do we hear the truth about the way humanitarianism is used for military and political objectives by the US-led military intervention? Do the media have access to the PRTs' relief and reconstruction projects that are, in fact, total failures and rejected by local populations? Why is there little reporting on the way humanitarianism is traded in return for the intelligence about Al-Qaida and Taliban from local communities?

Thirdly, the media's military embeddedness is a critical issue for humanitarianism in Afghanistan since reports from the frontlines often lack historical and geographical contextualisation. The focus on "security" reduces the challenges faced by Afghans to military ones, so marginalising the economic, cultural and religious dimensions of their struggles.

Moreover, there seem to be some well developed patterns in the way that Afghanistan is frequently reported by the media. For example, whenever there is a news item about the Afghan government it seems to be often about corruption or mismanagement. Such reporting gradually builds an overall assumption that Afghans will never be able to govern their own affairs. Also, whenever there is a rare report about a reconstruction project, it is often about an international NGO's work rather than those undertaken by many Afghan national and grassroots civil society organisations.

Alternatively, the reporting in the UK about the military operations is often about the "heroic" British forces and the way they are ready to sacrifice their lives in such a dangerous work. Isn't this true? Yes absolutely, but as pointed out earlier, the military's work in Afghanistan involves much more than frontline fighting, and the Western public needs to see more of it in the media. It is only in this way that it will be possible to talk about a fair and balanced coverage of what's really happening in Afghanistan and those humanitarian challenges faced by its population.

The conflict in Afghanistan has had a very heavy human toll and thus there is a moral responsibility for the Western media to try to become the voice of ordinary Afghans by covering their humanitarian and reconstruction challenges.

Conclusion

The war in Afghanistan fails to comply with international humanitarian law and humanitarian principles are usually subordinated to political interests. Aid agencies are becoming increasingly involved in complicated political emergencies and the subordination of humanitarian principles sets a dangerous precedent for future humanitarian crises. The use of reconstruction programmes for political and military objectives through PRT mechanisms poses a serious challenge to the basic principles of humanitarianism.

It is essential that reporting by the Western media should adopt a critical perspective. However, there appears little news about the intentions and work of PRTs in the British media. The priority is often given to those reports about the fighting carried out by the British forces against the Taliban and al-Qaida. The news of fighting and killing are clearly more suitable for headlines but, as those journalists who have been to Afghanistan would only know too well, the "story" is, in fact, much bigger than that.

The lack of contextualisation for such frontline reporting of military operations distorts the understanding of the issues of humanitarianism and state building in Afghanistan today. Embedded journalists may probably be considered as just trying to do their jobs, but it is important to bear in mind the cost of such embeddedness to humanitarianism.

References

Adams, Natasha (2009) *Policy options for state-building in Afghanistan: The role of NATO PRTs in Development in Afghanistan*, Washington, SAIS

Anderson, Mary (1996) *Do no harm: How aid can support peace or war*, Boulder, Lynne Rienner Publishers

El Bushra, Judith (1999) Neutrality and impartiality, Pirotte, Claire, Husson, Bernard and Grunewald, François (eds) *Responding to emergencies and fostering development: The dilemmas of humanitarian Aid*, London, Zed Books

Eronen, Oskari (2008) *PRT Models in Afghanistan: Approaches to civil-military integration*, Vol.1, No. 5, Finland, Crisis Management Centre

Jacobsen, Peter, Viggo (2005) *PRTs in Afghanistan: Successful but not sufficient*, No. 6, Copenhagen, Danish Institute for International Studies

Özerdem, Alpaslan and Rufini, Gianni (2005) Humanitarianism and the principles of humanitarian action in post-Cold War context, Barakat, Sultan (ed.) *After the conflict: Reconstruction and development in the aftermath of conflict*, London, I.B.Tauris pp 51-66

Sedra, Mark (2002) *Changing the warlord culture: Security sector reform in post-Taliban Afghanistan*, BICC Paper 25, Bonn, BICC

Suhrke, Astri, Harpviken, Kristian, Berg and Strand, Arne (2004) *Conflictual peacebuilding: Afghanistan two years after Bonn*, Bergen, Chr. Michelsen Institute

Note on the author

Alpaslan Özerdem is Professor at the Centre for Peace and Reconciliation Studies, at Coventry University. With field research experience in Afghanistan, Bosnia-Herzegovina, El Salvador, Kosovo, Lebanon, Liberia, Philippines, Sierra Leone, Sri Lanka and Turkey, he specialises in the politics of humanitarian interventions, peacekeeping, security sector reform, reintegration of former combatants and post-conflict state building. He is the co-author (with Tim Jacoby) of *Disaster management and civil society: Earthquake relief in Japan, Turkey, India* (I. B. Tauris 2006), author of *Post-war recovery: Disarmament, demobilization and reintegration* (I. B. Tauris 2008) and co-editor (with Richard Bowd) of *Participatory research methodologies in development and post-disaster/conflict reconstruction* (Ashgate 2010).

An "AfPak" weekend: US interest and *The New York Times'* news coverage

Oliver Boyd-Barrett examines in detail the coverage of Afghanistan and Pakistan in *The New York Times* over just one weekend at the start of May 2010 and concludes that the reports are in keeping with US/Nato foreign policy objectives, presenting US/Nato presence in the "AfPak" region as benign

This chapter analyses *The New York Times'* (*The NYT*) coverage of Afghanistan and Pakistan ("AfPak") over one weekend, 1-2 May 2010. Making no claim to being representative of *NYT* coverage, its purpose is to explore emerging issues concerning coverage of international conflicts in which *The NYT*'s own country is an important player. Such issues do emerge, concerning story selection, representation of place and players, narrative construction, sourcing, and ideology. Reports were selected according to whether they appeared in the full story listing on the web page of the global edition of *The NYT* as delivered to subscribers in the US on mornings (US EST) of the days sampled. In a larger study I am conducting, "AfPak" features and editorials have been included, but there were none this weekend.

The study is informed by a critical literature on coverage of international conflicts and terrorism (e.g. Barnett and Reynolds 2009; Cottle 2008; Edwards and Cromwell 2010; Moeller 2009). The focus is the US/Nato war against "Taliban", "al Qaeda", "insurgents", "militants", "guerrillas" or "terrorists" in "AfPak". Speech marks indicate my lack of conviction, as a reader, as to who exactly the "enemy" is and why, and whether this "enemy" has a homogeneous and structural identity. Such terms are likely constructed by association (e.g. with "9/11", "mistreatment of women", "drugs") to evoke negative connotations, conforming to usage by the political and military sources that media draw upon, and have propagandistic intent.

Terms such as "insurgents", "insurgency" or "militants" imply that fighters, so identified, oppose legitimate authority. "Legitimacy" in the context of foreign occupation is contentious. The Kabul-based regime of Hamid Karzai was slipped into power and sustained by occupying US/Nato troops, notwithstanding limited democratic process. Pentagon sources, spring 2010, testified, a decade following US/Nato invasion in fall 2001, that much of Afghanistan, especially the south, favoured the Taliban and/or rejected the legitimacy of Karzai's government (US Congress 2010).

Application of "Taliban" or "al-Qaeda" labels to any group, absent compelling evidence of its structural integration with either of these two distinctive (but fragmented/loosely-knit) movements, problematically identifies the group as a component of the "enemy," despite manifest complexity in the composition of local communities and forces and their respective aspirations. A *NYT* report of 30 April, on North and South Waziristan in Pakistan, refers to an "alphabet soup of dangerous militant groups", a "tangle of tribes" and "profound fracturing", including a Pakistani Taliban made up of several parts operating independently (Tavernise, Gall and Khan 2010).

Saturday 1 May 2010
Report 1: Suicide bomber kills 2 in Pakistan's Swat Valley (Anon 2010a)

From AP, this is posted 4.41am, datelined Mingora, Pakistan. It reports a suicide bomber blew himself up, killing two civilians. Six others were wounded. The principal source is a named police official. The incident occurred when the bomber was surrounded by police. The source initially said that a bomb had gone off. Later, he said that a "suicide bomber" detonated the bomb after being surrounded by police and asked to surrender. This was after one "militant" had been arrested and another killed by "security" forces, and after the police had received information that three "suicide bombers" had entered the area. The main part of the report comprises five short paragraphs. Four paragraphs follow, providing a recent history of conflict with the Taliban in this area. These do not refer to any of many local suicide bombings from the immediately preceding weeks and months. The final two paragraphs concern an entirely different incident, a roadside bomb explosion near a police vehicle which wounded seven people in Quetta, Baluchistan.

Why is this story selected?

These comments also apply to the second report. Many "AfPak" news developments occurred from 29 April to 1 May. Some were reported as 1 May; others carried 30 April deadlines even if not available to American readers until 1 May. Some earlier stories would easily have justified follow-up coverage on 1 May. But not in *The NYT*, whose choices, on criteria of area and topic significance, are less than self-explanatory. Alternative stories (appearing, for example, in the *Guardian*, Inter-Press Service, Anti-war.com and Wired), not mentioned in *The NYT* on 1 May, included a semi-annual Pentagon report, already cited, released on 28 April. This reported that Taliban dominated what Gareth Porter of Inter-Press Service called a "vast contiguous zone of heavily populated territory across Southern Afghanistan" and that 13 provinces were sympathetic to the "insurgents" (a word that could be substituted by "freedom fighters").

Porter argued that the Pentagon had understated local anger with opium eradication efforts, and the abusive behaviour of police and warlords. After nine years of war, the "Taliban" controlled the Pashtun south of the country. According to a Wired story by Nathan Hodge datelined 28 April, the report provided a "grim picture of the state of the nearly nine-year-old, US-led war". Indeed, "insurgents" considered 2009 their most successful year. Violence had increased 87 per cent between February 2009 and March 2010. US-backed forces had killed 87 civilians in the period January to March 2010, compared to 29 in the same period of 2009.

Richard Norton-Taylor, of the *Guardian*, quoted Nato's most senior civilian official in Afghanistan, Mark Sedwill, as warning of a "very tough" year ahead. Some 100 UK troops had already been killed and 150 injured in the previous year. This source anticipated that violent conflict would endure a further four years, with foreign troops remaining in Afghanistan for another 10 to 15 years. Sedwill estimated that three quarters of the "insurgents" were *allied* with, rather than fighting *for* the Taliban. An Anti-war.com (Ditz 2010) report, dated 30 April, quoted Centcom Commander General David Petraeus as predicting a lot more violence. The Iranian broadcaster Press TV, on 30 April, quoted a UN report that 2,400 civilians had been killed in Afghanistan in 2009, more than in 2001. Reuters reported, on 1 May, that the Obama administration sought an additional $20 billion for Afghan reconstruction (mainly for training Afghan soldiers), a 38 per cent increase on what had already been spent for this purpose since 2002, with the money being routed mainly through Afghan agencies.

For news of specific killings, several reports rivaled *The NYT* choice. Al Jazeera, on 30 April, reported French troops had admitted firing a missile, killing four civilians in Afghanistan – an incident occurring on 6 April but reported to Al Jazeera, April 29. Press TV, on 30 April, quoted an AFP report that US-led troops had killed two women and a child in southern Afghanistan and that the day before, foreign troops had killed a civilian when they were attacking the home of a member of parliament (an event also covered by the *Independent*, headlined "Afghan MP: US troops murdered my relative in raid"). Wired, May 1, reported that Afghan police were thought to have mistakenly killed between one and four UN employees, following a Taliban raid on a UN compound in Kabul, October 2009. The Chinese news agency, Xinhua, reported the killing of 15 militants and one security personnel in Orakzai tribal agency in the Mushti Shekhan area, in a Pakistani military campaign that started in March.

Why did *The NYT*, using an AP report, prioritise the "suicide bombing" in Pakistan? Was it the least dated? Possibly. Was it the most horrific or significant? Unlikely. It may have conformed best with how the US administration would want the public to view the area: a place of willful violence by religious extremists, in need of the "stability" that US-supported Pakistani police and "security forces", and their Afghan counterparts, can (allegedly) provide. It was a "success" in the sense that the bomber was killed (after what police claimed was fair warning). A *NYT* story of 30 April provides another clue. Stranger than any story analysed during the ensuing weekend, this lengthy report by Sabrina Tavernise, Carlotta Gall and Ismail Khan, starting on page one, has only *one* named – and not especially relevant source – towards the end. Its tone and purpose is suggested by the headline ("Pakistan in shift, weighs attack on militant *lair*" – author's italics) and the lead namely, "The Pakistani military, long reluctant to heed American urging that it attack Pakistani militant groups in their main base in North Waziristan, is coming around to the idea that it must do so, in its own interests." The story refers to unidentified "Western diplomats" and "security officials" in speculating the likelihood or otherwise of a Pakistani offensive, sowing concerns, along the way, about Pakistani military links to "militants."

Sources

There is only one source for the "suicide bombing" story, a senior police official, Qazi Ghulam Farooq. Why is one source deemed sufficient? Why is a police official's account assumed to be correct and disinterested? The story of the roadside bomb near Quetta also has one source, a named police official, Ghulam Nab. There are apparently no eyewitness accounts of these events.

Place

The story gently exoticises the location, noting that the Swat Valley, once favoured by tourists, has only recently been wrested from the Taliban by Pakistani military. An implication is that demonstration of a capacity for control of the region by US/Pakistani "authorities" is a test of the success or otherwise of the recent campaign, which in turn was part of a broader initiative against "militants" in the "volatile" northwest.

Players

The perpetrators, killed and wounded, are given no names. Much is unclear. Was the bomber intending to commit suicide, or did he detonate the bomb to avoid arrest? What was his relationship to the "militant" who had been arrested and the "militant" who had been killed? Were the "security forces" responsible for the arrest and killing, the same as the police who had surrounded the "suicide bomber"? What were the circumstances leading up to that arrest, and to that killing? Who initiated the violence in its immediate context? What are we to understand by the term "militant?"

The background detail mentions this is an area once cleared of the "Taliban", so can we assume the "militant" is "Taliban?" That would be quite a leap in a region populated by so many different "militant" groups, and in which the

"Taliban" is not a single, homogeneous entity. The anonymous treatment of the "militant" contrasts with the comparatively luxurious resonances attributed to the perpetrator of the roadside bomb in Quetta which, the report notes, is capital of Baluchistan province, where "ethnic Baluch nationalists have waged a slow-scale insurgency for years to demand more autonomy and a greater share of income from the area's natural resources". Did not the "suicide bomber" and his colleagues have comparable aspirations? Do Baluch "nationalists" have no religious affiliation with other Pakistanis or with "Taliban" (one Baluch group, Jundollah, is Sunni, like the Taliban, and targets Shia opponents – according to an anonymous report in Pakistan's *Daily Times*, 24 February 2010: see Anon 2010b)?

Contextualising paragraphs say nothing about "Taliban" objectives other than that in the past they have included demands for enforcement of "Islamic" laws. They tell us that the area fell under Taliban "sway" and later "insurgent control" from 2007 to 2009. During that time, some reports indicated that the "Taliban" attracted support from impoverished or oppressed locals. Pakistan features massive social injustices including the permanent bonding of labour to landowners and employees – a phenomenon that affects "millions" of labourers and their families, according to the US Department of Labor [1] or possibly up to eight million, according to human rights group Anti-caste.[2] The scope for leveraging local discontent is considerable, and doubtless comparable to Baluchistan.

Point

The immediate point centres on unattributed speculation that "the violence raised fears that the Taliban are returning" to a region that was supposedly "cleared" previously. We are not told whose fears these are. Were the "Taliban" ever really ousted from the area? A perhaps more important point, therefore, evident in the four paragraphs of contextualisation, is re-confirmation of the hegemonic narrative, relayed by Western media a year before today's event. After 2007, "authorities" (are they "authorities" when unable to exercise "authority"?) had tried talking peace with the "Taliban", but the "military" (Pakistani army, or the Pakistani army with encouragement and support from the US?) launched a major offensive when the "Taliban" began to "infiltrate" the Buner region just south of the Swat valley.

Assuming the term "Taliban" correctly and helpfully identifies particular armed groups, did these originate locally, did they move in from Afghanistan, or were they a mixture? This is a story about how the "Taliban" – commonly associated by Western politicians and media with responsibility for providing haven to "al Qaeda" before 9/11, therefore apparently but disputably bearing some responsibility for 9/11, as well as for having "extreme" Islamic views and being hostile to women and modernity – under military pressure from US, Nato and Afghan forces, have extended their influence in those areas of Pakistan least amenable to control by Pakistan's official government.

In this report, the Pakistan government supports US and Nato goals, whatever those are exactly and in face of the fact – evident in the second story analysed below – of deep-seated links between Pakistan's intelligence agency, ISI and the "Taliban". The dubious legitimacy of maintaining US and Nato occupation forces for nine years in a country in which their original enemy, "al Qaeda", no longer has a significant presence, is the eternal elephant in the room. To begin to unravel that mystery, so critical to hundreds of millions of people around the world, is perhaps too big a claim on Western media.

Report 2: Pakistani ex-intelligence officer killed (Tavernise and Shah 2010)

This thirteen paragraph report, by Sabrina Tavernise and Pir Zubair Shah, carries a 30 April date, although was still on *The NYT* site on 1 May. Datelined Islamabad, it concerns the finding of the corpse of a Pakistani ex-intelligence officer who had been kidnapped by "Taliban" some months previously. The first sentence describes him as having had "deep connections to the Taliban and al Qaeda". The second paragraph gives his name, Khalid Khawaja, and details where his body was found. He had been shot. This information is attributed to "Pakistani television," and to the victim's son (it is not clear whether the son talked directly to *The Times* or to Pakistani television).

The third paragraph contextualises the location with reference to the *"snarl* of militant networks" (author's italics) along Pakistan's Western border with Afghanistan. Other contextualisation includes information that Khawaja's links to militants originated during the Soviet occupation of Afghanistan. We learn that he was a "fast" (!) talker, and a former air force officer. Since defeat of the Soviets, the relationship of "militants" to the state of Pakistan had deteriorated. "Militants" who once enjoyed the support of the Pakistani state have now "turned on" it, forming a "dangerous patchwork of tribal, ethnic and sectarian alliances". Contextualisation continues into the fourth paragraph from which it appears that Khalid was a negotiator for Pakistani military during their siege of a "militant mosque" in Islamabad in 2007. This led to a split among "militant" groups with some ("half") – including a group known as Jaish-e-Muhammad, based in the Punjab – moving into "Taliban-controlled Waziristan" and declaring war on the state.

Paragraph five specifies sources that include a "religious leader familiar with the kidnapping", "Pakistani television" and "reports". Together, these inform us that the kidnappers called themselves "Asian Tigers", that they are linked to Jaish-e-Muhammad, speak Punjabi, and left a note on the body declaring that Khawaja had been killed because he sided with the government during the siege. No source is specified for the following one-sentence paragraph that says it is believed (by whom, is not clear) that Khawaja was killed because he persuaded one of the "militants" to escape during the siege wearing a burqa, so that the military could arrest the "militant".

The next paragraph, number seven, describes how Khawaja appeared in a video taken of him in captivity, confessing that he spied for the US and for Pakistan. There is reference to an "earlier report" that claimed he had been on a negotiating mission for the state. In paragraph eight an unnamed source for Pakistani intelligence denies that Khawaja had been on a state mission, and a "Western diplomat" claims that this would have been unlikely. Paragraph nine asserts that Pakistan cut ties with the "militants" after 2001, but that it is unknown how long Khawaja maintained links with the military. The author asserts that Khawaja provided "militant" contacts to Daniel Pearl, the *Wall Street*

Journal reporter who was assassinated in 2002. The following paragraph, ten, asserts that Khawaja was adamantly anti-American and opposed to the "AfPak" wars. Also, that he served the defense team of five Americans detained in 2009 on suspicion of seeking to wage jihad in Afghanistan, even though he had no law degree and was "self-appointed".

An anti-American quote is attributed to him from the previous December, in paragraph eleven. Khawaja is then quoted in paragraph twelve as saying that America is not held to account for its bombs and that suicide bombers are, in effect, justified. He is said to have claimed to be housing an Arab family whose father had been killed in Afghanistan. In the final paragraph, his son Osama is quoted as saying that his father loved martyrdom and that he is lucky to have achieved that status.

Why is this story selected?

There are several unusual features that may explain the choice, although it is likely not as significant as many of the others, already indicated, that could have been chosen or followed up on today, but were not. Any story that promises to shed further light on the shadowy inter-linkages between Pakistan's intelligence service, ISI, and the "Taliban" is likely to be newsworthy, in the context of the coercive alliance that the US imposed on Pakistan following 9/11 (Musharraf 2008), the history of both ISI and CIA cooperation with the Mujahidin during the Soviet occupation (Crile 2007) in distribution of weapons and in the nurture of militant versions of Islam that would best promote US foreign policy objectives (Chossudovsky 2002).

There are indications of ISI involvement in the events of 9/11 that may or may not have formed part of a US covert operation to provide a pretext for a radical up-scaling of US aggression in Central Asia (ibid; Griffin 2004; Ahmed 2005). Such matters are rarely subject to public discussion in Western media although occasionally hinted at obliquely (as in the movie depiction of the attempt to prevent the assassination of Daniel Pearl, *A Mighty Heart*, directed by Winterbottom 2007). The story provides substance to the contention that elements of ISI are sympathetic to the "Taliban" but also distances itself from that very same contention by appearing to foreground Pakistani denials that in his dealings with the "Taliban" Khawaja worked for the state.

Place

Khawaja's body was found between the towns of Mir Ali and Miranshah in the "militant-controlled" North Waziristan area. The discovery and state of his body is reported second-hand. The place names have no significance for most *Times* readers and the article does nothing to relieve them from obscurity. Khawaja's significance lies in other sources of iconicity: an intelligence officer (or ex-intelligence officer, as *The NYT* headline would invite us to believe) of the ISI, a victim of the "Taliban" (possibly), a man of mystery – did he work for the Americans and/or the Pakistani state, as the "Taliban" appear to have believed? Might he have been an exposed double-agent? Was he an anti-American fundamentalist sympathiser who somehow provoked the distrust of those with whose cause he identified? Other, unexplored variations present themselves. Who are the "Asian Tigers?" Why do they appear just now? Why do they need a new name? Could they be linked to US/Nato covert operations? Might they be a complete fiction? Who would know and who would really care? The sources quoted are almost all dubious to the extreme. The amount of independent *NYT* investigation appears inexcusably minimal.

Sources

For a sensitive story, it speaks volumes that the sourcing should be so unsatisfactory and one-sided. No attempt is made to help the reader assess the trustworthiness or credibility of "Pakistani television" – what is *that*? Is there just one television news service in Pakistan (actually there are several news channels), and what is Pakistan's record in television coverage of such instances (mixed, as one would expect)? No "militants" contribute their voices to this report, with the potential exception of a "religious" source "familiar with the kidnapping". No assessment of that source is offered, nor any indication as to the reasons for his anonymity. The tone makes it clear that "militants" are bad but that the Pakistani military is basically good.

Epithets such as "tribal," "ethnic" or "sectarian" are applied to "*them*" as though they could not be relevant to "*us*" and our allies. A reference is made to Jaish-e-Muhammad with virtually no background as to its nature and politics. No evaluation is offered of the 2007 siege of a so-called "militant" mosque (who determines when a mosque is "militant"?), or of the behaviour of either side in that conflict, or why it should have created a rift within the so-called "militant" community. What factors separate these groups? Much of the report has no source: recent historical background or context is presented without sourcing, as though it is non-contentious, public knowledge. Some of the sources are risibly opaque, notably the "Western diplomat".

Players

Here is a character who may have played a small part in the dramatic and tragic story of Daniel Pearl (though no less tragic than any other single death by violence in the "AfPak" region under US/Nato occupation). The report captures a few of the perplexities that Western powers confront in their dealings with the Pakistani state, including the complex interrelating powers of the ISI, Islam, the military, and the prickly but understandable interests that Pakistan has in its border with Afghanistan and in matters affecting the internal distribution of Afghani power. Who Khawaja was and what he represented is left almost entirely to attributions from deeply interested and compromised parties, to the exclusion of all voices from the side that it is presumed had perpetrated his murder. The "enemy" is voiceless, perhaps on this occasion by choice. Western journalists appear not to trouble themselves with even token attempts to redress this basically one-sided representation of events.

Point of the story

There is legitimate news interest in the fate of a man whose background has been one of negotiation or mediation between the Pakistani military and the "Taliban" (whoever exactly *they* are – conceivably any group of nationalists who resist occupying armies who massacre citizens with bombs and drones) and who *may* be still engaged in that enterprise up until his capture and death. (Note also persistent reports of US/Nato troops assisting the Taliban, e.g. Peled 2010). The story suggests there is little hope for reconciliation or a negotiated deal, unless special factors apply – such as reported "Taliban" suspicions as to Khawaja's goodwill and independence. From a Western point of view the story provides evidence of apparent continuing barbarity and unreasonableness of the "Taliban", whom the Pakistani army, with strong US and Nato encouragement if not participation, is (perhaps) attempting to liquidate.

The potential for more disturbing readings, such as the strength of anti-Western, nationalist sentiment in the Pakistani armed forces, and the possibility of Pakistani involvement in 9/11, is given short shrift, in part by seeming to suggest that Khawaja was possibly acting on his own, that he entertained ideas about Americans and of "suicide bombers" that would surely seem beyond the pail to most "civilised" US observers and that his links to Pakistani military may very likely have been terminated – even if it is not known exactly when. More assertive is the authors' contention that the Pakistani military had cut their links with militants after 9/11, which seems highly improbable in the face of a stream of reports over the years that would suggest the opposite.

Sunday, 2 May 2010
Report 1: Police seek man taped near Times Square bomb (Grynbaum, Rashbaum and Baker 2010)

This report updates a breaking news story from the previous evening, concerning a failed car bomb attempt near Times Square, New York. This would lead later in the week to the arrest and confession of the alleged bomber, Faisal Shahzad, and strong indications of his links to anti-American elements in Pakistan. The story would continue to dominate mainstream media headlines for much of the week. It was far from clear, as the story began to unfold, that this was, indeed, a report related to "AfPak".

According to the report, law enforcement officials have provided more detail of the failed car bomb, and of surveillance footage showing a "white man" in the area. The man, identified later as a "person of interest" to the police, had behaved "furtively," looking over his shoulder and removing a black shirt to reveal a red one underneath. It quotes senior police sources testifying to the damage that the bomb might have caused had it been successfully ignited. Apart from additional patrols, a significant increase in police presence is not envisaged. A Homeland Security source says there is no evidence of continued threat. Police say that the owner of the vehicle has been identified and that the police are seeking to interview him/her. There was no evidence to support a claim of responsibility from a "Pakistan Taliban group" with a record for "far-fetched" attempts to take credit for such attacks.

A separate tip was being followed up, but there were no suspects as yet. A police spokesman pointed out that a terrorist act did not need to be perpetrated by an institution, that an individual could act on his own. In the meantime, Times Square was undergoing an "uneasy return to normalcy" after a night of cancelled Broadway shows and use of a robot to investigate the parked Pathfinder car that had been used for the attempt. The report recalls that two street vendors had hailed a mounted police officer after noticing smoke coming from the car. The car had been brought to a forensics centre. No fingerprints had yet been found. Police were also trying to find where some of the bomb-related contents of the car had been purchased.

Most of the contents, the report later revealed, could have been purchased from a "home-supply store". The gun locker, it was believed, would be among the more easily traceable of the items. Ownership of the vehicle had been determined from the Vehicle Identification Number. Initial expectation as to the identity of the owner had proven incorrect. The car's licence plate was connected to a different vehicle. A repair shop owner was helping police with their inquiries. Attempts were being made to determine where the vehicle had entered Manhattan. The explosive device was on the back seat. This device was described, as were the reasons for why it had failed to explode. Investigators were looking into similarities with specified past incidents (Glasgow and London 2007) where similar devices had failed to explode. No link to these had been established.

The mayor of New York said there was no evidence, so far, linking the event to a recognised terrorist organisation. A Homeland Security official said that the TSA had heightened security outside airports. A conference call had been arranged for Sunday night. Police were also viewing surveillance footage from 80 cameras as well as video footage shot by a tourist; police were flying to Philadelphia to interview the tourist. A call had been received at 4:00am warning that the car bomb was a diversion before a greater explosion. Because the car had been parked near the headquarters of Viacom, there was speculation, not ruled out by the police, that the motive might be related to a controversial episode of a Viacom entertainment property, South Park, that had portrayed the Prophet Muhammad.

Why is this report selected?

Of all the reports included in this study, this one requires the least explanation. It barely needs comparison with other possible "AfPak" stories, and fits usual Western criteria of newsworthiness. It is of clear relevance and importance to the newspaper's immediate New York constituency and beyond. It may signify an escalation in terrorist attempts on American soil. Three things stand out from the narrative construction:

- First, there is considerable emphasis on the rapid and sophisticated progress that police are making to identify the perpetrator.
- Secondly, there is a distinct effort by sources to distance the event from "AfPak", even though a "Pakistan Taliban group" (not identified) has claimed responsibility. The reliability of the group's claims is ridiculed (without specification of previous instances of such claims).
- Thirdly, there is an emphasis on quick restoration of "normalcy:" no significant additional police presence is anticipated; Broadway shows are expected to open as usual that evening. Authority, in this perspective, has everything under control, is responding quickly and efficiently. While the danger was great, it has past. There is no comfort here for the enemy.

Sources

The report is attributed to Michael Grynbaum, William Rashbaum and Al Baker. This is a law enforcement story, drawing on both identified and anonymous law officers. There are four named authoritative or official sources: they include the New York City police commissioner, the Police Department's chief spokesman, the Homeland Security secretary and New York City major. The other official sources, and it seems there are many, are anonymous. "FBI agents and detectives", of whom at least some are from the "Joint Terrorist Task Force" (which is not otherwise described), "police and FBI officials", "investigators", "police", "officials", "authorities", a "Homeland Security official". There is only one civilian source, the car repair shop owner, one Wayne Le Blanc. Curiously, there are no interviews with the street vendors who alerted the police originally, nor with the mounted policeman who was first to be alerted by the vendors, nor with any of the eyewitnesses or passers-by.

Place

The location, close to Times Square, is given considerable emphasis, with references and maps – unsurprising, given its iconic status in US history and culture. This is the location where television networks celebrate the welcoming of each New Year from the first time zone of the US to enter it. This is the iconic and actual center of the nation's news and entertainment industries, many of them having their headquarters in and around Times Square. The location is leveraged both by the terrorist, who has heightened the shock of his intended act on that account, and by the media, for whom the location comes to represent the nation's good fortune, professionalism, resilience.

Players

The principal players are undoubtedly the police and the numerous investigations they are conducting and the actions they are taking to determine who was guilty. The story emphasises their alertness, commitment, expertise. Everything else, everyone else, is marginal.

The point of the story

The point of the story, in addition to simply keeping the public informed of a specific and significant act of (planned) terrorism, appears to be to highlight the potential menace of terrorism, while at the same calming fears, parading the concerned and competent leadership of major public officials, encouraging public trust in police competence, and rubbishing the credibility of attempts by a Pakistani "Taliban" group to claim responsibility.

Report 2: Afghans die in bombing, as toll rises for civilians (Oppel and Wafa 2010)

In the first paragraph, it is reported that seven people were killed when a bus struck a roadside bomb in eastern Afghanistan near the border with Pakistan. The second paragraph reports that as many as 14 other Afghans were wounded. A police source in the third paragraph claims that most of the victims were women and children. The fourth paragraph notes that the blast took place shortly after a gun battle between "Taliban" and Afghan "security" forces: the relationship between these events is not established.

Fifth and sixth paragraphs provide some context in terms of the rising number of Afghan civilians being killed, mostly from roadside bombs and suicide attacks. A seventh paragraph attributes most of the killings to "insurgents" but notes that some, accidental, deaths were due to the stepped-up activities of American and Nato troops. An eighth paragraph predicts that there will be a certain increase during the summer when fighting is at its most intense and because of a planned American and Nato offensive for Kandahar that "was the center of power when the Taliban led the country". A ninth paragraph observes that 173 American and NATO troops have been killed "here" (Kandahar? Afghanistan?) in 2010, an increase of almost 90 per cent over the previous year. The final paragraph notes that the most recent death was of a British soldier who was providing protection for other troops returning from patrol.

Why is this story selected?

Apart from the Times Square attempted car bombing this is the only other "AfPak" story in *The NYT* this Sunday. Had it been a relatively quiet weekend in that part of the world? No. Stories becoming available on the Sunday through various sources, including Antiwar.com, dated from April 29 onwards, embraced the following:

AP, 30 April: Private Afghan security guards protecting Nato supply convoys in southern Kandahar fire wildly into villages they pass hindering coalition efforts to build local support ahead of the planner summer offensive (Abbot 2010a).

AP, 29 April: A congressional hearing into the legalities over "America's undeclared drone war in Pakistan" which a prominent law professor has suggested could, in theory, lead to criminal prosecution for "war crimes" (placed in speech marks in the article) (Hodge 2010).

Wired, 30 April: a State Department counter-narcotics air force that also runs missions for the government of Pakistan, staffed by mercenaries working for DynCorp, in the airspace along the Afghanistan/Pakistan border, and extremely controversial in Pakistan, as revealed in a recently released State Department Inspector General report (ibid).

Antiwar.com, 30 April: "Atrocities in Afghanistan: A troubling timetable", reports on Bills in the US Congress and Senate favouring a timetable for withdrawal of US forces from Afghanistan, and is concerned with "disturbing patterns of misinformation regarding US/Nato attacks against Afghan civilians, whereby US/Nato officials first distribute misleading information about victims of an attack and later acknowledge that the victims were unarmed civilians. The story chronicles all such stories that had occurred in recent months (Kelly and Pearson 2010).

Antiwar.com, 1 May: A Pentagon source is quoted to the effect that the US military has sent so many of its UAVs to the Middle East that other operating theatres are going without (Anon 2010c).

Times Online, UK, 1 May: Rapid acceleration in the growth of Afghan security forces in Kabul and a recent improvement in security across the capital. But some "Western officers" are concerned that corners are being cut to meet ambitious targets: quality controls have been set low and quality reduced, and Afghan forces have been infiltrated by Taliban (Coghlan 2010).

Los Angeles Times, 1 May: Ammonium nitrate, a fertiliser that serves as a main ingredient in Taliban roadside bombs, is shipped into Afghanistan in large quantities, where it is banned, by Pakistani businessmen who buy off large numbers of police and officials (Rodriguez 2010).

Los Angeles Times, 1 May: A US Army captain bolstering the authority of a district governor in Maiwind, Kandahar, who relies on him almost completely for financial resources and credibility (Abbot 2010b).

Wired, 30 April: An Afghan National Army sergeant working with British troops who has apparently found 177 Improvised Explosive Devices (IEDs) during a three-year period in Helmand (Shactman 2010).

AFP, 2 May: A fire in the US chancery building in Islamabad (Anon 2010d).

PressTV, 2 May: The killing of at least two children, and at least six people wounded in a US missile attack in eastern Afghanistan (Anon 2010e).

PressTV, 2 May: The killing of at least two Nato soldiers in separate incidents in Afghanistan (Anon 2010f).

Many of these could potentially rival the story selected by *The NYT*, on the basis of standard journalistic criteria. What makes *The NYT* selection special is that it emphasises the number of civilian deaths which it claims are due to "enemy" actions, as against the much more modest number of (allegedly) accidental deaths of civilians caused by US and Nato troops. It also predicts an increase of such casualties during the summer months. 173 civilians were killed from roadside and suicide bombs in a one-month period in 2010, as against 72 killed by US/Nato action in a three-month period. It does not seem far-fetched to suggest that the story is intended to lift some weight of responsibility for civilian deaths from US/Nato troops. The report seeks to place these in comparative "context" and to prepare the public for a rise in civilian deaths in a planned US/Nato operation in Kandahar designed to rid the area of "Taliban".

Sources

The report is attributed to Richard Oppel and Abdul Waheed Wafa, and datelined Kabul. The source for information about the roadside bomb attack on a bus is a named Afghan police spokesman. There are no eyewitnesses, no first hand accounts. A named Interior Ministry spokesman is quoted as source for the numbers of civilians being killed. The story offers no insight into the reliability of this source, or the methodology that is used to collect such figures, which likely come from the half-yearly Pentagon report released the previous Wednesday. "Afghan officials" and "Nato officials" are quoted for the assertion that "insurgents" are causing most civilian deaths. There is no indication that such sources would have a strong vested interest in downplaying deaths caused by US/Nato and exaggerating those caused by "enemy" action. Speculation as to the likelihood that numbers will increase during the summer is not sourced. A British "military spokesman" is quoted for information relating to the recent death of a British soldier who is said to have died heroically protecting fellow soldiers.

Place

Datelined Kabul, the actual location is Paktia Province, in eastern Afghanistan near the border with Pakistan. Few American readers will have any idea about Paktia Province. The story offers them little assistance: no details, for example, as to the relative strength of the Taliban in that area, the presence or otherwise of local "warlords", the mood of the people towards the Kabul regime, the Afghan military or the US and Nato occupying force or any local demographic information. But the relationship of the province to Pakistan appears likely to strike a chord with American readers, who may be aware that the US has extended its "war against the Taliban" (if that is the most accurate descriptor of US activity, at least open to doubt) into Pakistan. Stories of violence from the border may remind Americans of the porous nature of the border and perhaps help confirm in their minds the "necessity" for US involvement in the two countries.

The players

The victims who are the initial focus have no personhood, barely any humanity other than the information provided by a police spokesman that the majority are women and children. It is not clear to whom responsibility for the bomb should be attributed. In such a murky conflict there is no room for confidence that just because IEDs are commonly associated in mainstream media reports with the "Taliban" that therefore all such devices must originate from the "Taliban". There is an indirect indication that the explosion had some relationship to earlier fighting that day between Taliban "guerillas" and Afghan "security forces".

These labels appear to attribute legitimacy to the Kabul regime and the Afghan army, implying that only they have the capability of establishing "security," even though it is obvious there is little if any security in this region for ordinary civilian bus passengers, and even though the "Taliban", whatever their faults and limitations, had for a period during the 1990s established sufficient "security" in Afghanistan for the Clinton administration to want to deal with them as the guarantors of oil and gas pipelines (Chossudovsky op cit).

The main players in this report are the statistics about casualties and the role these play in manipulation of perceptions about which party to the conflict is most "responsible" for civilian as well as other deaths. "Insurgents" and "militants" are identified as the principle culprits. Among their favourite tools are those of "roadside bombs" and "suicide attacks". There is no comparative reference to the far more sophisticated and devastating weapons available to occupying troops. In the sources' calculation of "responsibility", the role of the occupation itself and the "stepping-up" of its operations is not included: the unstated presumption is that their role is benign. It is further asserted that deaths of civilians caused by occupying troops are "accidental" which appears no more nor less likely than that civilian deaths caused by Taliban are "accidental".

The point of the story

As suggested earlier, this appears essentially to be a report about casualty trends. The story is pegged to a report of a recent roadside bomb incident in which Afghan civilians are killed by what may (but may not be) a "Taliban" bomb, and ends with reference to the death of a British soldier in what is suggested, indirectly, was in noble circumstances. Almost any roadside bomb and Afghan deaths would have done as a pretext for a story that attributes most of a recent increase in civilian deaths to "Taliban insurgents" and "suicide bombers" and prepares the readers for an increase in civilian deaths in the wake of "stepped up" operations planned by the occupying powers. Paradoxically, but likely unintentionally, this establishes a causal link between anticipated civilian deaths and the policies of the occupying powers: the paradox seems unremarkable, however, in the context of reporting whose underlying presumption is that the occupying forces have a benign role.

Conclusion

The evidence from this limited investigation of *NYT* coverage of international conflicts suggests that reports routinely demonstrate significant problems of selection, narrative construction, stereotyping, and sourcing, such that at least one by-product, possibly intentional, is news coverage that is in keeping with US/Nato foreign policy objectives and that presents US/Nato presence in the "AfPak" region as benign.

Notes

[1] See http://www.dol.gov/ilab/media/reports/iclp/sweat/pakistan.htm, accessed on 22 May 2010

[2] See http://www.anti-caste.org/pakistan, accessed on 22 May 2010

References

Abbot, Sebastian. (2010a) Reckless behavior of private companies protecting Nato convoys, APNews, April 30. Available online at http://hosted.ap.org/dynamic/stories/A/AS_AFGHAN_SECURITY_CONTRA CTORS?SITE=TXMID&SECTION=HOME&TEMPLATE=DEFAULT&CTIM E=2010-04-30-19-05-13, accessed on 22 May 2010

Abbot, Sebastian (2010b) US Army captain who sets out to build local Afghan government known as a king, AP News, *Los Angeles Times,* 1 May. Available online at http://articles.latimes.com/keyword/afghanistan, accessed on 22 May 2010

Ahmed, Nafeez (2005) *The War on Truth: 9/11, Disinformation and the Anatomy of Terrorism,* New York, Oliver Branch Press

Anon (2010a) Suicide bomber kills 2 in Pakistan's Swat Valley, AP, *New York Times*, 1 May. Available online at http://www.ajc.com/news/nation-world/suicide-bomber-kills-2-508225.html, accessed on 22 May 2010

Anon (2010b) Iran arrests Jundollah leader Abdolmalek Rigi, *Daily Times*, 24 February. Available online at http://www.dailytimes.com.pk/default.asp?page=2010%5C02%5C24%5Cstory_24-2 2010_pg7_12, accessed on 22 May 2010

Anon (2010c) Afghan surge strips UAVs from forces elsewhere, Antiwar.com, http://www.airforcetimes.com/news/2010/05/defense_uavs_centcom_050110/, accessed on 22 May 2010

Anon (2010d) Fire at US embassy in Pakistan: Spokesman, AFP, 1 May. Available online at http://news.yahoo.com/s/afp/20100502/wl_sthasia_afp/pakistanusfire, accessed on 22 May 2010

Anon (2010e) US-led troops kill 3 Afghan citizens, 30 April. Available online at http://www.presstv.ir/, accessed on 22 May 2010

Anon (2010f) Two US-led troops fall, PressTV, 2 May. Available online at http://www.presstv.ir/detail.aspx?id=125190&sectionid=351020403, accessed on 22 May 2010

Barnett, Brooke and Reynolds, Amy (2009) *Terrorism and the Press: An Uneasy Relationship*, New York, Peter Lang

Chossudovsky, Michel (2002) *War and Globalization: The Truth behind September 11*, Shanty Bay, Ontario, Global Outlook

Cottle, Simon (2008) *Global Crisis Reporting*, Milton Keynes, Open University Press

Coughlan, Tom (2010) Full speed ahead: but drive to bolster Afghan security carries risks, Times Online, 1 May. Available online at http://www.timesonline.co.uk/tol/news/world/afghanistan/article7113422.ece, accessed on 22 May 2010

Crile, George (2007) *Charlie Wilson's War: The Extraordinary Story of How the Wildest Man in Congress and a Rogue CIA Agent Changed the History of Our Times*, New York, Grove Press

Ditz, Jason (2010) Petraeus: Tough Times Ahead in Kandahar, Anti-war.com, 30 April. Available online at http://news.antiwar.com/2010/04/30/petraeus-tough-times-ahead-in-kandahar/, accessed on 22 May 2010

Edwards, David and Cromwell, David (2010) *Newspeak in the 21st Century*, London, Pluto

Griffin, David (2004) *The new Pearl Harbor: Disturbing questions about the Bush Administration and 9/11*, New York, Interlink Books

Grynbaum, Michael, Rashbaum, William and Baker, Al (2010) Police seek man taped near Times Square, *New York Times*, 2 May. Available online at http://www.timesonline.co.uk/tol/news/world/afghanistan/article7113422.ece, accessed on 22 May 2010

Hodge, Nathan (2010) Does This Video Show Afghan Cops Killing UN Guard? Wired, Available online at http://www.wired.com/dangerroom/2010/04/did-afghan-cops-kill-un-security-guard/, accessed on 22 May 2010

Hodge, Nathan (2010) State Department flies mercenary air force over Pakistan, AP, 30 April. Available online at http://www.wired.com/dangerroom/2010/04/state-department-flies-mercenary-air-force-over-pakistan/ accessed on 22 May 2010

Kelly, Kathy and Pearson, Dan (2010, April 30) Atrocities in Afghanistan: A troubling timetable, Antiwar.com, 30 April. Available online at http://original.antiwar.com/kelly-pearson/2010/04/30/atrocities-in-afghanistan-a-troubling-timetable/, accessed on 22 May 2010

Moeller, Susan (2009) *Packaging Terrorism: Co-opting the News for Politics and Profit*, New York, Wiley-Blackwell

Musharraf, Pervez (2008) *In the Line of Fire: A Memoir.* New York, Free Press

Norton-Taylor, Richard (2010) Afghanistan forces face four more years of combat, warns Nato official, *Guardian*, 29 April. Available online at http://www.guardian.co.uk/world/2010/apr/29/afghanistan-combat-nato-official, accessed on 22 May 2010

Oppel, Richard and Wafa, Abdul (2010) Afghans die in bombing as toll rises for civilians, *New York Times*, 2 May. Available online at http://www.nytimes.com/2010/05/03/world/asia/03afghan.html, accessed on 22 May 2010

Peled, Daniella (2010) Afghans believe US is funding Taliban, *Guardian*, 25 May. Available online at http://www.guardian.co.uk/commentisfree/cifamerica/2010/may/25/afghans-believe-us-funding-taliban, accessed on 27 May 2010

Porter, Gareth (2010) Pentagon map shows wide Taliban zone in the South, Inter-Press Service, 30 April. Available online at
http://ipsnews.net/news.asp?idnews=51274, accessed on May 2010

Rodriguez, Alex (2010, May 1) Potential smugglers supplying Afghan bombmakers, *Los Angeles Times*, 1 May. Available online at
http://articles.latimes.com/2010/may/01/world/la-fg-pakistan-fertilizer-20100501, accessed on 22 May 2010

Tavernise, Sabrina and Shah, Pir Zubair (2010) Pakistani ex-intelligence officer is killed, *New York Times*, 30 April. Available online at
http://www.nytimes.com/2010/05/01/world/asia/01pstan.html, accessed on May 2010

Tavernise, Sabrina, Gall, Carlotta. and Khan, Ismail (2010) Pakistan in shift, weighs attack on militant lair, *New York Times*, 30 April p. A1

US Congress (2010) On Progress Toward Security and Stability in Afghanistan. Report to Congress in Accordance with the 2008 National Defense Authorization Act, Section 1230, Public Law 110-181

Winterbottom, Michael (2007) Director: *A Mighty Heart*, Paramount Vintage

Note on the author

Oliver Boyd-Barrett graduated from Exeter University (UK) and acquired his PhD from the Open University (UK). He has published extensively on international communication, particularly concerning the operations of the international and national news agencies. In recent years he has turned his attention to media coverage of the "war on terror". Boyd-Barrett was founding director of the graduate distance learning programme of the Centre for Mass Communication Research at the University of Leicester (UK). He is currently Professor of Journalism at Bowling Green State University, Ohio.

Section 4. Deeper meaning

Deconstructing "Hero Harry" coverage and the dilemmas of reporting secret warfare

Richard Lance Keeble

Amidst all the celebratory reporting of "Our Boys" and "Our Heroes" in Afghanistan, there suddenly appeared in March 2008 in the UK mainstream media a flurry of stories about "Hero" Prince Harry. In December 2007, the prince had been deployed to Helmand Province, in southern Afghanistan, and following an agreement between the Ministry of Defence and the Society of Editors, the media simply went mum. It was feared his presence on the frontline would put the lives of other soldiers at risk.

And amazingly, in this age of transparency, tabloid hysteria and surveillance, when it appears hardly any secrets can be held for any length of time, the global embargo last ten weeks! While an Australian women's magazine, *New Idea*, first leaked the story on 7 January 2008, the global embargo was not lifted until Matt Drudge's notorious US gossip website, the Drudge Report (www.drudgereport.com) spilled the beans on 28 February 2008. So poor Harry had to quit the front – and the international media went immediately bananas.

How can we explain this explosion of patriotic fervour around Harry? Well, in considering the history and function of the UKs military covenant, John Tulloch examines the "Hero Harry" propaganda. And he suggests:

> An ancient myth of redemption is being worked out. Just as much as Shakespeare's Prince Hal, the worthless Harry symbolises the rebirth of the military covenant. He represents the mystical body of the sovereign which itself embodies the mystical nation. He is presented as assuming equal risks with ordinary squaddies – therefore, a hero communing like King Henry with the army, as one of the boys or rather, *our* boys. He is presented as running the risk of sacrifice, shedding his boyish Prince Hal

image and becoming a professional capable of undertaking...er fire control.

In the context of recent press representations of British soldiers in Afghanistan and their relation to the imagined community of the nation, Tulloch also examines shifting concepts of the citizen soldier versus military elites. And he explores the ways in which the Afghan war has reanimated debates, going back to the Victorian army and beyond, about reciprocal rights and duties in the relationship between soldiers and civilians.

Promoting the interests of the military/industrial/media complex

In my own chapter I argue that Fleet Street's coverage of the Afghan conflict has served largely to promote the interests of the military/industrial/media complex. The chapter also considers Fleet Street's editorial stances on the Afghanistan war – which was costing the UK £5 billion a year – and the ways in which the views of the public (most of whom consistently call for the withdrawal of troops from Afghanistan) have been marginalised. I draw on a range of alternative media reports and analyses (ignored by Fleet Street and the academy) to critique mainstream coverage.

Next, David Edwards and David Cromwell, of the award-winning media monitoring website, Media Lens, argue that mainstream media coverage of the Afghan conflict has failed to convey the horror of continuing civilian casualties – largely because they are operating as a filter and booster system for powerful interests. Drawing on a detailed critique of BBC and Fleet Street reporting, they argue: "A range of incentives and disincentives ensures that there are many more compelling reasons for the corporate media to promote stories that are inoffensive to, or favoured by, powerful interests."

Finally in this section, Donald Matheson, argues that the reporting of New Zealand's special forces in Afghanistan, by far the country's most significant military commitment outside of peacekeeping for 20 years, has been largely hidden under a blanket of secrecy. Moreover, he suggests that this lack of scrutiny of the New Zealand military is of wider significance for the country's political direction. In mobilising certain historic ideals of the Kiwi male, the government and the military have successfully aestheticised politics, aligning New Zealandness with loyalty to a Western world order through nostalgic appeal.

Soldiers and citizens: the Afghan conflict, the press, the military and the breaking of the "military covenant"

John Tulloch considers the history and function of the UK's "military covenant" in the context of recent press representations of British soldiers in Afghanistan and their relation to the imagined community of the nation. He also examines shifting concepts of the "citizen soldier" versus military elites and ways in which the Afghan war has reanimated debates, going back to the Victorian army and beyond, about reciprocal rights and duties in the relationship between soldiers and civilians

Introduction

The so-called "military covenant", on which so much media attention in the UK has been focused since 2007 to the present day, forms part of the official British army doctrine and appears on the website of the Ministry of Defence (MoD).[1]

It was authored in 1998 by Major General Sebastian Roberts, whose responsibilities had included: the command of the Household Division – two regiments of cavalry and five of footguards who form the monarch's bodyguard and the centre piece of military ceremonials; heading up the army's security, recruiting, and training efforts in London; and working as the army's public relations officer (see Roberts 2000). Religion is listed as his leading interest and he was educated at Ampleforth, a leading Catholic public school, and Balliol College, Oxford. In other words, he was a modern major general with strong Royal and Christian connections and skills in public presentation. He retired in March 2010.[2]

The doctrine had sat harmlessly on the MoD website until an unprecedented campaign was launched in September 2007 by that most seemingly apolitical, established and familiar organisation in British life, the Royal British Legion. The campaign raised important constitutional issues about the relationship between the British army, the state and the government of the day (Royal British Legion 2007).

So uncontroversial was the Military Covenant at its inception that Major General Roberts was able to confide to an Oxford college alumni magazine in 2006 that writing, as he put it, at Wellington's old desk, he "had in my mind always, and literally on my desk, a variety of touchstones of literature and other works". He kept by him, for example, the Rule of St Benedict. "The words have not changed in 1, 500 years," he says, and he compares the tract to "ethical regimental standing orders." He also relied on the American Constitution for inspiration. "It is based on ideals that mattered terribly," he says. "And it is beautifully written" (*Balliol College News* 2006).

The Arnoldian cadence of "touchstones" alerts us to the fact that we are in the presence of fine writing. And the obvious signals that come from "doctrine" and "covenant" are important. We are in an aesthetised region of religion, faith, the invention of tradition, an active process of imagining an ideal narrative for the nation: in Tom Nairn's suggestive Tennyson quotation, an "enchanted glass" (Nairn 1990; Hobsbawm 1992) in which, as for the Lady of Shalott, "Shadows of the world appear" (Tennyson 1965). Let us look therein.

Sacrifice, service, nation...

The relevant section that outlines the covenant is this:

> Soldiers will be called upon to make personal sacrifices – including the ultimate sacrifice – in the service of the Nation. In putting the needs of the nation and the Army before their own, they forgo some of the rights enjoyed by those outside the Armed Forces. In return, British soldiers must always be able to expect fair treatment, to be valued and respected as individuals, and that they (and their families) will be sustained and rewarded by commensurate terms and conditions of service. In the same way the unique nature of military land operations means that the Army differs from all other institutions, and must be sustained and provided for accordingly by the Nation. This mutual obligation forms the Military

Covenant between the Nation, the Army and each individual soldier; an unbreakable common bond of identity, loyalty and responsibility which has sustained the Army throughout its history. It has perhaps its greatest manifestation in the annual commemoration of Armistice Day, when the Nation keeps covenant with those who have made the ultimate sacrifice, giving their lives in action (Roberts op cit).

References to this document were comparatively sparse in 2000. *The Times* noted that the army had published a Moral Code:

> …in return for commitment and dedication, soldiers must have the reassurance that in bearing arms for their country, "the nation will look after them and their families". The code, drawn up during the past three years by senior officers led by a brigadier, states: "This mutual obligation is the essence of the military covenant" (*The Times*, 3 April 2000).

However, although operating from the same Wapping stable, the late Richard Stott at the *News of the World* took an altogether more robust line:

> The Army has brought out a new moral code for soldiers, emphasising that they will be called upon "to make personal sacrifices-including the ultimate sacrifice-in the service of the nation". Fair enough.

In return, "the nation will look after them and their families. This mutual obligation is the essence of the military covenant". Cobblers.

> To save money the Army is getting rid of vital welfare services by closing down places such as the Services Cotswold Centre where families with problems, usually brought on by the strains of service life, can be looked after by skilled staff (*News of the World*, 9 April 2000).

We might note that the Covenant, perhaps, unwisely claims Armistice Day as the site of national obligation. Armistice Day, of course, commemorates a truce, a stopping of hostilities by mutual consent. Indeed, between 1919 and 1945, remembrance ceremonies in Britain were held on Armistice Day; but were then moved to Remembrance Sunday, the closest Sunday to the 11th day of the 11th month. However, since 1995, ceremonies have been held on both days. Remembrance Sunday was established as a popular communion of a nation with its dead through the voluntary agency of the Royal British Legion, founded in 1921, royalled in 1971, and styling itself "the nation's custodian of remembrance".[3]

The covenant, however, only became an issue in March 2007 when the *Independent on Sunday* launched a campaign based on it, using the case of former Lance Corporal Justin Smith, medically discharged from the army with post traumatic stress disorder. Mr Smith had achieved prominence when he rounded on the prime minister on a local television programme, telling him: "I have lost my house, my security and any self-belief. I want to know what the government is going to do for people suffering the same as me?" He told the newspaper: "I always believed it [the army] was a big family. But the family has turned its back" (*IoS*, 11 March 2007). The paper added:

> More than 17, 000 troops are estimated to be suffering from anxiety and depression, and around 3, 500 reservists are thought to be facing similar problems. Yet, between January 2003 and October 2006, only 2,123 military personnel received treatment for mental health conditions from the MoD; of these, 328 were diagnosed with PTSD. Specialists at King's College, London, estimate that up to one in four soldiers suffers from mental problems after returning from Iraq and Afghanistan (ibid.).

Also in the article, however, is a reference to the historic roots of the covenant as "first drafted in the times of the Duke of Wellington" a mysterious reference since Wellington survived for 52 years into the 19th century. This canard cropped up speedily in the *Daily Mail* in March 2007: "The military covenant was drafted in the 19th century at the time of Wellington and was last reviewed in 2005" (*Daily Mail*, 12 March 2007).

Constructing a myth

Although there is some historical evidence that reformers achieved improvements in army conditions in the first half of the nineteenth century they mainly had to fight the Iron Duke and the conservative military establishment he embodied. As Richard Holmes notes, many of Wellington's Peninsular veterans ended their days begging on the London streets (Holmes 1994 [1985], 402). Peter Burroughs observes:

> Traditionalists disparaged the rank and file as incorrigibly idle, dissolute, vicious reprobates who required stern discipline to restrain their natural instincts. Any misguided attempt to improve their minds, morals, or conditions of service would undermine discipline by fostering dissatisfaction and insubordination. Paternalists and reformers, in contrast, evinced a more benevolent view of human nature and potentialities. They emphasised the environmental factors that influenced soldiers' conduct: the severe disciplinary code, the monotonous routine, the insanitary living conditions, the inducements to drunkenness and trouble-making. They believed that the State had a duty to promote the well-being of the ordinary soldier through material and moral improvements in army life (Burroughs 1994: 171).

Evangelical Christianity, of course, was a major factor here and many were exercised by the question: "Tommy, 'ow's yer soul?" (Kipling 1892). Flogging, in particular, aroused much parliamentary concern, and the army authorities were gradually forced to reduce the rates of punishment. In 1829, maximum sentences of general or district courts martial were restricted to 500 lashes and regimental courts to 300. In 1836, the totals were cut again to 200, 150, and 100. In 1846, sentences were cut to a maximum of 50 strokes. Corporal punishment was only finally abolished in 1881 (Burroughs op cit: 174).

But the essential fact was that Britain's small mercenary army was decidedly unpopular at home. Gerard Manley Hopkins might exclaim in a poem: "Why do we all, seeing a soldier, bless him? Bless/Our redcoats, our tars?" (Hopkins 1967) but his sentimentality was untypical in the public sphere. The real value placed in Victorian society on soldiers can be gauged by the resources devoted to barracks: as Correlli Barnett observes, a convict enjoyed 1000 cubic feet of air, a soldier 400.

> The British people provided their soldiers with one pound of bread and three-quarters of a pound of meat a day, and supplied two coppers to boil the meat in – the only cooking equipment. Just before the Crimean War in 1854, a third daily meal was provided – at the soldier's own expense (Barnett 1970: 280).

The notion that a prototype military covenant was being hatched "during Wellington's time" is to employ a pair of sentimental binoculars constructed in the wake of the blooding of Britain's first truly citizen army, the mass participation force constructed from volunteers, and then conscripts, after the destruction of Britain's old regular army in 1914, and the birth, with the British Legion, of a culture of remembrance in the 1920s which, as formal religion has declined, has paradoxically become stronger.

It is not the thin red line of the Victorian army that has this insidious power to move British people – although the Crimean War (1854-1856) and its journalistic fallout, plus the skills of Victorian artists like Lady Butler, Rudyard Kipling and the appalling poet Sir Henry Newbolt , all served to humanise and sentimentalise the late Victorian Tommy Atkins. Rather, it is the fading photo of our father, grandfather or great grandfather in uniform, the visit to Ypres or the Somme, the sound of the bugles of the Belgian fire brigade at the Menin Gate. It is the mass entry of citizens into the armed forces, and the political demands that flow from that, that allowed the British to identify with soldiers, not as a guild or warrior elite, but as a people in arms.

Of course, the concept of the Covenant has nothing to do with citizenship. Its initial formulation is based on a notion that soldiering embodies the *surrender* of rights, the abrogation of discussion and the potential for sacrifice that is supposed to generate a sense of public obligation. Yet what is the nature of the concept? Legal/ethical commentary struggles with its inherent unlimited liability (e.g. Mileham 2010). And British newspaper coverage has struggled with a variety of definitions. According to the *Sunday Times*:

> The [British] legion has made significant progress by reminding the government and the country of the military covenant, the understanding by which soldiers, in return for risking their lives, are promised appropriate service and respect at home by the government and the country (*Sunday Times*, 30 September 2007)

It's about *respect*, thought *The Times*:

> The military covenant…stated that soldiers called upon to make personal sacrifices in the service of the nation could in return expect that they and their families would be valued and respected (*The Times*, 5 January 2007).

The Press Association described it as a *guarantee*:

> There is growing anger that the Military Covenant – which guarantees soldiers fair treatment in return for forgoing other rights – is not being upheld (Press Association, 15 August 2007).

In the hands of the then Under Secretary of State for Defence, Derek Twigg, it was nothing as crude as a contract but, in cosy vernacular, a *"deal"* entered into by the *"nation"*:

> The Military Covenant is about the nation keeping its side of the deal. It is about taking responsibility for ensuring that those who have given service receive the recognition and support they deserve for the commitments and risks that they have taken on. It is a responsibility that falls principally on the Government – on behalf of the nation (Twigg 2008).

This struggle for definition reflects the fact that the formulation was less a concept than an invitation to inhabit a state of feeling – an invitation to construct our own narrative of sacrifice and obligation. And it poses a question:

what should be the appropriate relationship of a modern state and country to its army?

The Major General's ideal narrative presents the army as an apolitical and silent repository of duty and sacrifice. This is totally in line with traditional military thinking. Soldiers *cannot* be citizens. Human rights in an army will lead to disaster. The classic touchstone here is Clausewitz, who in his work *On War* observed that:

> No matter how clearly we see the citizen and the soldier in the same man, how strongly we conceive of war as the business of the entire nation, opposed diametrically to the pattern set by the *condottieri* of former times, the business of war will always remain individual and distinct. Consequently for as long as they practice this activity, soldiers will think of themselves as members of a kind of guild, in whose regulations, laws, and customs the spirit of war is given pride of place (Clausewitz 1993 [1832]: Book 3, Ch.5).

This perception of the *specialness* of the military, the distinction of soldiers from ordinary citizens, is still passionately argued by many commentators. Britain's leading military historian and populariser of things military, Richard Holmes, is also a Colonel in the Princess of Wales Royal Regiment. He says:

> Soldiers do things, which are inherently different to those done by the rest of society…they have an unlimited liability contract which takes them into the jaws of death. To do this they need particular qualities and a particular ethos, and there is a "necessary gap" between their organisation and behaviour and that of almost any other social group. They must, in the final analysis, be value-dominated, not interest dominated (Holmes 2006b).

Getting people not to run away but to stand their ground is the basic requirement of any army. The organised armies that first developed in the Middle East around 1000 BC depended on a concept of discipline which includes acting in a uniform fashion, and obeying a commander. Richard

Holmes, with John Keegan, outlines four ways in which this discipline can be imposed.

There is the religious duty to a god or god-like ruler. There is the private contract of the mercenary, hired for a limited period. (The Swiss pikemen feared throughout Europe were known to negotiate pay rises on the 14th century battlefields.) There is the "system, organization and tradition" which underlay the Roman Army and earned its participants Roman citizenship and a pension – such as the veterans who constituted the original citizens of Lindum Colonia – modern day Lincoln. And finally there is the "social duty" that citizens acknowledge to their fellow citizens (Keegan and Holmes 1985: 23-24).

Of course, these are not mutually exclusive. One might argue that England was never keen on number one, except during the Civil War of the 1640s and 1650s, in the psalm singing regiments of the New Model Army. That it moved to number two – a mercenary army – but aspired to number three: the civilising legions of the British Empire and its liberal internationalist successor articulated by former Prime Minister Blair, under a US umbrella. And that it only advanced to number four in two world wars, "people's wars" that required people's armies.

The result is a crisis of governance in relation to the army. As a culture, the British have been proffered representations of a warrior elite. But fighting the escalating asymmetric wars of liberal interventionism requires a controllable people's army rather than a killing machine – citizens in uniform, under the umbrella of human rights law, who might conceivably have development skills, and senior officers who know their place, compliant to a political elite.

Renewed interest in the representation of soldiers and soldiering

The launching of two asymmetric conflicts in Iraq and Afghanistan by Western invasions since 9/11, under the banner of the so-called "war on terrorism", has created a renewed interest in the representation of soldiers and soldiering, of an intensity last seen during the Vietnam War and in the case of Britain, the Falklands/Malvinas conflict of 1982. In Britain, this was given a distinctive political spin, in the run-up to 9/11, by the adoption of a rhetoric by Tony Blair and New Labour promoting a foreign policy of liberal interventionism in Africa and former Yugoslavia – a distinctive break with a previous Conservative rhetoric foregrounding British interests rather than human rights.

This is more than a mere academic or political interest. In a way arguably unsuspected by the political elite which launched the process, it has decisively transformed the structure of national feeling and engaged and reanimated powerful underlying themes and public rituals embedded in British culture and connected with the experience of two world wars. The rituals memorialise sacrifice and loss and celebrate the relationship between the imagined community of a nation united in struggle and its armed forces. The experiences, and in particular, the "heroism" and death, of young people, and the burden of loss and remembrance borne by their family members, is the organising narrative which links the various practices of "remembrance".

Whilst susceptible to management by political elites intent on maintaining Western global hegemony, and easily dismissable in a left critique as media "mythmaking", at root this is a popular process and, therefore, at some level involves a struggle between competing and oppositional interpretations. In this process, the comfortable posturing of a Military Covenant handed down by a political/military elite in 2000 became transformed into a series of demands – for reliable equipment, decent conditions and pay, support for families and injured soldiers – which, like a homegrown IED, possesses the explosive capability to derail the smoothest political operator.

The crucial change – first in Iraq and then in Afghanistan – was, of course, the consecutive transitions from a "war" against two failed and crippled states to an "insurgency". The first could be presented as a media event, a mythic adventure based on the virtually casualty-free deployment of smart weaponry and mercenary soldiers, and the ignoring of, or systematic lying about, the inevitable huge civilian casualties. The "insurgency", conducted by irregular forces with ambush and IED, is, of course, "a real war" involving substantial casualties by the coalition forces, even though they remain a tiny fraction of the continuing toll on civilians. The "real war" involves the dreary mechanisms of imperial policing – taking and holding strong points, denying resources to the enemy, supporting a Quisling and corrupt government and invoking the need to "win hearts and minds".

Paradoxically, it has occurred at a time when the British armed forces have never been smaller. Despite the salience of weapons manufacture in the British economy (Keeble 1997, 2004), as Richard Holmes points out, the British army is the smallest it has been as a proportion of the population since the early 17th century. In numbers, it is the smallest it has been since 1838 (Holmes 2006b). At an emotional level, if you have family links or, indeed, children of a certain age it is hard to escape the mixture of anxiety and guilt that must be the lot of any parent with a child serving in Iraq of Afghanistan. In part this is a "middle class" guilt. As is evident with the *Guardian's* eminent commentator, Polly Toynbee:

> If you have a son the same age as these boys, it does help concentrate the mind. It is also a crisp reminder that most of us live in worlds where no one has a boy anywhere near the armed forces, which have become dangerously detached from most peoples' ordinary experience – neither the Sandhurst type or the squaddie drawn mainly from poorer places (*Guardian*, 21 August 2007 p. 29).[4]

Although, as an elite, liberal metropolitan journalist, Polly Toynbee's sphere of "most people" has stretched to working undercover as a low paid worker (Toynbee 2003), the drawing of that confident but hackneyed cliché of Sandhurst versus the delicately alluded to, "poorer places" smacks problematically of Bloomsbury.

Press coverage of soldiers and war-fighting

In exploring press coverage of soldiering over four years (2006-2010), an attempt was made to construct a typology that describes the broad themes into which news and comment has fallen, based on a close reading for 'themes' of sample of 280 items from five daily and five Sunday British national newspapers. The most salient themes are the following:

Milestones in the wars: significant numbers, "firsts", "records" (e.g. "The bloodiest day, eight UK soldiers killed in 24 hours", *Guardian*, 11 July 2009 p. 1).

Tributes to the fallen including profiles – e.g. death of Lt Col Rupert Thorneloe (Harding 2009), Staff Sergeant Olaf Schmid (Drury 2009) – and to "heroism" in the frontline e.g. bomb disposal experts (Hardman 2009).

"Frontline" accounts by embedded reporters e.g. from Helmand (Walsh 2007).

Personal tragedies – the bereavement experience of families and loved ones – e.g. "Wearing his poignant souvenir, a little boy says farewell as town salutes Paras who fell" (Levy 2008).

Comment by elite military actors about conditions or public attitudes – e.g. army chief Sir Richard Dannatt's comments on need to "embrace" returning troops (Norton-Taylor 2007).

"Gaffes" by political figures and agents of the state – e.g the row over Prime Minister Gordon Brown's allegedly wrongly spelt letter to "grieving forces mum" Jacqui Janes (Newton Dunn 2009).

Scandals regarding alleged inadequate support for soldiers and families – housing, hospitals, public respect – e.g. Cenotaph ban on wounded war heroes (*Observer* 2007).

Prejudice against soldiers and opposition to the military from elements within British society – e.g. National Union of Teachers "militants" who want to end promotional visits to schools by the army (Wooding 2008) or a hotel that refused a corporal a bed and makes a "groveling apology after public outrage" (*Daily Mirror*, 5 September 2009) or the protests in Luton against returning soldiers marching through the town (Bracchi 2009).

Scandals regarding "kit" – alleged lack, inadequacy of battlefield equipment e.g. helicopters, armoured vehicles (e.g. Townsend 2009).

After-effects of serving in the army – jail (Doward 2008), alcoholism (Laurance 2010, mental illness (Taylor 2008).

The role of the Royals – in particular, Prince Harry's brief sojourn in Afghanistan.

I will examine four examples: milestones; tributes; personal tragedies and, finally, the royals in the shape of Harry.

"Another bloody milestone…"

Much of the coverage in 2006-2010 was dominated by the routine reporting of casualties. Compared to any major conflict in which Britain has been involved, it has to be said that these were comparatively small, but they bulked hugely in the coverage (King 2010). A rhetoric of numbers was deployed, tied to the memorialisation of the individual casualty and the creation of a human interest story as a "hook" for the figures. For example, on the occasion of the 100th British casualty in Iraq, Corporal Gordon Pritchard, the *Daily Telegraph* (1 February 2006 p. 1) printed his full face, uniformed image across its entire front page beneath the headline:

SACRIFICE
100TH BRITISH SERVICEMEN DIES IN IRAQ

Similar tactics were employed by the *Daily Mail* and the *Independent*. Such pages memorialise loss, and draw on certain well-established images in memorial iconography, aping the formal structure and severity of the war memorial. For example, the *Independent's* page recalls the look of the Vietnam war memorial in Washington. The *Telegraph* opts for an austere layout reminiscent of the Cenotaph.

Most of the papers also used the device of the page or spread – a macabre wall full of faces. The *Guardian* was typical, accompanying each face in its "Eyewitness" page with a paragraph devoted to the dead individual (*Guardian*, 1 February 2006). This tactic, brought to a high degree of human interest impact during the Iraq conflict, has been continued as the numbers of British dead have mounted in Afghanistan. For example, on page one of the *Daily Mail* of Monday 9 June 2009, when 100 passport-size pictures, framed in black, memorialised the 100th death in Afghanistan, beneath the headline: "Salute to 100 fallen heroes".

There has also been a concern with "firsts" – for example, the first woman to die in Iraq, Flight Lieutenant Sarah-Jayne Mulvihill, the first Fijian, Private Joseva Lewalcel, and, indeed, in July 2006 , Lance Corporal Jabron Hashmi, claimed as the first British Muslim soldier killed fighting the Taliban. Frequently the "firsts" are now linked to a reported deficiency in equipment, training or tactics. Corporal Sarah Bryant, the first British woman soldier to be killed in Afghanistan in June 2008, was the half-page, smiling image in front of a union flag around which the *Guardian* ran: "Unfit vehicles, lack of kit and poor training – failings that led to the death of Corporal Bryant" (*Guardian*, 2 March 2010 p. 11).

Quantities also figure of course : for example, the *most* casualties in a week. And the point at which the British Afghan death toll overtook that of Iraq – 11 July 2009. But the style of this coverage generates a recurring critique within the newspapers themselves. For example, a column by Tom Sutcliffe, in the *Independent* in February 2006 is headed "Sad numbers games" and says "This kind of numerology really shouldn't be applied to the deaths of human beings…if the media need a hook on which to hang a discussion of the human cost of the war what's wrong with that old journalistic standby, the anniversary?" (*Independent*, 7 February 2006, p14).

Tributes and remembrance

Many stories fall into this category, geared to memorial services. Much has been made of the emergence of Wootton Bassett, the small Wiltshire town through which corteges pass on their way from the airbase where the dead are landed. But also striking is the extensive use of many other tributes –a notable example is the treatment of the Westminster Abbey tribute to fallen Mercians in Afghanistan in the *Guardian*. This starts:

Nine candles were lit for the fallen and carried from the Grave of the Unknown Warrior to the high altar of Westminster Abbey yesterday. Each was in remembrance of a member of the 2nd Battalion the Mercian Regiment (Worcesters and Foresters) who died during a six month tour of Afghanistan this year (*Guardian*, 11 December 2007 p11).

This invokes the solemn rhetoric of Remembrance Sunday and the 1920s and also regimental tradition, the moral cement that is popularly supposed to hold the British army together. But the second battalion of the Mercians, in fact, conceals a story which sums up a current and central problematic for the army – extensive reorganisations have tended to undermine the identity of regimental formations. The structure of the infantry has been under its latest review since 2004. Regiments might be seen in the British military as giving a sense of belonging, a history, continuity, and a battle hoard of celebrated soldiers and actions: the reality is that they are recruiting across enormous areas and are the products of successive amalgamations.

Thus, in an enthusiastic play of geographical fancy, the Mercian Regiment is described on its website as "the regiment of the modern heart of England's – confident, diverse and forward looking". Big-hearted, indeed. This regiment was formed as recently as 16 December 2004 as part of the restructuring of the infantry through the merger of four single battalion regiments: the Cheshire Regiment (1881); the Worcestershire and Sherwood Foresters Regiment (formed in 1970 from two older regiments); the Staffordshire Regiment (formed in 1959) and the West Midlands Regiment (formed in 1988).[5]

Personal tragedies

Grieving families have rounded on the authorities during the current conflicts in an unprecedented fashion, and delivered potent human interest stories into the hands of the press, backed by a burgeoning network of charities and support organisations. [6] The *Independent's* powerful page from September 2006 about a young casualty from Iraq signalled the start of this trend. It was headlined: "Why did Blair send my teenage son to fight an illegal and dishonest war?" (*Independent*, 2 September 2006 p 15). In such stories, the youth of the soldier casualties is a constantly reiterated motif, within a frame which announces betrayal: a major theme of children being misled. Take, for instance, this report from the *Daily Mail*:

TALE OF TWO BOY SOLDIERS

Painfully young, they joined up together and, at barely 18, were sent out to Afghanistan. On their first day of action, they were still together when a Taliban rocket struck. Today, one lies wounded. The other is coming home in a Union Jack draped coffin…When the rocket struck, fate flipped a coin. One friend was wounded but survived. The other did not (*Daily Mail*, 10 July 2009 pp 1, 4-5).

Emphasising their youth and maybe naivety within an emblematic structure including chance and fate (larger forces outside their understanding) and the macabre echo of an old popular song ("Two little boys…") powerfully suggests that they are the unfortunate nation's children for whom we all have responsibility. It also has the effect of infantilising the subject. As with Polly Toynbee, the soldiers are somehow presented as working class mugs and losers who have got themselves killed, whilst the more fortunate middle classes have well-paid jobs at home.

In similar vein the *Sun* reported the deaths of three soldiers in June 2008: "Three fresh-faced lads who each earned less than a traffic warden…the latest to lay down their young lives for freedom in Afghanistan." And the headline ran: "THE BABES OF WAR" (*Sun*, 10 June 2008 p. 1). We learn that "Nathan Cuthbertson and David Murray were just 19 and Daniel Gamble 22 [when] they laid down their lives after it was revealed squaddies earn less than traffic wardens".

Of course, since World War One the youthfulness of service personnel has been a staple of twentieth century war literature and reportage (see Fussell 1975), and a recurrent source of guilty reflection. But the literature of war also celebrates its role as a maturing force. Although it is a central to recruiting literature, youth attaining maturity or manhood was a muted theme of the coverage examined, until the apotheosis of Prince Harry in Helmand in February 2008.

"Hero" Harry in Afghanistan

In physical terms, this attracted by far the greatest volume of coverage over the four years – 11 pages in the *Mail*, nine in the *Sun*, eight in the *Mirror*. Even the *Telegraph* gave it five full broadsheet pages in February 2008.

What is the function of the Harry coverage? One can't of course underrate in this deluge of bad news the sheer desire for a good news story. But much more is involved than that. The symbolism of Harry being sent to Afghanistan is complicated, although the PR story is a simple tale of media manipulation. Harry, beset by scandals about his drinking (e.g HARRY POTTY: Boozy Prince in snapper bust-up, *Sun*, 22 October 2004 p. 1) and casual racism (e.g. HARRY RACIST VIDEO SHAME, *News of the World*, 11 January 2009 p. 1) is desperate to "serve". The army is desperate not to have him shot. A compromise is reached, brokered by the UK's Society of Editors. A story is spun that he wanted to go to Iraq and has been grounded. Harry secretly goes to Afghanistan for a brief sojourn. The press agrees to secrecy on the understanding that a big picture story will eventuate. The cover is blown early and his pictures flood the tabloids (*Press Gazette* 2008).

But why go to the trouble for such a transparent piece of propaganda? An ancient myth of redemption is being worked out. Just as much as Shakespeare's Prince Hal, the worthless Harry symbolises the rebirth of the military covenant. He represents the mystical body of the sovereign which itself embodies the mystical nation. He is presented as assuming equal risks with ordinary squaddies – therefore, a hero communing like King Henry with the army, as one of the boys or rather, *our* boys. He is presented as running the risk of sacrifice, shedding his boyish Prince Hal image and becoming a professional capable of undertaking…er fire control.

So far so bizarre. Something quite ancient is being celebrated. But, of course, the modern function of this coverage is to dissociate the royals from the despised political class who have got "our" troops stuck there, provide a positive story from Afghanistan and restore the image of the army. Afghanistan becomes an adventure. Instead of the mirror of our limitations and society's decadence, the army becomes, again, the mystical mirror of society in which a warrior elite redeems us and "Britishness".

Harry, like Prince Hal, is groomed to be the author of our redemption. Indeed, a founding myth of Britishness is Shakespeare's Hal renouncing Falstaff and becoming a military leader, and the camp he strides through, you will recall, includes Welsh, Irish and Scottish soldiers, as well as English.

What does this really mean? Of course, it is a PR stunt, with the complicity of the press. It *means* nothing. Or rather, it represents a quest for meaning. "Contemporary war is both a pragmatic exercise in risk management and an attempt to recover a sense of historical purpose," observes Philip Hammond (Hammond 2007: 122). One does not have to be a mad postmodernist to see that meaning has somehow to be injected into a meaningless war. Or we might say, a sense of meaning has to be rescued.

Conclusion

Risk theory is the new conventional academic wisdom. If war is, indeed, a continuation of politics by other means (or as Baudrillard has it the continuation of a lack of politics by other means) it figures that the forms of military action will broadly reflect the world view of particular periods. A plausible argument can be made for categorising the current generation of wars as essentially undertaken as 'risk management' exercises (ibid; Heng 2006).

Battle, John Keegan observed, may become so intolerable for participants that it is abolished (Keegan 1976). Some hope. More likely is that, despite the spectacle, it will be rendered uninviting for recruits and intolerable for home populations. That points, of course, to a distinctly post-modern mode of warfare, the so-called "risk transfer war" (Shaw 2005): really only the 18th century rewritten. The extensive use of mercenary soldiers from the poorer parts of Europe or Asia , conjoined with robot combat vehicles, remote surveillance and command. Like the Roman legionaries or the Gurkhas, citizenship may be the most potent recruiting device.

According to recruiting officers, Poles living in Britain want to follow their ancestors by joining a hard-pressed British army…short of 5,000 soldiers…the assumption that you have to be a British citizen to join the army and swear an oath of loyalty to Queen and country is not entirely correct. In a statement yesterday the MoD said stiffly: "We have no plans to change our recruitment rules…The army says that the Irish are a special case…" (*Guardian*, 19 March 2008 p. 3).

But meanwhile, as unemployment worsens and the universities await 20 per cent cuts, recruitment is surging…

Notes

[1] See http://www.army.mod.uk/join/terms/3111.aspx, accessed on 9 June 2010

[2] See http://www.london-gazette.co.uk/issues/59355/supplements/4054 and http://www.worldsecuritynetwork.com/_dsp/dsp_authorBio3.cfm?authID=559, both accessed on 9 June 2010

[3] See http://www.britishlegion.org.uk/remembrance, accessed on 10 June 2010

[4] In writing *Hard Work*, Toynbee worked as a hospital porter, a dinner lady in a primary school, a nursery assistant, a call-centre employee, a cake factory worker and a care home assistant. See http://en.wikipedia.org/wiki/Polly_Toynbee, accessed on 9 June 2010

[5] See http://www.army.mod.uk/infantry/regiments/mercian.aspx, accessed on 10 June 2010

[6] e.g. Help for Heroes, a charity founded in October 2007 by Bryn and Emma Parry, is sponsored by a number of high profile media figures (e.g. Jeremy Clarkson) and retired military officers and supported by the *Sun*. See http://www.helpforheroes.org.uk/sun_campaign.html, accessed on 9 June 2010

References

Appleton, Josie (2003) Back to Baudrillard, spiked-online.com. Available online at http://www.spiked-online.com/Articles/00000006DD41.htm, accessed 28 March 2008

Balliol College News (2006) Old Members Around the World, June. Available online at http://alumni.balliol.ox.ac.uk/news/fd2006/old_members.asp, accessed on 9 June 2010

Barnett, Correlli (1970) *Britain and Her Army 1509-1970*, London, Allen Lane, the Penguin Press

Bracchi, Paul (2009) Britons who hate Britain: This was the scene that greeted homecoming soldiers in Luton this week, *Daily Mail*, 14 March pp 24-25

Burroughs, Peter (1994) An Unreformed Army? 1815-1868, Chandler, David and Beckett, Ian (eds) *The Oxford Illustrated History of the British Army*, Oxford, Oxford University Press

von Clausewitz, Carl (1993 [1832]) *On War*, edited and translated by Howard, Michael and Paret, Peter, London, Everyman's Library

Doward, Jamie (2008) Record numbers of ex-soldiers in jail as combat leaves mental scars, *Observer*, 31 August 2008 p. 11

Drury, Ian (2009) Legendary soldier who defused 64 Taliban bombs is blown up on his last day on the front line, *Daily Mail*, 3 November 2009 p. 7

Fussell, Paul (1975) *The Great War and Modern Memory*, Oxford, Oxford University Press

Grey, Stephen (2009) *Operation Snakebite*, London, Viking

Harding, Thomas (2009) Death of a leader, *Daily Telegraph*, 3 July 2009 p.1

Heng, Yee-Kuang (2006) *War as Risk Management: Strategy and Conflict in an Age of Globalised Risks*, Abingdon, Routledge

Hammond, Philip (2007) *Media, War and Postmodernity*, Abingdon, Routledge

Hardman, Robert (2009) The most dangerous job on earth, *Daily Mail*, 14 April pp 28-29

Hobsbawm, Eric (1992) *The Invention of Tradition*, Cambridge, Cambridge University Press, Canto edition

Holmes, Richard (1994 [1985]) *Firing Line*, London: Pimlico paperback. Previously published in hardback, London, Jonathan Cape

Holmes, Richard (2006a) *Dusty Warriors*, London, Harper Press

Holmes, Richard (2006b) Soldiers and Society: Liddell Hart Annual Lecture, King's College, London, 10 May 2006. Available online at http://www.kcl.ac.uk/content/1/c6/01/45/60/LiddellHartLecture0702.pdf, accessed on 30 March 2008

Hopkins, Gerard Manley (1967 [1918]) *Poems*, Gardner, W.H. and Mackenzie, N.H. (eds), 4th edition, Oxford, Oxford University Press

Independent on Sunday (2007) The betrayal of British fighting men and women, 11 March. Available online at http://www.independent.co.uk/news/uk/politics/the-betrayal-of-british-fighting-men-amp-women-439784.html, accessed on 31 March 2008

Independent (2006) Soldier born in Fiji joins list of British servicemen killed while serving in Iraq, 16 May p.8

Keeble, Richard (1997) *Secret State, Silent Press: New Militarism, the Gulf and the Modern Image of Warfare*, Luton, John Libbey

Keeble, Richard (2004) Information warfare in an age of hyper-militarism, Allan, Stuart and Zelizer, Barbie (eds) *Reporting War*, London: Routledge pp 43-58

Keegan, John (1976) *The Face of Battle*, London, Jonathan Cape

Keegan, John and Holmes, Richard (1985) *Soldiers: A History of Men in Battle*, London, Hamish Hamilton

King, Anthony (2010) The Afghan War and "post-modern" memory: Commemoration and the dead of Helmand, *The British Journal of Sociology*, Vol.61, No. 1

Kipling, Rudyard (1974 [1892]) *The Complete Barrack Room Ballads*, Carrington, Charles (ed.) London, Methuen

Laurance, Jeremy (2010) Alcohol a problem for war veterans, study finds, *Independent*, 13 May p. 22

Levy, Andrew (2008) My hero brother: Wearing his poignant souvenir, a little boy says farewell as town salutes Paras who fell, *Daily Mail*, 31 October p. 39

Nairn, Tom (1990) *The Enchanted Glass: Britain and Its Monarchy*, London, Picador

Newton Dunn, Tom (2008) Exclusive: Army Chief talks to the *Sun:* Soldiers risk life yet earn less than a traffic warden, *Sun*, 5 June pp 14-15

Newton Dunn, Tom (2009) What PM told dead soldier's mother in 13-min phone row, *Sun*, 10 November pp 1, 4-6

Norton-Taylor, Richard (2007) Embrace returning troops, pleads army chief:General Dannatt calls for homecoming parades. Alarm at growing gulf between army and nation, *Guardian*, 22 September p. 4

Mileham, Patrick (2001) But will they fight and will they die? *International Affairs*, Vol. 77. No 3. Available online at http://www.jstor.org/stable/3095441, accessed on 9 June 2010

Mileham, Patrick (2010) Unlimited liability and the military covenant, *Journal of Military Ethics*, Vol. 9, No. 1, March pp 23-40

Roberts, Sebastian et al (2000) Soldiering: The military covenant, *Army Doctrine Publication*, Vol 5, par 0103,GD&D/18/34/71 Army Code No. 7164, February.

Press Gazette (2008) Prince Harry news blackout "was justified", 7 March. Available online at http://www.pressgazette.co.uk/story.asp?storyCode=40505&sectioncode=1, accessed on 6 June 2010

Royal British Legion (2007) Legion launches campaign: "It's time to honour the Covenant", 13 September. Available online at http://www.britishlegion.org.uk/news/index.cfm?fuseaction=newsdetail&asset_id =517232, accessed on 15 February 2008

Shaw, Martin (2005) *The New Western Way of War: Risk-Transfer War and its Crisis in Iraq*, Cambridge, Polity

Taylor, Matthew (2008) Mental illness cases in British forces neared 4,000 last year, *Guardian*, 5 November 2008 p. 14

Tennyson, Alfred (1965 [1912]) *Poems and Plays*, Oxford, Oxford University Press. Also available online at http://www.poetry-online.org/tennyson_the_lady_of_shallot.htm, accessed on 8 June 2010

Townsend, Mark (2009) We don't have the right kit to fight a war, warn troops, *Observer*, 9 August p. 7

Toynbee, Polly (2003) *Hard Work: Life in Low Pay Britain*, London, Bloomsbury

Twigg, Derek (2008) Speech by Under Secretary of State for Defence, Derek Twigg at Veterans UK 2008 Conference, 13 March. Available online at: http://www.mod.uk/defenceinternet/aboutdefence/people/speeches, accessed on 8 June 2010

Walsh, Declan (2007) With the Brits in Helmand, *Guardian*, 1 May, G2 pp 10-15

Wooding, David (2008) "Kick army out of schools" say sirs: Ranting militants try to end goodwill visits, *Sun*, 26 March p. 6

Note on the author

John Tulloch is Professor of Journalism and Head of the School of Journalism, University of Lincoln. Previously he was chair of the Department of Journalism and Mass Communication at the University of Westminster. Recent work includes jointly editing, with Colin Sparks, *Tabloid Tales* (Rowman and Littlefield, 2000) to which he contributed the essay "The eternal recurrence of the New Journalism". He has written on press regulation, official news management, popular television and the press's coverage of the "war on terror". He has also had a chapter on the journalism of Charles Dickens in *The Journalistic Imagination: Literary Journalists from Defoe to Capote and Carter* (edited by Richard Keeble and Sharon Wheeler, Routledge, 2007) and a chapter on the newspaper treatment of pacifists and conscientious objectors 1939-1940 in *Peace Journalism, War and Conflict Resolution* (edited by Richard Keeble, John Tulloch and Florian Zollmann, Peter Lang, 2010).

Operation Moshtarak and the manufacture of credible, "heroic" warfare

Richard Lance Keeble argues that Fleet Street's coverage of the Afghan conflict has served largely to promote the interests of the military/industrial/media complex – and marginalise the views of the public who have consistently appealed in polls for the troops to be brought back home

Introduction

This chapter examines Fleet Street's coverage of the US-led Operation Moshtarak in Afghanistan in 2010. It outlines the major strands of US/UK military strategy since the 1980s (defined here as New Militarist) and argues that the conflict in Afghanistan, as currently represented in the mainstream media, is no war at all: rather it's a series of manufactured, media-hyped "operations" led by a nation with the largest and most heavily resourced fighting force in history, against a pitifully under-resourced and yet skilful and merciless guerrilla movement in one of the most impoverished countries in the world.

So the role of the media embedded with the military is to manufacture the image of legitimate, heroic "warfare" against a credible threat. In the process the reality of the conflict, the appalling suffering of the Afghan people, is kept secret from the British public. The chapter also considers Fleet Street's editorial stances on the Afghanistan war – which was costing the UK £5billion a year (see Norton-Taylor 2010a) [1] – and the ways in which the views of the public (most of whom consistently call for the withdrawal of troops from Afghanistan) have been marginalised. The study draws on a range of alternative media to critique mainstream coverage.

Secret warfare

There are three major strands to New Militarist strategy – each accompanied by a particular form of media coverage. Firstly the most important strategy is conducted in complete secrecy away from the glare of the media. This involves in the case of Afghanistan during 2010:

- the targeted assassinations in both Afghanistan and over the border in Pakistan of alleged Taliban leaders (Walsh 2010a);

- the night raids by the CIA and some of its 56,000 Special Forces, such as the Green Berets and Navy SEALS, Special Boat teams, Air Force Special Tactics Teams and Marine Corps Special Operations Battalions (see Gopal 2010; Turse and Engelhardt 2010; Porter 2010a; Grey 2009a); [2]

- the secret detention and torture centres; the secret and massively expensive installation of almost 400 US and coalition military bases in Afghanistan and at least 300 Afghan National Army (ANA) and Afghan National Police (ANP) bases. According to investigative reporter Nick Turse (2010): "Existing in the shadows, rarely reported on and little talked about, this base-building programme is nonetheless staggering in size and scope…It has added significantly to the already long secret list of Pentagon property overseas and raises questions about just how long, after the planned beginning of a drawdown of American forces in 2011, the US will still be garrisoning Afghanistan."[3]

- the many disappearances;

- the increasing and largely secret use of pilotless drones to attack targets in Afghanistan and over the border in Pakistan; [4] In a celebratory feature on Britain's £124 million drones programme, Rob Waugh (2010) commented: "Autonomous machines save money, save pilots' lives and point to a future where Stealth-enabled unmanned fighters and ultra-long-endurance surveillance planes can almost remove human beings from the aerial battlefield. But this technology has largely appeared without governments or the public questioning it."

- the penetration of allied and enemy governments by the CIA/MI6. In October 2009, for instance, it was revealed that the brother of Afghan president, Ahmed Wali Karzai, long alleged to be a powerful drug lord, had been on the CIA's payroll for almost eight years (Borger 2009). Leaks of this kind reflected the rivalries amongst the US's 16 intelligence agencies (see MacAskill, Nasaw and Boone 2010a);

- and the Pakistan military offensives against the Taliban and al-Qaeda, instigated by Washington, which have claimed thousands of lives and displaced over a million people in the northwestern tribal areas (see Cockburn 2010a, 2010b). In particular, there are the little reported attacks by the army against the rising independence movement in Baluchistan. This is Pakistan's largest province, covering 44 per cent of the country's area but where 60 per cent of the population live in abject poverty (Khan and Prasad 2010). Yet on 7 June 2010, it was reported that Pakistan planned to increase its military budget to a massive 442 billion rupees (the equivalent of £3.59bn) (*Morning Star* 2010).

On 7 June 2010, the *Independent* reported that US special forces were operating in more than 75 countries – from Colombia to the Philippines. The "secret war" had vastly increased in scope and size under President Obama (Sengupta 2010a). No other information was forthcoming. Columnist Sam Leith (2010), in the London *Evening Standard*, commented critically: "It sounds...cool. But how, in principle – that is, in terms of accountability and respect for law – does dropping bombs from drones or fielding teams of assassins in other countries differ from the secret bombing of Cambodia in Kissinger's day?"

UK battles: beyond the glare of the media

In fact, since 1945 the UK and the US have deployed troops somewhere in the globe at least once every year – most of them far away from the gaze of the media. As Steve Peak (1982: 10) pointed out, the Falklands "war" of 1982 was the 88th deployment of British troops since 1945. These deployments took place in 51 countries and nearly all of them in Africa, the Middle East, South-East Asia, the Far East and around the Caribbean. Newsinger (1989) describes British intervention in Indonesia in 1945-1946 as a "forgotten war". Britain's longest running post-1945 campaign (leaving aside Northern Ireland) was in Malaya from 1948 to 1960. But this was never described as a war. Rose (1986) argued that British troops had been involved in more wars in more places across the globe than any other country since 1945.

In the case of the US, the investment in secret warfare is still greater than that of the UK. Cecil Currey (1991: 72-73) argued that since 1950, America had used either force or its threat about 500 times, mostly in Third World countries. Former CIA agent John Stockwell (1991: 70-73) suggests that the agency had been involved in 3,000 major operations and 10,000 minor operations which had led to the deaths of 6m people worldwide – mainly in Korea, Vietnam, Cambodia, Africa and Central and South America. It had overthrown functioning democracies in more than 20 countries and manipulated dozens of elections. During the 1980s, secret support from CIA and MI6 (the UK's foreign intelligence service) for the mujahedin in their fight against Soviet occupiers in Afghanistan ultimately helped in the creation of the "Taliban" (not an organisation with a convention command structure but a disparate insurgency involving many, largely Pashtun, groups) and al-Qaeda. As John Pilger recorded (2003):

> For 17 years, Washington poured $4bn into the pockets of some of the most brutal men on earth – with the overall aim of exhausting and ultimately destroying the Soviet Union in a futile war. One of them, Gulbuddin Hekmatyar, a warlord particularly favoured by the CIA, received tens of millions of dollars. His speciality was trafficking opium and throwing acid in the faces of women who refused to wear the veil. In 1994, he agreed to stop attacking Kabul on condition he was made prime minister – which he was.

Special forces, such as the UK's SAS and the American Navy Seals, which are so crucial to secret warfare strategies, reportedly played important roles in the build up to the 1991 Iraq conflict and during them. They were the subject of a series of "inordinately flattering" features in the US and UK media (Ray and Schaap 1991:. 11). Yet accounts of their daring deeds of courage and endurance, since they were shrouded in almost total secrecy, amount to a form of fiction (see de la Billière 1995: 319-338; Hunter 1995: 169-175; Kemp 1994: 191-197).

By 2010, covert military action lay at the heart of US/Nato strategy in Afghanistan, the Middle East, the Horn of Africa and elsewhere. On 26 May 2010, both the *Guardian* and *Independent* followed up a report in the previous day's *New York Times* that General David Petraeus, head of the US's Central Command, had signed a directive (called the Joint Unconventional Warfare Task Force Execute Order) on 30 September 2009. Under its provisions, special forces such as Navy Seals and the Army's Delta Force would be able to "penetrate, disrupt, defeat or destroy" terrorist organisations, allowing for the assassination of US citizens abroad suspected of being terrorists (Cornwell 2010a; MacAskill 2010).[5] Significantly, America's top commander in Afghanistan in 2010, Gen. Stanley McChrystal, had headed the Joint Special Operations Command between 2003 and 2008.

In an accompanying comment piece, Rupert Cornwell, in the *Independent*, expressed support for the move. By following in the footsteps of President George Bush in his expansion of special force operations, US President Barack Obama had shown that he was "above all a realist and a pragmatist" (Cornwell 2010b). He continued: "Politically, Mr Obama must be seen as tough on national security. And if the CIA has many critics, no one doubts the quality of the US military." An unsigned, hagiographic profile of McChrystal in the *Sunday Times* of 4 October 2009 described him as a "ruthless US special forces hunter killer", a "mild, thoughtful and at times humorous soldier" and a "gaunt ascetic who rises at 4.30 am, eats one meal a day and jogs for an hour". [6]

Low Intensity Conflict (LIC)

The second New Militarist strategy is known in militaryspeak as Low Intensity Conflict (LIC): this involves the day to day grind of long-drawn-out engagement; occasional small-scale skirmishes with the enemy, sometimes involving pilotless drones and Apache helicopters; the taking out of snipers and the removal of roadside bombs. The regular reporting from Afghanistan of British soldier casualties ("our Heroes"), more than 300 by June 2010, is part of the sporadic coverage of this LIC, counter-insurgency strategy.

Pentagon adviser John M. Collins, in his seminal analysis of LIC, points out (1991: 4): "All LICs are contingencies and technically transpire in peacetime because none have yet been declared wars." Focusing on just 60 examples over the last century, Collins shows that 33 per cent of his sample exceeded 10 years while 57 per cent lasted less than five years. A feature of American strategy since the beginning of the 20th century, it developed still further as an offshoot of the nuclear stand-off between East and West during the Cold War and in response to the US defeat in Vietnam.

As Halliday (1989: 72) argued: "LIC theorists insisted that US combat forces should not be involved in the long-run, Vietnam style operations. The 'lesson' drawn here from Vietnam was that the US effort failed because it was too direct and too large." Significantly Collins' sample showed LICs mounting substantially in the post Vietnam, New Militarist era. During the 1980s, LIC strategists "came out" in the US and UK, numerous conferences were held and strategy documents were compiled exploring the concepts. But the LIC debate was largely ignored by the mainstream media.

Manufactured "wars" and "operations"

Finally, there are the occasional manufactured, media-hyped "operations" such as the attack on Musa Qala in December 2007, dubbed "Operation Snake Bite" (Grey 2009b),[7] "Operation Panther's Claw", focusing on Garmsir, Nad-e-Ali and Khanashin, in June 2009. And the one dubbed "Moshtarak", launched in February 2010. In these "operations", the nation with the largest and most heavily resourced fighting force in history, faces a comparatively small movement – though one which is highly skilled in guerrilla tactics – in one of the most impoverished countries in the world. These "operations" are then spectacular, essentially PR events providing the theatre in which the US and its allies can claim their so-called "victories".

They emerge from a long history of changing military strategies (driven by capitalism's relentless drive for minerals and foreign markets) which can be dated back to the mid-nineteenth century.[8] MacKenzie (1984) has described the "spectacular theatre" of 19th century British militarism when press representations of heroic imperialist adventures in distant colonies had a considerable entertainment element. Featherstone, too (1993; 1993a) has identified the way in which the Victorian "small" wars of imperial expansion in Africa and India were glorified for a doting public by correspondents such as William Russell, G. A. Henty, Archibald Forbes and H.M. Stanley.

But Victorian newspapers and magazines did not have the social penetration of the mass media of today. And Victorian militarism was reinforced through a wide range of institutions and social activities: the Salvation Army, Church Army and uniformed youth organisations, rifle clubs, ceremonial and drill units in factories. "In all these ways, a very large proportion of the population came to have some connection with military and paramilitary organisations" (MacKenzie op cit: 5-6). By the 1980s, this institutional and social militarism had given way to a new mediacentric, consumerist, entertainment militarism in which the mass media, ideologically aligned to a strong and increasingly secretive state, had assumed a dominant ideological role.

The traditional, industrialised militarism of the First and Second World Wars, in which the mass of the population participated in the war effort, either as soldiers or civilians, was founded on the widespread fear that the British state faced serious threats to its very existence. By the 1980s the supposed "threats" to Western interests came from puny Third World countries: and so the role of the media in these New Militarist adventures became even more critical in manufacturing the enemy as a credible "threat". During the 1980s, the military adventures of the UK in the Falklands (1982), the US in Grenada (1983), Libya (1986) and Panama (1989), culminating the Iraq conflict of 1991, all bore the hallmarks of this new military/media strategy.

- The threats posed to US/Western interests, in all these military interventions were either grossly exaggerated or non-existent. Significantly, the failure of the Soviet Union to intervene militarily in Poland in 1981 to crush the Solidarity movement under the leadership of Lech Walesa proved to the Western elites that the threat posed by their traditional "enemy" was waning. And so the permanent war economies of Britain and America (with their military/industrial complexes) needed the manufacture of "big enemies" to legitimise the continued massive expenditure on the weapons of war. Hence the massive displays of US/UK force in all these adventures bore little relation to the threats posed.

- They were all quickie attacks. The Libya bombings lasted just 11 minutes. All the others were over within days.

- They were all largely risk free and fought from the air. Since reporters were banned from accompanying pilots on the fighter jets, then the crucial air conflicts were conducted largely in secret.

- All the attacks resulted in appalling civilian casualties. Yet the propaganda, in Orwellian style, claimed the raids were essentially for peaceful purposes. Casualty figures were covered up and the military hardware was constantly represented as "precise", "surgical", "modern" and "clean".

- Central to the new strategy was the demonisation of the enemy leaders. In the absence of any serious military force, this demonisation served to represent the enemy states as credible threats.

- Media pools were deployed largely to keep journalists away from any action.

- All the invasions were celebrated in ecstatic language throughout the mainstream media. The editorial consensus remained firmly behind the military attacks. Administration lies were rarely challenged just as the global protests against the actions were largely ignored.

Defeat in Vietnam had proved to be a terrible trauma to the American military and political elites. With the waning of Soviet power in the 1980s, American imperialism could operate largely unchallenged. Victories were celebrated – and yet they were gained against largely puny Third World countries. The "Vietnam syndrome" could only be kicked in a "big" war. And Iraq's invasion of Kuwait in August 1990 was to prove the perfect opportunity for the manufacture of this perfect "big" war.

The New Militarist strategy was to continue well into the new century. Media-hyped, spectacular "wars" were waged – as in Somalia (1992-93), Serbia (1999), Afghanistan (2001) and Iraq (2003). With reporters embedded alongside the military, coverage remained tightly controlled. By 2010, low intensity conflicts were continuing in Somalia, Afghanistan and Iraq – and occasionally "major operations", where the US-led forces could claim victories against strangely shadowy enemies, were celebrated in the press.

No basis in international law

The Afghanistan conflict launched in 2001 following the 9/11 outrages in the US clearly had little basis in international law. So, in these "operations", the essential role of the media embedded with the military and constrained by the enormous risks involved in reporting from such a lawless country, is to manufacture the image of legitimate, heroic so-called "warfare" against a credible threat. In other words, the conventional language of the military is deployed to describe completely asymmetrical conflict. As Bishop points out (op cit: 13):

> Wars with insurgents were always unbalanced. One side had modern conventional weapons. The other fought with what was cheap, portable and easily improvised. But in Afghanistan the scale of the asymmetry at times seemed blackly absurd.

In the process the reality of the conflict, the high-tech violence of the invading forces, the appalling suffering of the Afghan people, is kept secret from the British public. We know precisely how many Coalition troops are killed (all of them, indeed, tragic and unnecessary), their names, their family histories – and how many have been wounded. As James Cogan noted on 23 April (2010): "Since 2001, the lives of 1,733 US and Nato troops have been squandered in Afghanistan...At least another 8,000 have been wounded in action, including more than 5,000 Americans. Thousands more have suffered non-battle injuries and illness." In 2009 alone, there were 1,400 British casualties flown from Afghanistan to the UK, 212 in a critical condition (Willetts 2010).[9] But the Afghan casualties of US/UK and Taliban attacks remain largely nameless and unknown. According to a report in *Le Monde* (Follorou 2010), almost 5,000 (grossly under-funded) Afghan policemen , with more than 70 per cent of them estimated to be illiterate, had been killed since 2003. [10] Moreover, the Marjah offensive had created an estimated 27,000 internal refugees – but these are hardly ever reported in the media (Boone and Norton-Taylor 2010).

Indeed, the Taliban, supported by their al-Qaeda allies, are distinguished largely by their invisibility in the media. They lay booby traps and roadside bombs otherwise known as improvised explosive devices (IEDs: usually home-made from fertiliser[11]), snipe at their enemy – and flee (often on battered motorbikes). In the military jargon, this is known as "shoot and scoot" (Bishop op cit: 73). Over the six-month period up to June 2010, British soldiers had come across more than 500 IEDs and engaged in more than 1,300 gunfights in central Helmand (Norton-Taylor 2010c). IEDs were accounting for 80 per cent of British injuries and fatalities (Rayment 2010). Many of the guns the Taliban were using date back to the 1890s (Sengupta 2010b). As Turse and Engelhardt stress (op cit):

> Al-Qaeda has no tanks, Humvees, nuclear submarines, or aircraft carriers, no fleets of attack helicopters or fighter jets…Al-Qaeda specialises in low-budget operations ranging from the incredibly deadly to the incredibly ineffectual…In the present war on terror, called by whatever name (or, as at present, by no name at all), the two "sides" might as well be in different worlds. After all, al-Qaeda today isn't even an organisation in the normal sense of the term, no less a fighting bureaucracy. It is a loose collection of ideas and a looser collection of individuals waging open source warfare.

Suicide bomb attacks and assaults on areas suspected of siding with the occupying forces have been other Taliban guerrilla tactics. In 2003 there were only two suicide attacks in Afghanistan. In 2006, there were at least 136, six times more than the year before. Eighty were directed at military targets but killed eight times as many civilians as soldiers or policemen (ibid: 130-131). The Taliban also terrorise individuals and communities suspected of siding with the occupation forces. According to Julius Cavendish (2010a), the insurgents executed two civilians whom they suspected of aiding government and international forces every three days during 2009.

Journalists have also been targeted. The decapitation of Afghan reporter Ajmal Naqshbandi, in 2007, was filmed and distributed on the internet [12]– but this did not receive the global media attention given to the similar decapitation of the *Wall Street Journal*'s Daniel Pearl, in February 2002.[13] The *Guardian*'s foreign correspondent Ghaith Abdul-Ahad was released along with two other journalists in December 2009 after being held hostage for six days in a remote region of Afghanistan (Taylor 2009). In January 2010, Rupert Hamer, embedded with US Marines at Nawa in Helmand for the *Sunday Mirror*, became the first UK journalist to be killed in Afghanistan. And this received massive media coverage. The front page of the *Daily Mirror* of 11 January carried a large photograph of Hamer smiling in front of troops with the headline: "Fine, fearless, dedicated" (Hughes 2010). [14]

The Taliban's basic weapon is an AK-47 rifle of Second World War design, augmented by machine guns and latterly home-made roadside bombs. In addition, the "legacy mines" left over since the time of the Soviet occupation (1979-1989) pose a durable threat. Facing them, the US-led troops have state-of-the-art satellites, spy planes and unmanned drones. Writing in 2009, Patrick Bishop commented in his book celebrating the heroics of 3 Para Battlegroup in Afghanistan (op cit: 12):

> Anti-American rebels had made great use of IEDs and suicide bombs in Iraq but they had been late arriving in Afghanistan [since 2006]. Together they now kept the troops in a constant state of alertness and anxiety. The insurgents' new methods carried less risk to themselves than did their previous confrontational tactics. Even when they suffered losses, though, there seemed to be no shortage of replacements.

With Osama bin Laden and Mullah Omar having mysteriously fled into the unknown following the US invasion of 2001, the Taliban in 2010 had no leader – such as the "mad dog" Gaddafi, of Libya, or the "new Hitler, Butcher of

Baghdad" Saddam or the "Butcher of Belgrade", "Slobo" Milosevic – on whom our patriotic editors safe in their Fleet Street bunkers and the military could direct their venom. The Taliban had no headquarters which US precision-guided missiles could "take out".

On 17 February 2010, the media reported American claims that the actual head of the Taliban's military operations had been seized in Karachi: a certain Mullah Abdul Ghani Baradar.[15] But like the rest of the Taliban, Mullah Abdul remains a shadowy, unknown figure. Significantly, no photographs of Taliban's toppled No 2 accompanied the reports.

Moshtarak: billed as the "biggest US offensive since 2001"

Operation Moshtarak, launched on 12 February in Afghanistan, was billed as "the biggest US military offensive since the US invasion of 2001" (note how PR-ish superlatives always accompany every new assault by the American military).

The 15,000 Coalition forces drawn from the US, the UK, Canada, Denmark, Estonia and most significantly Afghanistan were equipped with a vast arsenal – including Apache, Chinook and Cobra, Black Hawk attack helicopters and unmanned predator aircraft – all of it backed up by ranks of military intelligence operatives and information gathering hi-tech satellites. But whom were they "battling"? Possibly just 400 Taliban, according to some US officers (Lamb 2010). On 7 February, the *Sunday Times* predicted just 1,000 Taliban would be facing the 4,000 crack British troops (Colvin 2010). For the follow-up Kandahar offensive planned for the summer, military intelligence were said to be expecting between just "500 and 1,000" insurgents (Kirkup 2010).

So this is an "operation": not real warfare. Rather, it's a simulated, mediacentric event providing a symbolic show of US/UK military strength and proof that the new Afghan army is capable of taking over once the occupying forces withdraw. The operation had certainly no credible strategic legitimacy. The target of the US-led assaults was Marjah in Helmand province in the south of the country. But as reporter Anand Gopal told the progressive Democracy Now! radio station Marjah was "a very tiny town". Gopal continued:

It's more a show of force by the Coalition forces, something they can offer their home audiences of how they've gone into a village and retaken some Taliban. But beyond that, nothing will really change on the ground, regardless of what happens in Marjah. It's just business as usual.[16]

Investigative reporter Gareth Porter (2010b: 8) claimed that the picture of Marjah presented by military officials and obediently reported by major news media was "one of the clearest and most dramatic pieces of misinformation of the entire war, apparently aimed at hyping the offensive as a historic turning point in the conflict". On 2 February 2010, Associated Press quoted "Marine commanders" saying they expected 400 to 1,000 insurgents to be "holed up" in the southern Afghan town of 80,000 people". According to Porter, "that language evoked an image of house-to-house urban street fighting". On 14 February, the second day of the "offensive", Lt Josh Diddams said the Marines were "in the majority of the city at this point". He also used the language that conjured images of urban fighting, claiming the insurgents were hold some "neighbourhoods". Yet, as Porter stressed, Marjah is not a city nor even a real town but either a few clusters of farmers' homes or a large agricultural area covering much of the southern Helmand River Valley.

Maintaining the myth of warfare

Predictably the Coalition forces were reported as "storming" Marjah. More superlatives appeared in the press to manufacture the image of credible warfare: the town was suspected of being "one of the biggest, most dangerous minefields Nato forces had ever faced" (Martin 2010). Brig Gen. Larry Nicholson, commander of the Marines in southern Afghanistan, was quoted as saying: "This may be the largest IED threat and largest minefield that Nato has ever faced." while the US military were reported as saying that "hundreds of beleaguered insurgents could insist to fight until death" (ibid).

On 13 February Gulab Mangal, governor of Helmand, was reported as saying it was "the most successful operation we have ever carried out". Duncan Larcombe (2010), embedded with the Fire Support Company, 1st battalion, the Royal Welsh, in the *Sun* of 15 February trumpeted: "Our boys are in high spirits after successfully pulling off the largest helicopter assaults in British military history." Oliver Harvey (2010), embedded with 3 Platoon Queen's Company for the *Sun*, celebrated the flying of the Afghan national flag at the "Taliban stronghold Marjah" as a "sign of hope".

Always the myth of warfare survives: usually as a future danger. So the *Sun* of 11 February reported: "Fighting …in Helmand is expected to be ferocious." In the *Sunday Times* of 14 February Miles Amoore and Marie Colvin reported (2010): "Most Taliban appear to have scattered before the onslaught which was strongly signalled in advance. However, military commanders expect them to regroup and attack in the weeks ahead." And Jon Boone (2010b) in the *Guardian* of 10 March quoted Commanding Officer Major Joseph Brannon on the Taliban: "They know we are making a difference here so we are expecting a pretty strong fight."

But as John Pilger (2010) commented: "The recent 'liberation of the city of Marja' from the Taliban's 'command and control structure' was pure Hollywood. Marja is not a city – there was no Taliban command and control. The heroic liberators killed the usual civilians, the poorest of the poor. Otherwise it was fake. A war of perception is meant to provide fake news for the folks back home to make a failed colonial adventure seem worthwhile and patriotic."

The celebritisation of "heroic" warfare
One way in which the media hide the reality of the horror of warfare is to celebrate the visits of celebrities from the world of politics and entertainment to the troops on the frontlines. The events are pure PR – being usually accompanied by photographs of the smiling visitors shaking hands with equally smiling troops or trying some of the military hardware for the cameras. The language used is always positive and uplifting. Typical, then, was the coverage given to President Barack Obama on 29 March 2010 on his first visit to the war zone since ordering a "surge" of 30,000 extra US troops in Afghanistan in November 2009. Stephen Foley (2010), in the *Independent*, quoted the President: "I'm encouraged by the *progress* that's been made…One of the main reasons I am here is just to say than you for the *extraordinary efforts* of our troops."

On 24 May, the *Daily Mail* along with the rest of Fleet Street reported David Beckham, England football "hero", dropping in on the troops in Camp bastion, Afghanistan. He told troops of his "huge admiration" for them.[17]

Fleet Street backs Moshtarak offensive – despite massive public opposition

Virtually all the New Militarist attacks have won the overall support of Fleet Street editors: Operation Moshtarak, involving 9,500 British troops, was no exception. For the 1991 conflict all Fleet Street newspapers backed the military response together with 95 per cent of columnists. For the 1993 and 1998 attacks on Iraq the consensus fractured with the *Guardian*, *Independent* and *Express* coming out against the attacks. Then for the Nato attacks on Serbia in 1999 virtually all of Fleet Street backed the action, even calling for the deployment of ground troops (which not even the generals dared adopt as policy). There was one exception – the *Independent on Sunday* – and its editor, Kim Fletcher, left the paper just weeks after the end of the conflict. But there was far more debate amongst columnists. A survey I conducted showed 33 out of 99 prominent columnists opposed military action against Serbia. For the attacks on Afghanistan and the toppling of the Taliban, the whole of Fleet Street backed the action – but again there was a wide-ranging debate amongst columnists and letter writers (Keeble 2004 and 2007).

In 2003, with significant opposition to the rush to war being expressed by politicians, lawyers, intelligence agents, celebrities, religious leaders, charities and human rights campaigners – together with massive street protests – both nationally and internationally, the breakdown in Fleet Street's consensus was inevitable. Yet still for the invasion of Iraq, the vast bulk of Fleet Street backed the action (though columnists and letter writers were divided). The *Independents*, carrying prominently the dissident views of foreign correspondent Robert Fisk, were the most hostile. Following the massive global street protests on 15 February, the *Independent on Sunday* editorialised: "Millions show this is a war that mustn't happen."

The *Guardian* did not criticise military action on principle but opposed the US/UK rush to war and promoted a wide range of critical opinions. The *Mirror*s were also "anti" in the run up to the conflict (perhaps more for marketing reasons since the Murdoch press was always going to be firmly for the invasion) with the veteran dissident campaigning journalists John Pilger and Paul Foot given prominent coverage. But then, after editor in chief Piers Morgan claimed his papers' stance attracted thousands of protesting letters from readers, their opposition softened. And the *Mail*s managed to stand on the fence mixing both criticism of the rush to military action with fervent patriotic support for the troops during the conflict.

In 2010, most of Fleet Street was still backing the Nato "war" in Afghanistan. On 6 December 2009, the *Sunday Times* editorial, titled "Prepare for the long haul in Afghanistan", welcomed President Obama's "surge" strategy: "He took his time, but President Barack Obama reached the right decision with his announcement last week the United States is to send 30,000 more troops and 250 helicopters to Afghanistan." On 14 February the same newspaper was hailing, cautiously, Operation Moshtarak: "Maybe this is the end of the beginning". According to the *Independent*'s editorial of 9 February 2010, the strategy of General Stanley McChrystal, to put Afghan troops alongside Western troops, had "logic" and "should at least be given an opportunity to prove itself".

On 2 June, the *Daily Telegraph* editorialised: "The heroic work undertaken by the British forces these past four years has laid the foundations for the new American-led strategy." The *Guardian*'s editorial on the following day suggested the British government "could make a bold decision – to withdraw troops from the front, use them to secure Kabul and set themselves the more modest aim of doing things that work". But by 24 June 2010, the *Guardian* was describing the war as "dysfunctional" and "unwinnable". According to *The Times*' editorial of 10 June 2010, the new Prime Minister, David Cameron "to his credit...has chosen to reaffirm the importance of success in Afghanistan and to offer unbridled support to the military". A follow-up leader the next day concluded, firmly, that "at a time of austerity, it is imperative that this nation spends more on its defence". But as during the Nato attacks on Serbia in 1999, the *Independent on Sunday* dared to stand outside the consensus. On Remembrance Sunday, 8 November 2009, its editorial commented:

> It is time, on this solemn day on which we remember the sacrifice of those who gave their lives for our freedom and security, for a change in policy. It is time to say that this war was ill-conceived, unwinnable and counterproductive. It is time to start planning a phased withdrawal of British troops.

Fleet Street's general support for the UK government's Afghan strategy did not match the public mood with polls consistently calling for troops to be withdrawn (Milne 2009). In July 2009, the BBC/*Guardian*, ITN, *The Times* and *Independent* all published polls showing Britons wanted immediate or rapid withdrawal of troops. Yet Polina Aksamentova argued (2009) that the media largely downplayed their findings. For instance, the ICM study, reported in the *Guardian* on 11 July, found 42 per cent wanted Britain to pull out immediately and 14 per cent by the end of the year. The *Guardian*, however, titled the article "Public support for Afghanistan is firm, despite deaths". It stressed that support for the war had increased from 30 per cent in 2006 to 46 per cent but left the call for withdrawal to the last three sentences of the article. Few of the newspapers wrote about any of the other polls.

On 11 November 2009, the *Independent* published a vote showing four out of five did not believe the government's main justification – and did not believe that British involvement was keeping the streets of Britain safe from terrorist attacks. Some 46 per cent felt the war actually increased the threat of attacks by creating anger and resentment among the Muslim population (Sengupta and Morris 2010). Even while Operation Moshtarak was under way, another poll by ComRes for the *Independent* and ITV News showed that almost three-quarters of electors viewed the conflict as unwinnable – and more than half said they did not understand why British troops were still in Afghanistan (Morris 2010). Similar massive public opposition to the war was being recorded in the US. A *Washington Post*/ABC poll released in June 2010 showed 53 per cent of respondents saying the war was "not worth fighting" – the highest percentage in three years. [18]

Opposition has appeared in the mainstream media from a number of prominent columnists – such as Simon Jenkins, Seamus Milne, Peter Preston (all *Guardian*), Andreas Whittam Smith, Johann Hari (*Independent*), Max Hastings and Andrew Alexander (*Daily Mail*), Jeff Randall (*Daily Telegraph*), Peter Beaumont (*Observer*) and Denis McShane MP. But, intriguingly, the loudest protests in the media have come largely from those calling for still more investment in the war. The *Sun*, *Mail*, *Express* and *Telegraph*, to name but a few of Fleet Street's most hawkish members, criticised loudly the supposed failures of the Gordon Brown New Labour government to equip "our heroes" properly. Particular attention has focused on the alleged failings of the Snatch Land Rover (Sturke 2008; Bulstrode 2010). The claims of a Catholic bishop at a military funeral that soldiers in Afghanistan urgently needed more helicopters and vehicles in late April 2010 received substantial media coverage (e.g Bowcott 2010).

The row promoted an illusion of critical media holding the rulers to account. And yet the controversy was entirely manufactured. The US military have spent around one trillion dollars on its post 9/11 wars so far (Stiglitz and Bilmes 2009); it has 1.4 million active duty men and women and another 1.3 million reserve personnel; it employs more than 700,000 civilians in support roles while there are estimated 100,000 members in its civilian intelligence community. Its military budget in 2009 amounted to $661 billion. [19] In June 2010, Congress was set to approve an "emergency" supplemental financing Bill including more than $33 billion, mainly for funding the American military "surge" in Afghanistan (Astore 2010). Britain had already spent £9.4 billion on its Afghanistan operations by 2010 (Turse and Engelhardt op cit; see also Turse 2008). Its annual military spending was the equivalent of $53.8 billion, the fourth highest in the world (after the US, France and China).[20] So much for under-resourcing.

"Operations" certainly help provide a "theatre" in which some of these massively expensive weapons and the various branches of the military (army, navy, air force, special forces, satellites, intelligence and so on) can be tested. Significantly, Adam Ingram, a former Armed Forces Minister, suggested that a desire within the army to try out a new range of recently purchased Apache helicopters was a factor in the deployment of British troops to Helmand in 2006

(Haynes 2010). Before the 3,000 British troops arrived, the province had been "relatively quiet", according to Andrew Krepinevich, who served on the personal staff of three US secretaries of defence, but their arrival "stirred up a hornet's nest" (Evans 2010).

The contradictions of New Militarism and the failure of Operation Moshtarak

Central to manufacture of New Militarist "operations" is the celebration of "victory" to applauding home audiences usually just days after their launch. But since 2001 and the US/UK invasions of Afghanistan and Iraq, the New Militarist strategy has faced significant setbacks. The occupations of Iraq and Afghanistan have attracted massive opposition from local forces and, by 2010, substantial majorities in the UK were calling for the troops to be withdrawn from Afghanistan.

Thus while the US/UK military remained committed to the launch of media-hyped "operations", by 2010 they were often no longer achieving their desired results. In the case of Operation Moshtarak, its launch was given predictably massive media coverage yet its conclusion was hardly covered at all. Almost immediately after, the focus shifted to US plans to take over Kandahar, Afghanistan's second city, in the summer. Typical was the report by Julius Cavendish (2010), in the *Independent* of 21 April 2010. Buried in the coverage of the assassination of the deputy mayor of Kandahar in a mosque was a comment from provincial council member Haji Moqtar Ahmed on Operation Moshtarak: "My thinking is [there was] no result. It failed...If they start without consulting ordinary people, thousands of families will move to Kandahar city. There will be great misery." And Cavendish added:

> Nato's strategy for Kandahar was partly tested in its campaign to restore government control over the town of Marjah in neighbouring Helmand. The campaign, which began in February, has been held up by the Taliban.

The *Morning Star* reported in early May 2010 that resistance forces continued to operate in Marjah and that locals had largely refused to collaborate with occupation troops or Karzai government officials (Mellen 2010). Kim Sengupta

(2010e) reported on 28 May 2010 claims by Hajj Mohammad Hassan, a local tribal elder, that there remained no security in Helmand. "By day there is government. By night it's the Taliban." The *Guardian*'s editorial of 3 June 2010 commented: "The Marjah campaign, which was designed as a blueprint for how the Taliban could be rolled back, has become – in Gen. McChrystal's words – a bleeding ulcer of the campaign. There could be bigger wounds yet." On 9 June 2010, the BBC reported Nato and Afghan official claiming "success" for the Marjah campaign, but there were reports of continuing violence and Taliban intimidation.[21] And by 17 June, the writer and historian, William Dalrymple (2010), reported:

> …it appears that the Taliban have regained control of the opium-growing centre of Marjah in Helmand province, only three months after being driven out by McChrystal's forces amid much gung-ho cheerleading in the US media

Serious splits over strategy for the planned summer, follow-up "operation" in Kandahar, amongst military and civilian leaders in both the UK and US, also surfaced prominently in the media (e.g. Helm and Beaumont 2010; Sengupta 2010c).[22] They culminated (amazingly) in the sacking of Gen. McChrystal by President Obama on 23 June 2010 after his outspoken criticisms of the civilian leadership of the US were published in *Rolling Stone* magazine. Moreover, Nato officials were warning that there were no quick, New Militarist fixes in Afghanistan with British and foreign troops expected to be engaged in a combat role there for at least three or four more years (Norton-Taylor 2010d).

The performance of local Afghan forces in Operation Moshtarak was also disappointing, according to reports. It was thrown into further disarray with the resignations of two of the "most internationally respected" members of Karzai's government – interior minister Hanif Atmar and spy chief Amrullah Saleh – after a gathering of 1,600 leaders in Kabul came under Taliban rocket attack (Boone 2010). Moreover, a survey of 1,994 people in Afghanistan, commissioned by Gen. McChrystal, found that 85 per cent viewed the Taliban as "our Afghan brothers". More than two thirds said they viewed Karzai's government as totally corrupt while the occupying forces and Afghan police were considered the greatest threat to personal security by 56 per cent (Cogan op cit).

Missing from the coverage: the massive, global opposition

Largely missing from the Moshtarak coverage is any acknowledgement of the views and protests of the massive anti-war movement in this country and globally. CND, the Anti-War Coalition, War Resisters International, the Peace Pledge Union, Pax Christi, Campaign Against the Arms Trade, Respect are but a handful of the many groups in the UK largely ignored by the mainstream. On 3 April 2010, for instance, PressTV reported that thousands of peace activists had taken to the streets in 30 towns and cities across Germany demanding an immediate end to the country's unpopular presence in Afghanistan. [23]

While the mainstream media, with a few notable exceptions (such as veteran reporter Kathy Gannon of Associated Press, Patrick Cockburn and Robert Fisk, of the *Independent*, Jonathan Steele, of the *Guardian*) are failing in their coverage of Afghanistan there are still some excellent reports in alternative media to be accessed via the internet. To name but two: TomDispatch.com, edited by the US historian Tom Engelhardt, has carried a series of excellent investigative pieces on the conflict contextualising it historically and highlighting the vast military industrial complex which is promoting it. The Indian journal *Frontline* (at www.frontlineonnet.com) has also a history of covering US imperialistic adventures with a detailed and critical eye (while other useful websites are listed towards the end of this chapter). For journalism students and critical media consumers there are, indeed, many models out there of good, brave reporting to admire and learn from.

Richard Lance Keeble
wishes to acknowledge the comments made by Prof John Tulloch on a draft, but remains entirely responsible for this final copy. It is based on the talk he gave on 18 March 2010 to an international conference on the Afghan media coverage organised by John Mair, of the journalism department at Coventry University.

Notes

---

[1] At a time of general spending cuts (imposed by the government as a response to the global credit crisis and in an attempt to reduce the massive national debt) the defence budget was due to be increased in 2010 by more than £500 million to £38 billion (Norton-Taylor 2010b). David Swanson (2010) reported that Congress was expected to vote on $33 billion extra war funding for the Afghan troop "surge". According to the Congressional Budget Office, Congress had already approved $345 billion for the war in Afghanistan and $708 billion for the Iraq war. Government figures released on 19 June 2010 showed that Britain had spent at least £9.24 billion in Iraq and £11.1 billion since 2001. The actual cost, which did not include soliders' salaries or caring for the wounded, was expected to be much higher (see http://news.bbc.co.uk/1/hi/uk/10359548.stm, accessed on 20 June 2010). The Pentagon also spends an enormous amount on fuel. In 2009 alone, according to the Pentagon's Defense Energy Support Centre, the military spent $3. 8 billion on 31.3 million barrels (around 1.3 billion gallons) of oil consumed at posts, camps and bases overseas. Another $974 million was spent by the ground-fuels division just on the Afghan war in 2009. Also in 2009, the military awarded $22.5 billion in energy contracts. The largest contractor was BP which received more than $2.2 billion – almost 12 per cent of all petroleum-contract dollars awarded (see http://www.lobelog.com/tomgram-nick-turse-bp-and-the-pentagons-dirty-little-secret/, accessed on 18 June 2010)

[2] After the killings of civilians during a night raid provoked massive protests in eastern Afghanistan, Nato commander Gen. Stanley McChrystal ordered his troops to avoid night raids (see Afghanistan: Protest erupts over Nato killings, *Morning Star*, 15-16 May 2010). Nato spokesman Gen. Joseph Blotz claimed in June 2010 civilian casualties had fallen by 44.4 per cent over the previous three months due to more stringent rules of engagement (see: http://news.bbc.co.uk/1/hi/world/asia_pacific/10356741.stm)

[3] According to Turse (2010), quoting Colonel Kevin Wilson, head of the building operations in southern Afghanistan for the US Army Corps of Engineers, the Americans were spending $3 billion on base-building in Afghanistan in 2010. In Iraq in August 2009, there were still almost 300 American bases and outposts. In

addition to those in Iraq and Afghanistan, the Pentagon listed 716 overseas sites across the globe – especially in the Middle East, Europe, Japan and South Korea.
[4] See Evans and Norton-Taylor (2010). A freedom of Information request by the *Guardian* revealed that the RAF had fired 845 missiles from reaper drones since they were first deployed in June 2008. They plan to double the number of drones in use over the next two years. The drones are launched from a base in Kandahar by a squadron of 90 RAF personnel at Creech US Air Force base in Nevada. Harvey (2009) reported that Predator drones were to rack up 1 million flight hours and that there were 35 Predators in the air at any one time. Harvey described the drones as being "so successful in the fight against the Taleban and a-Qaeda". Focusing on the new Avenger drone, Harvey said it could fly practically undetected at 60,000ft and was being "fine-tuned" at Gray Butte flight operations facility of General Atomics Aeronautical Systems, Inc. But citing figures compiled by Pakistan's Interior Ministry, the Karachi-based daily, *News International*, reported that "Afghanistan-based US Predators carried out a record number of 12 deadly missile strikes in the tribal areas of Pakistan in January 2010, of which 10 went wrong and failed to hit their targets, killing 123 innocent Pakistanis" (van Auken 2010). Significantly, the US claimed in January 2010 that a drone attack had killed the head of the Pakistan Taliban, Hakimullah Mehsud in North Warzirstan. But in April 2010, new intelligence suggested that he had escaped – as the Taliban had always insisted (Buncombe and Waraich 2010; Walsh 2010a). In May 2010, the Americans claimed that Mustafa Abu al-Yazid, prominent in al-Qaeda in Afghanistan (and arrested over the killing of the Eyptian President Anwar Sadat in 1981), had been assassinated by missiles fired from a drone in Pakistan (Sengupta 2010d). His wife, three daughters and a granddaughter were all said to have also died in the attack. Al-Yazid was erroneously reported dead by Pakistan officials after a drone strike in August 2008 (Walsh 2010b)
[5] Kim Sengupta (2010b) reported that the law on assassinations was aimed specifically at future attempts to target Anwar al-Awlaki, suspected of being the mentor to the 2009 Christmas Day "underpants bomber" Umar Farouk Abdulmuttallab and US Army Major Nidal Malik Hasan who killed 13 people at Fort Hood in Texas in November 2009
[6] See http://www.iiss.org/whats-new/iiss-in-the-press/october-2009/profile-stanley-mcchrystal/, accessed on 1 May 2010

[7] A substantial genre of books has emerged celebrating the heroics of "Our Boys" in Afghanistan. They include Moore (2003), Scott (2008), Kemp, Hughes (2009) and Junger (2010). Geoff Dyer (2010) argues that writing in this non-fiction genre is best able to capture the essence of US-style warfare today: "Reportage, long-form reporting – call it what you will – has left the novel looking superfluous. The fiction lobby might respond: it's too soon to tell." He adds: "We are moving beyond the non-fiction novel to different kinds of narrative art, different forms of cognition. Loaded with moral and political point, narrative has been recalibrated to record, honour and protest the latest, historically specific instance of futility and mess"

[8] Significantly, the Mail Foreign Service reported on 15 June 2010 that untapped ore – including huge veins of gold, iron, copper, cobalt and industrial metals such as lithium – valued at more than £820 billion had been discovered by geologists in Afghanistan. The article commented that the find "will also raise question marks over the motives behind the long and costly war launched in the wake of the 9/11 attacks". Later in the same week, the Americans tripled the estimated value of the untapped mineral wealth to $3 trillion

[9] Some 23 of the 55 British deaths in Afghanistan from January to June 2010 had taken place around Sangin. Of the total Nato casualties of 1,849 on 21 June 2010 (drawn from the 25 countries of he coalition and including 125 US women), 1,125 were American, 147 Canadian, 44 French and 42 German (see Higginson, John, "Highest price must be paid", *Metro*, 22 June). Soldiers were also suffering major psychological problems. In June 2010, some 20,000 ex-servicemen were in prison or on probation in Britain – one in ten of the jail population. Since of 1982, 264 veterans of the Falklands conflict of that year have committed suicide, compared with 255 who died in action (Newton Dunn 2010)

[10] The Americans, in addition to funding the Afghan police, had directed $1 million on building up private security forces (see Follorou 2010). Yet these companies were operating in a "culture of impunity" that was encouraging lawlessness and corruption, according to Britain's most senior commander in southern Afghanistan, Major General Nick Carter (Richard Norton-Taylor 2010e). According to investigative reporter Pratap Chatterjee (2010), the US had spent $7 billion on police training since 2003 but had left "the country of 33 million people with a strikingly ineffective and remarkably corrupt police force. Its terrible habits and reputation have led the inhabitants of many Afghan communities to turn to the Taliban for

security". Fears were also growing that the Taliban had infiltrated the Afghan police (Wintour and Norton-Taylor 2010)

[11] Accord to the *Sun*: "Evil Taliban improvised bombs are usually packed with filth – the the hope those they fail to kill outright die later from infection" (Willetts op cit). A UN Security Council report in June 2010 said that over the previous four months roadside bomb attackls rose by 94 per cent compared with the same period in 2009 while there were three suicide bombings every week. See: http://news.bbc.co.uk/1/hi/world/asia_pacific/10356741.stm

[12] See http://www.democracynow.org/2009/8/17/fixer_the_taking_of_ajmal_naqshband i, accessed on 1 May 2010

[13] See http://www.truthtube.tv/play.php?vid=2795, accessed on 1 May 2010

[14] Colin Hughes, of the *Daily Mirror*, was later sent death threats after he posted a blog that criticised a charity motorbike ride through Wootton Bassett, through which pass the hearses carrying the bodies of repatriated soldiers (Milmo 2010). After more than 5,000 Facebook members called for a boycott of the *Mirror*, the newspaper apologised for Hughes' posting

[15] Soon after the arrest of Baradar Pakistan arrested two more senior Taliban figures, Mullah Abdul Salam and Mullah Mir Mohammad. Mystery surrounded the arrests. Some commentators considered that Islamabad was shifting away from its secret support for the Taliban. But as Shah (2010) commented in the *Guardian*: "A more cynical interpretation suggested that instead of turning its back on the Taliban, Pakistan was simply putting pressure on them to come to the negotiating table"

[16] See http://www.medialens.org/forum/viewtopic.php?t=3070&sid=76d871d7f9209d50 c8b991fc950f2a5d, accessed on 3 June 2010

[17] See also Patrick Mulchrone's report on Beckham's visit and his praise for the "fallen heroes" in the *Daily Mirror*, available online at http://www.mirror.co.uk/celebs/news/2010/05/24/becks-silence-for-the-fallen-115875-22280836/, accessed on I June 2010

[18] See http://www.wsws.org/articles/2010/jun2010/afgh-j19.shtml, accessed on 19 June 2010

[19] See http://www.globalfirepower.com/defense-spending-budget.asp, accessed on 4 June 2010. Britain's figure represented a $3.7 billion increase on the previous year.

Guardian columnist Simon Jenkins (2010) called for all the £45 billion defence spending "against fantasy enemies" to be cut

[20] ibid

[21] See http://news.bbc.co.uk/1/hi/world/south_asia/10274262.stm, accessed on 9 June 2010

[22] Nato strategy in Afghanistan was thrown into further disarray with the resignation of the German President, Hörst Kohler, after he had suggested that military deployments were central to the country's economic interests (Connolly 2010)

[23] See inthesetimes.com/2010/04/03/german-easter-rallies-decry-afghanistan-killings, accessed on 4 May 2010

References

Aksamentova, Polina (2009) Withdrawal majority censored, *Peace News*, September, No 2513

Amoore, Miles and Colvin, Marie (2010) British spearhead allied offensive, *Sunday Times*, 14 February

Astore, William, J. (2010) Doubling Down in Afghanistan, 3 June. Available online at http://www.tomdispatch.com/archive/175256/, accessed on 2 June 2010

van Auken (2010) Obama's surge: killing spree on both sides of Afpak border. Available online at http://www.wsws.org/articles/2010/feb2010/afpk-f03.shtml, accessed on 1 May 2010

de la Billière, Sir Peter (1995) *Looking for Trouble: SAS to Gulf Command*, London, HarperCollins

Bishop, Patrick (2010) *Ground truth: Back on Afghanistan's frontline – 3 Para's epic new challenge*, London, Harper Press

Boone, Jon (2010a) Afghan minister resigns over *jirga* attack, *Guardian*, 7 June

Boone, Jon (2010b) Afghanistan: 24-hour patrols in Kandahar to win hearts and find mines, *Guardian*, 10 March

Boone, Jon and Norton-Taylor, Richard (2010) Poppy town that became deathtrap for British army, *Guardian*, 22 June

Bowcott, Owen (2010) Army shortages cost lives, bishop warns, *Guardian*, 29 April

Bulstrode, Mark (2010) Snatch Land Rovers blamed for dozens of deaths, *Independent*, 9 March

Buncombe, Andrew and Waraich, Omar (2010) Taliban leader was not killed by drone strike, says Pakistan, *Independent*, 30 April

Borger, Julian (2009) Karzai's brother in pay of CIA for eight years, US officials claim, *Guardian*, 29 October

Cavendish, Julius (2010b) Mosque murder leaves Kandahar on edge, *Independent*, 21 April

Cavendish, Julius (2010b) Fighters switch back to Taliban after "broken promises", *Independent*, 23 April

Chatterjee, Pratap (2010) Policing Afghanistan: How Afghan police training became a train wreck, 21 March. Available online at www.tomdispatch.com/blog/175220/, accessed on 3 June 2010

Cockburn, Patrick (2010a) The secret war – and the hidden lair of the Taliban, *Independent*, 16 April

Cockburn, Patrick (2010b) Caught in the crossfire of Pakistan's secret war, *Independent*, 22April

Cogan, James (2010) Afghanistan: Another massacre as a bloody summer loons in Kandahar, 23 April. Available online at www.wsws.org/articles/2010/apr2010/afgh-a23.shtml, accessed on 24 April 2010

Collins, John M. (1991) *America's Small Wars*, London/Washington, Brasseys (US)

Colvin, Marie (2010) Special forces assassins infiltrate Taliban strongholds in Afghanistan, *Sunday Times*, 7 February

Cornwell, Rupert (2010a) US to launch covert strikes on terror targets, *Independent*, 26 May 2010

Cornwell, Rupert (2010b) When it comes to terrorism, Obama is following Bush's lead, *Independent*, 26 May

Connelly, Kate (2010) German president quits amid accusations of 'gunboat diplomacy' after Afghanistan gaffe, *Guardian*, 1 June

Currey, Cecil (1991) Vietnam: lessons learned, Helling, Phil and Roper, Jon (eds) *America, France and Vietnam: Cultural history and ideas of conflict*, Aldershot, Avebury pp 71-90

Dalrymple, William (2010) The British army overwhelmed by Afghan warriors. No, not today but in 1842. So can we learn lessons of history before it happens again?, *Dail Mail*, 17 June

Dyer, Geoff (2010) The human heart of the matter, *Guardian*, 12 June

Evans, Michael (2010) Complacent British ignored advice that force was too small. Say Pentagon officials, *The Times*, 10 June

Evans, Rob and Norton-Taylor, Richard (2010) RAF strategy in Afghanistan shifts to drones, *Guardian*, 8 February

Featherstone, Donald (1993a) *Victorian Colonial Warfare: Africa*, London, Blandford

Featherstone, Donald (1993b) *Victorian Colonial Warfare: India*, London, Blandford

Foley, Stephen (2010) Obama rallies the troops on surprise visit to Afghanistan, *Independent*, 29 March

Follorou, Jacques (2010) Le état d'âmes des policicers afghan, privés de moyens et minés par la corruption, *Le Monde*, 9 June

Gopal, Anand (2010) Afraid of the dark in Afghanistan, 28 January. Available online at www.tomdispatch.com/dialogs/print/?id=175197, accessed on 29 January 2010

Grey, Stephen (2009a) *Operation Snake Bite: The explosive true story of an Afghan desert siege*, London, Viking

Grey, Stephen (2009b) New elite force for Helmand, *Sunday Times*, 6 September

Halliday, Fred (1989) *Cold War, Third World: An Essay on Soviet-American Relations*, London, Radius

Harvey, Mike (2009) Avenger of the skies: next wave of drones takes off, *Times*, 3 October

Harvey, Oliver (2010) The Sun goes into Helmand with our brave army medics, *Sun*, 26 February

Haynes, Deborah (2010) The Whitehall brass and mandarins who set up the bloodiest mission since Korea, *The Times*, 10 June

Helm, Toby and Beaumont, Peter (2010) Cameron calls Chequers summit as strains grow over coalition's aims in Afghanistan, *Observer*, 30 May

Hughes, Chris (2010) Fine, fearless, dedicated, *Daily Mirror*, 11 January

Hunter, Robin (1995) *True stories of the SAS*, London, Virgin

Jenkins, Simon (2010) My once-in-ia-generation cut? The armed forces. All of them, *Guardian*, 9 June

Junger, Sebastian (2010) *War*, London, Fourth Estate

Keeble, Richard (2004) Information warfare in an age of hyper-militarism, Allan, Stuart and Zelizer, Barbie (eds) (2004) *Reporting War: Journalism in Wartime*, London and New York, Abingdon, Oxon pp 43-58

Keeble, Richard (2007) The necessary spectacular "victories": New Militarism, the mainstream media and the manufacture of the Two Gulf Conflicts 1991 and 2003, Maltby, Sarah and Keeble, Richard (eds) *Communicating War: Memory, Media and Military*, Bury St Edmunds, Arima pp 200-212

Kemp, Anthony (1995) *The SAS: Savage Wars of Peace*, London, Signet

Kemp, Col. Richard and Hughes, Chris (2009) *Attack State: Taking the fight to the enemy. The awesome untold story of a landmark tour of duty in Afghanistan*, London and New York, Michael Joseph

Khan, Sartaj and Prasad, Yuri (2010) Crisis and conflict in Pakistan, *International Socialism*, Vol. 126, 14 April. Available online at http://www.isj.org.uk/index.php4?id=636&issue=126, accessed on 12 May 2010

Kirkup, James (2010) Kandahar offensive to target 1,000 Taliban, *Daily Telegraph*, 2 June

Lamb, Christina (2010) Battle for town is small step on the path to victory, *Sunday Times*, 14 February

Larcombe, Duncan (2010) Mud 'guts, the *Sun*, 15 February

Leith, Sam (2010) The secret war on terror sets a bad example, *Evening Standard*, 7 June

MacAskill, Ewen (2010) US sends more soldiers on covert mission, *Guardian*, 26 May

McAskill, Ewen, Nasaw, Daniel and Boone, Jon (2010) CIA agents in Afghanistan are "menace to themselves", former operatives claim, *Guardian*, 6 January

Martin, Patrick (2010) US military noose tightens on Afghanistan town, 12 February. Available online at http://www.wsws.org/articles/2010/feb2010/afgh-f12.shtml, accessed on 13 February 2010

McKenzie, John (1984) *Propaganda and Empire: The Manipulation of British Public Opinion 1880-1960*, Manchester, Manchester University Press

Mellen, Tom (2010) Afghans "not ready to fight yet", *Morning Star*, 8-9 May

Milne, Seamus (2009) In a war for democracy, why worry about public opinion, *Guardian*, 15 October

Milmo, Cahal (2010) Forces of Facebook turn on the *Daily Mirror*, *Independent*, 19 March

Moore, Robin (2003) *Taskforce Dagger: The Hunt for Bin Laden*, New York, Random House

Morris, Nigel (2010) Afghan war is unwinnable and we should pull it now, say voters, *Independent*, 21 April

Morning Star (nb) (2010) Pakistani military gets 17% boost to spending, 7 June

Newsinger, John (1995) The myth of the SAS, *Lobster*, Vol. 30 pp 32-36

Newton Dunn, Tom (2010) Troops to get trauma help, *Sun*, 7 June

Norton-Talor, Richard (2010a) British troops may leave Helmand as tension grows over Afghan role, *Guardian*, 22 April

Norton-Taylor, Richard (2010b) Cost of war in Afghanistan soars to £2.5bn, *Guardian*, 13 February

Norton-Taylor, Richard (2010c) Afghan police failings fuelling Taliban, say UK army chiefs, *Guardian*, 4 June

Norton-Taylor, Richard (2010d) Four more years of Afghan war, warns Nato official, *Guardian*, 30 April

Norton-Taylor, Richard (2010e) Afghan private security firms 'fuelling corruption', *Guardian*, 14 May

Peak, Steve (1982) Britain's military adventures, *The Pacifist*, Vol. 20 p 10

Pilger, John (2003) What good friends left behind, *Guardian Weekend*, 20 September pp 43-49

Pilger, John (2010) A predatory ideology in denial, *Morning Star*, 27-28 March pp 10-11

Porter, Gareth (2010a) Night raids belie McChrystal's new image, *Asia Times*, 2 April. Available online at inthesetimes.com/2010/04/03/night-raids-belie-mcchrystals-new-image/#more-11017

Porter, Gareth (2010b) Marja, the city that never was, the Coldtype Reader p 8-9. Available online at http://www.coldtype.net/Assets.10/Pdfs/0410.Reader45.pdf, accessed on 22 May 2010

Ray, Ellen and Schaap, William H. (1991) Disinformation and covert action, *Covert Action Information Bulletin*, No. 37, summer pp 9-13

Rayment, Sean (2010) The hidden victims of war: 1,000 casualties of the Afghan conflict, *Sunday Telegraph*, 21 February

Rose, Stephen (1986) Spend, spend, spend – on military only, *New Statesman*, 3 January

Scott, Jake (2008) *Blood Clot: In combat with the Patrols Platoon, 3 Para, Afghanistan, 2006*, Solihull, Helion and Company

Sengupta, Kim (2010a) US cruise missile parts found in Yemeni village where 52 died, *Independent*, 7 June

Sengupta, Kim (2010b) Army given new rifles to engage enemies from further away, *Independent*, 7 June

Sengupta, Kim (2010c) British military split over plan to move troops to Kandahar, *Independent*, 27 April

Sengupta, Kim (2010d) UN asks drone attacks to be taken out of CIA's hands, *Independent*, 3 June 2010

Senguta, Kim (2010e) Warning to politicians about early Afghan troop pull-out, *Independent*, 28 May

Sengupta, Kim and Morris, Nigel (2010) Afghan war is bad for security, voters say, *Independent*, 11 November 2009

Shah, Saeed (2010) Taliban arrests in Pakistan amid talk of policy shift, *Guardian*, 19 February

Stiglitz, Joseph and Bilmes, Linda (2009) *The three trillion dollar war*, London, Penguin

Sturcke, James (2008) SAS commander quits in Snatch Land Rover row, *Guardian*, 1 November. Available online at http://www.guardian.co.uk/uk/2008/nov/01/sas-commander-quits-afghanistan, accessed on 1 May 2009

Swanson, David (2010) Afghan escalation funding, 11 May. Available online at http://www.tomdispatch.com/blog/175246/tomgram%3A_david_swanson,_did_you_say_$33_billion__/, accessed on 12 May 2010

Taylor, Matthew (2009) Kidnapped Guardian journalist released, *Guardian*, 17 December

Turse, Nick (2008) The trillion dollar tag sale, 26 October. Available online at http://www.nickturse.com/articles/tom_trillion.html, accessed on 1 May 2009

Turse, Nick (2010) The 700 military bases of Afghanistan, 9 February. Available online at http://www.tomdispatch.com/blog/175204/tomgram:_nick_turse,_america's_shadowy_base_world/, accessed on 10 February 2010

Turse, Nick and Engelhardt, Tom (2010) Shooting gnats with a machine, 14 January. Available online at www.tomdispatch.com/dialogs/print/?id=175191

Walsh, David (2010) US military's private spy and murder ring continues to operate in Afghanistan, Pakistan, 18 May. Available online at www.wsws.org/articles/2010/may2010/cont-m18.shtml, accessed on 20 May 2010

Walsh, Declan (2010a) Taliban leaderin Pakistan survived CIA drone strike said to have killed him, spy agency says, *Guardian*, 29 April

Walsh, Declan (2010b) US hails 'big victory' after Islamist website confirms drone strike killed al-Qaida veteran, *Guardian*, 2 June

Waught, Rob (2010) The rise of the robo-fighters, *Daily Mail*, 5 May

Willetts, David (2010) A wing and a prayer, *Sun*, 7 June

Wintour, Patrick and Norton-Taylor, Richard (2010) Commanders fearTaliban infiltration as troops hunt assassin, *Guardian*, 11 May

Websites

http://afpak.foreignpolicy.com/ – critical readings on Afghanistan and Pakistan

www.anandgopal.com – site of distinguished journalist specialising in Afghanistan

http://www.afghanistannewscenter.com/ – excellent round up of news from a range of sources (e.g. BBC, Xinhua news agency, Press Trust of India, McClatchy Newspapers, *Guardian*)

www.theatlanticwire.com – US-based site with useful range of features on Afghanistan

www.juancole.com – invaluable Informed Comment blog

http://rethinkafghanistan.com/blog/ – progressive US commentaries on Afghanistan

www.stephengrey.com – distinguished freelance, investigative reporter specialising in "war on terror" and Guantanamo Bay

www.warincontext.org– commentary by Paul Woodward particularly useful

Afghanistan – Civilian casualties of the PR war

David Edwards and David Cromwell, of the media monitoring website Media Lens, argue that mainstream media coverage of the Afghan conflict has failed to convey the horror of continuing civilian casualties – largely because they are operating as a filter and booster system for powerful interests

Spinning for Edelman

Reports that former BBC director of news Richard Sambrook had found new employment in February 2010 were delivered with perfect timing. *The Times* commented on 16 February: "He was 30 years at the BBC, but in May, Richard Sambrook will start a new life spinning for Edelman, the world's biggest independent public relations company."

It seemed a natural career move. In 2002 and 2003, in the lead-up to the invasion of Iraq, Sambrook's BBC news team spun heaven and earth to lend an air of respectability to one of history's most brazen campaigns of state-orchestrated lying. Their performance was summed up well by BBC "rotweiller" Jeremy Paxman, host of the flagship *Newsnight* programme, when he said in 2009:

> ... when Colin Powell sat down at the UN General Assembly and unveiled what he said was cast-iron evidence of things like mobile, biological weapon facilities and the like [in Iraq]...When I saw all of that, I thought, well, 'We know that Colin Powell is an intelligent, thoughtful man, and a sceptical man. If he believes all this to be the case, then, you know, he's seen the evidence; I haven't. [1]

Naivety is one thing but, in this case, the naivety all went one way – no BBC journalist deferred so meekly to dissidents *challenging* pro-war propaganda. Consider *Newsnight*'s response to the vast anti-war march of February 2003, when some 2 million protestors flooded the centre of London – the biggest protest march in British history. *Newsnight's* political correspondent David Grossman asked: "The people have spoken, or have they? What about the millions who didn't march? Was going to the DIY store or watching the football on Saturday a demonstration of support for the government?" (David Grossman, BBC 2, *Newsnight*, 17 February 2003).

Massive public opposition to unilateral military action

And yet, one month earlier, it was widely reported that fully 81 per cent of the British public was opposed to unilateral military action by the US and UK, with 47 per cent opposed to war in all circumstances. Only 10 per cent of those polled believed that the war should be waged regardless of UN backing (Travis 2003).

As news of Sambrook's move arrived, his former colleagues at the BBC were once again deferring to the "intelligent", "thoughtful", "sceptical" politicians hyping the latest US-UK offensive in Afghanistan, Operation Moshtarak. As the media were keen to remind us, "moshtarak" means "together" in the Dari language.

On 14 February 2010, 12 Afghan civilians, six of them children, died "moshtarak" when a High Mobility Artillery Rocket System (HIMARS), designed for use against tanks and infantry, hit their home. HIMARS allows operators to launch at targets and then quickly change position before enemy artillery can pinpoint the source of fire – a vital component in Nato's armoury facing the massed ranks of Taliban tank and missile regiments. There had been at least 60 documented civilian deaths over the preceding week.

As journalists occasionally recognised, it was hard to be sure of the extent to which the Afghan population was brought "together" by Operation Moshtarak. The problem being that journalists were universally embedded with Nato military forces – there were no embeds with the insurgents known as "the Taliban". And so Nato was free to proclaim the "aims", "progress" and "success" of the offensive without significant challenge from the media. In his letter of resignation of 10 September 2009, Kabul-based US Foreign Service Officer Matthew P. Hoh challenged even the idea that Nato was fighting the Taliban:

> The Pashtun insurgency, which is composed of multiple, seemingly infinite, local groups, is fed by what is perceived by the Pashtun people as a continued and sustained assault, going back centuries, on Pashtun land, culture, traditions and religion by internal and external enemies. The US and Nato presence and operations in Pashtun valleys and villages, as well as Afghan army and police units that are led and composed of non-Pashtun soldiers and police, provide an occupation force against which the insurgency is justified...I have observed that the bulk of the insurgency fights not for the white banner of the Taliban, but rather against the presence of foreign soldiers and taxes imposed by an unrepresentative government in Kabul. The United States military presence in Afghanistan greatly contributes to the legitimacy and strategic message of the Pashtun insurgency (Hoh 2009).

Our LexisNexis media database search (25 February 2010) found 13 mentions of Hoh's resignation in the entire UK national print media.

Operation Moshtarak – more a PR exercise than a fight

Operation Moshtarak had been telegraphed to the world, including the insurgents, several weeks earlier, suggesting this was to be a PR exercise rather than a fight. In his familiar supportive style, the BBC's Mark Urban wrote an article entitled: "Why Moshtarak might succeed where Soviet army failed":

> It was never likely that the Taliban would not [sic] contest Operation Moshtarak in a major way. When 36 Sea Stallion helicopters land around your farm (as happened in Marjah), each of them carrying 30 or more US marines, even the most ardent guerrilla fighter knows it is time to strike the pose of a peaceful farmer (Urban 2010).

More to the point, why would an ardent guerrilla be anywhere near the farm when he had known for several weeks that the helicopters would be arriving? As with any product, profitable selling of a PR war requires that features, advantages and benefits be clearly signalled to consumers. The BBC's Frank Gardner (2010a) reported on 13 February Nato Commander Maj. Gen. Nick Carter's view that "11 objectives had already been taken" and "the offensive had been 'so far extremely successful... Indeed it would appear that we've caught the insurgents on the hop – he appears to be completely dislocated'".

Further good news arrived with the announcement that "the top Taliban military commander" Mullah Abdul Ghani Baradar, had been captured in Pakistan. The comic aspects of "the capture" were inadvertently highlighted in an *Independent* leader which noted:

> It is not clear...how far it is accurate to say that he was taken prisoner and how far he might have been detained with a view to opening talks with the Afghan government... Nor has it been revealed whether Mullah Baradar's capture was the result of new intelligence, gleaned either by the United States or Pakistan, or whether his whereabouts were known, at least to the Pakistan authorities, and it was simply a question of their lifting any immunity he might have enjoyed.

In other words, the "capture" was in all likelihood a carefully timed PR stunt. Julius Cavendish (2010) understood the required message in the *Independent* on February 17: "The capture of Mullah Abdul Ghani Baradar, the Taliban's top strategist, deals a psychological blow to the insurgents currently fighting British troops in southern Afghanistan." The BBC's Frank Gardner (2010b) commented on the prospects for ultimate success: "It all depends on whether the coalition can hold the ground and bring lasting security and good governance to the population of central Helmand."

Taking for granted the coalition's aims

Gardner took for granted that it was the intention of the coalition to "bring lasting security and good governance" to Afghanistan. Journalists operating with the Soviet occupiers of Afghanistan from 1979 to 1989 worked on similar assumptions. Propaganda organs such as *Krasnaya Zvezda* insisted that their invasion was required "to help the hapless Afghan people to defend their freedom, their future" (*Krasnaya Zvezda*, 5 January 1988). In 1986, the newspaper, *Izvestiya*, declared that Soviet soldiers were fighting "for a just cause and happy new life for all Afghan people" (*Izvestiya*, 14 January 1986).

On ITV news, anchor Mary Nightingale reported on a newly opened girls' school in Afghanistan, saying: "Here's a reminder of why British and American troops are in Afghanistan" (Mary Nightingale, ITV *News at Ten*, 18 February 2010).

Craig Murray, former British ambassador to Uzbekistan, reviewed Frank Gardner's performance:

> Yet again his grave but reassuring features have been delivering smooth propaganda, this time from the comic opera re-re-re-re-re-re-re-reinvasion of parts of Helmand – an operation which is costing the UK taxpayer £2 billion this month, and the US taxpayer very much more...One of Gardner's favourite tricks is to call ordinary Afghan courtyard houses "Taliban compounds". It is not a compound, it is a house. Perhaps Afghans don't live in things we would recognise in Acacia Drive – but they are their homes. (Craig Murray, Weblog, 15 February 2010, see http://www.craigmurray.org.uk/weblog.html)

The *Guardian*'s Declan Walsh and Stephen Bates (2010) on 14 February 2010 morphed from independent media watchdogs to military spokespeople, commenting: "Operation Moshtarak must succeed not only on the battlefield but in the follow-through by Afghan civilian and security forces."

Innocent enough, one might think, until we imagine a German journalist writing in similar terms of Operation Barbarossa in June 1941, or an Iraqi journalist reporting the invasion of Kuwait in August 1990.

Freelance journalist Ian Sinclair challenged Walsh on his habit of describing areas of Afghanistan as "Taliban-infested": "In the article I was dismayed to see you refer to 'Previous sweeps into Taliban-infested corners of Kandahar and Helmand'. [2] As you are fully aware an infestation' is something normally associated with a place being overrun by rats or other rodents and pests that are seen as harmful to human beings. This hardly seems to be neutral or objective or indeed useful language. Surely you could have used a better word such as "Taliban-dominated" instead?" [3] We also wrote to Walsh asking: "Would you refer to areas of Helmand province as 'Nato-infested'?" [4] An unthinkable thought, of course, for our scrupulously impartial "free press". Predictably, Walsh did not respond.

The PR surge

By contrast, speaking on the Real News website (http://www.therealnews.com), investigative journalist Gareth Porter offered a rare, honest view of Operation Moshtarak. Porter argued that the offensive was primarily intended to prepare American public opinion to accept negotiations with the Taliban:

> Well, in my view, this offensive has to be viewed as more of an effort to shape public opinion in the United States than to shape the politics of the future of Afghanistan, the reason being that no matter how you slice it, this is too small a slice of Afghanistan, even too small a slice of that part of Afghanistan that is controlled by the Taliban, to really make a difference in the long run, to shape, to make a difference in terms of the kind of negotiations that are going to take place, inevitably, to settle this war (Porter 2010a).

Porter pointed out that some 15,000 troops were being used to control a community of just 80,000 people. The offensive was intended to be one of a series of propaganda victories at home that would enable the US to appear to be negotiating with the Taliban from a position of strength: "I think that's what's going to happen 18 months from now, exactly, or 17 or 16 months from now...I think they're going to try to do this over a period of time to build up some sense in the US public that, well, this administration's been doing something positive on the ground, and therefore they should be able to negotiate from strength" (ibid).

In the *Washington Post*, Greg Jaffe and Craig Whitlock reported that the primary goal of the offensive was to "convince Americans that a new era has arrived in the eight-year long war". US military officials "hope a large and loud victory in Marja will convince the American public that they deserve more time to demonstrate that extra troops and new tactics can yield better results on the battlefield" (cited in Porter 2010b). Porter noted that Centcom Chief Gen. David Petraeus appeared to be presenting Operation Moshtarak as a pivotal battle as well as a successful model for the kind of operations to follow:

> As top commander in Iraq in 2007-2008, Petraeus established a new model for re-establishing public support for a war after it had declined precipitously. Through constant briefings to journalists and Congressional delegations, he and his staff convinced political elites and public opinion that his counterinsurgency plan had been responsible for the reduction in insurgent activities that occurred during this command. Evidence from unofficial sources indicates, however, that the dynamics of Sunni-Shi'a sectarian conflict and Shi'a politics were far more important than US military operations in producing that result (ibid).

This was genuinely independent journalism – reporting that did not accept the claimed intentions, benevolence and achievements of power at face value.

Civilian casualties and the PR problem

In March 2010, the WikiLeaks website released a classified CIA document describing possible PR-strategies to promote public support for the war in Afghanistan in Germany and France. CIA concerns were heightened after the February 2010 fall of the Dutch government over the participation of Dutch troops in the conflict. The CIA became worried that similar problems might afflict France and Germany, countries that contribute the largest number of troops to the war after the US and Britain. The CIA report commented:

The fall of the Dutch Government over its troop commitment to Afghanistan demonstrates the fragility of European support for the Nato-led ISAF mission. Some Nato states, notably France and Germany, have counted on public apathy about Afghanistan to increase their contributions to the mission, but indifference might turn into active hostility if spring and summer fighting results in an upsurge in military or Afghan civilian casualties and if a Dutch-style debate spills over into other states contributing troops.[5]

Civilian casualties, then, are a key issue. Also in March, military officials in Kabul admitted that US and Nato troops had killed thirty Afghans and wounded eighty more in or near military checkpoints since the previous summer. Military commander General Stanley McChrystal said: "We have shot an amazing number of people, but to my knowledge, none has ever proven to be a threat" (Oppel Jr. 2010). The importance of civilian casualties to the war effort helps explain both the lack of information on casualties, and the lack of media interest in the issue.

A striking example was provided in January 2010, when rare media reports claimed that American-led troops had dragged Afghan children from their beds and shot them during a night raid in Kunar province in eastern Afghanistan on 27 December 2009. Ten people were killed, including eight schoolboys from one family. The atrocity was almost wholly ignored by the corporate media, including the BBC. Two months after these disturbing allegations surfaced, *The Times* correspondent Jerome Starkey (2010a) sought out two local men whose children and other relatives had been killed. Starkey invited the men to Kabul where they "provided pictures of their dead sons, a sketched map of the compound and copies of the compensation claim forms signed by local officials detailing their sons' names, relatives and positions at school. Their story was supported by Western military sources" (ibid).

After its initial attempts to deny culpability, Nato subsequently asserted that the raid had been carried out on the basis of faulty intelligence and should never have been authorised: "Knowing what we know now, it would probably not have been a justifiable attack. We don't now believe that we busted a major ring." Starkey reported the testimony of Mohammed Taleb Abdul Ajan, father of three of the boys who were killed: "When I entered their room I saw four people lying in a heap," said Taleb. "I shook them and shouted their names but they didn't respond. Some of them were shot in the head. Some of them were shot in the chest. I was praying that in the next room maybe they were still alive but when I went in I saw everyone was dead. I saw blood on their necks. I became crazy. I don't remember what I felt" (Starkey 2010b). However, a *Times* editorial on the same day managed to portray the atrocity in the required context of a "just war": "The legitimacy of the cause in Afghanistan is called into question by civilian deaths. The conflict needs to be conducted with regard for the native population." [6]

The stated benign aims of Western governments have to be taken on trust; just as the Soviet government portrayed its invasion of Afghanistan in 1979 as an act of humanitarian intervention initiated at the "request of the [Afghan] government". The aim of that earlier occupation, the Soviet people were assured, was "to prevent the establishment of...a terrorist regime and to protect the Afghan people from genocide" and to provide "aid in stabilising the situation and the repulsion of possible external aggression". [7]

The final payoff line from *The Times* leader could have come from a *Pravda* editorial of thirty years ago: "In order to defeat our enemies we must be seen to be better than them." Meanwhile, the rest of the corporate media averted its gaze from the bloodied remains of dead Afghan schoolchildren.

The malodorous myth of BBC balance

In December 2009, BBC news online had posted these two brief 'balanced' reports of the US-led killing of the Afghan schoolchildren. [8] In the first of these reports, the BBC observed: "Nato said it had no record of operations or deaths in the area." And: "The BBC's Peter Greste in Kabul says Kunar province is remote, snowbound and dominated by the Taliban, so the investigation into Saturday's alleged incident will be difficult." The second report commented: "The BBC's Peter Greste in Kabul says it is impossible to verify either account.

He says it is possible that both are broadly correct – and that the victims might well have been school students, but that they helped the insurgency."

When Media Lens readers challenged the BBC's failure to report the allegations fully and responsibly, the corporation responded: "It's worth noting that the circumstances of the incident are disputed, unlike some previous examples of civilians killed by coalition forces. The Afghan government and the UN believe that civilians were killed as the result of the US operation in Kunar. Nato still does not accept this and strongly argues that US forces killed insurgents." [9] Evidence of a massacre soon became even stronger, and yet we are not aware of *any* subsequent BBC news reports, or any corrections or apologies.

On 27 February 2010, we emailed two senior BBC editors: Helen Boaden, director of BBC News, and Steve Herrmann, who is responsible for BBC news online. We pointed out that Jerome Starkey, of *The Times*, had now been able to verify the reports that Afghan schoolchildren had been shot dead in the December raid involving US forces. We asked the BBC editors, in light of *The Times'* revelations:"What will you and your colleagues be doing to follow up your previous reports? With the resources that the BBC has available, why were you apparently unable to do what Mr Starkey has done and investigate – and now indeed verify – the initial disturbing allegations of Afghan schoolchildren being shot? How will these latest revelations affect how you deal with Nato statements in future?" [10] We received no response from Boaden or Herrmann.

We emailed the same questions to BBC reporter Peter Greste, who forwarded our inquiry to the BBC's bureau editor in Kabul. A banal response was finally sent to us by Sean Moss, a "divisional advisor" at BBC complaints: "As I'm sure you will appreciate, it is not feasible for the Kabul bureau to enter into a dialogue with individuals. If you would like to make a complaint, you need to do so through the webform at www.bbc.co.uk/complaints." [11]

As many of our readers have observed, the BBC's "complaints procedure" is a magnificent exercise in headless bureaucracy. The BBC *does* respond to complaints – that is, it does acknowledge their receipt and send a response. But the responses rarely have anything meaningful to say about the actual complaint and nothing changes as a result. Another ironic echo of the Soviet invasion of Afghanistan.

Conclusions: A curious pattern of reporting

Meanwhile, the killing, and the propaganda campaign, continued. In March 2010, Jerome Starkey (2010c) reported in *The Times* that another night raid carried out by US and Afghan gunmen that month had led to the deaths of two pregnant women, a teenage girl and two local officials – an atrocity which Nato then tried to cover up. The family was offered "American compensation" – $2,000 per victim. Bibi Sabsparie, the mother of two of the dead, responded: "There's no value on human life. They killed our family, then they came and brought us money. Money won't bring our family back."

Again, this horror was buried out of sight by the UK media. Our search of the LexisNexis media database (14 June 2010) found no press mentions of the killing outside of *The Times*. The fact that this story was covered by the Murdoch-owned *Times* and yet ignored by reputedly more liberal media like the *Guardian* and the *Independent* may seem curious. We asked the Israel-based, former *Guardian* journalist Jonathan Cook for his opinion on this pattern of reporting. He agreed with us that it was "revealing":

> One thing worth noting is that even rightwing media like *The Times* sometimes manage to go out on a limb to report important human interest stories that embarrass our powerful elites. But the special context and circumstances in these cases should be understood. Starkey, like many war correspondents in similar situations, was probably driven to chase the story out of a mix of motives: a genuine concern for civilian suffering; the adrenaline rush of a dangerous story; and a chance to make his name and career. *The Times* news desk had similar interests in allowing him to cover the story, not least because it proves their investigative credentials and gives them a chance to win an award for their paper. That's doubtless why Starkey is still chasing this story. BUT *The Times'* executives have a different interest: they need to minimise the fallout over the story from

powerful elites. Thus, the importance of providing the "context" that it was a terrible accident, a one-off event etc. [12]

By contrast, Cook noted, there was little glory to be gained for other newspapers following up a story broken by *The Times* (in fact, doing so would have highlighted their own failure to break the story). And if they had covered it, they, like *The Times*, would risk suffering the fallout. So instead they took the safest course of action, which was to ignore the story. Cook added a crucial point: "The significance of their decision can be understood if we imagine that *The Times* had found an exclusive that supported Western state interests: for instance, proof that Iran is meddling in Afghanistan. Then, far from being ignored, *The Times* exclusive would have been followed up relentlessly by the wires and every other media outlet."

This, then, is another indication of how the mainstream media simultaneously functions as a filter and booster system for powerful interests. A range of incentives and disincentives ensures that there are many more compelling reasons for the corporate media to promote stories that are inoffensive to, or favoured by, powerful interests.

Notes

[1] See Coventry University podcasts, Is there a crisis in world journalism? Jeremy Paxman, 29 October 2009. Available online at
http://coventryuniversity.podbean.com/2009/10/29/is-there-a-crisis-in-world-journalism-jeremy-paxman/), accessed on 3 December 2009
[2] See http://www.guardian.co.uk/world/2010/feb/12/afghanistan-allies-attack-helmand, accessed on 15 February 2010
[3] Email to Declan Walsh, forwarded to Media Lens, 15 February 2010
[4] Media Lens email to Declan Walsh, 17 February 2010
[5] See CIA report into shoring up Afghan war support in Western Europe, WikiLeaks, March 26, 2010; http://file.wikileaks.org/file/cia-afghanistan.pdf, accessed on 27 March 2010

[6] See Editorial, Just War, *The Times*, 25 February 2010. Available online at
http://www.timesonline.co.uk/tol/comment/leading_article/article7040089.ece,
accessed on 26 February 2010

[7] See Nikolai Lanine and Media Lens, Invasion: A comparison of Soviet and
Western Media performance, 20 November 2007. Available online at
http://www.medialens.org/alerts/07/071120_invasion_a_comparison.php

[8] Afghanistan children killed "during Western operation", 28 December 2009.
Available online at
http://news.bbc.co.uk/1/hi/world/south_asia/8432653.stm, accessed on 1 January
2010. And Afghan MP accuses US troops of killing schoolchildren, 30 December
2009. Available online at
http://news.bbc.co.uk/1/hi/world/south_asia/8434800.stm, accessed on 1 January
2010

[9] Email from BBC complaints to Media Lens reader, 19 February 2010

[10] Media Lens, email to Helen Boaden and Steve Herrmann, 27 February 2010

[11] Email to Media Lens from BBC Complaints, 15 March 2010

[12] Email, Jonathan Cook to Media Lens, 17 March 2010

References

Cavendish, Julius (2010) Nato has struck a blow, but the war isn't yet won,
Independent, 17 February. Available online at
http://www.independent.co.uk/news/world/asia/nato-has-struck-a-blow-but-the-
war-isnt-yet-won-1901748.html, accessed on 25 February 2010

Gardner, Frank (2010a) Afghanistan offensive on Taliban in Helmand, BBC Online,
13 February. Available online at
http://news.bbc.co.uk/2/hi/south_asia/8513849.stm, accessed on 25 February
2010

Gardner, Frank (2010b) Afghanistan offensive on Taliban in Helmand, BBC Online,
13 February 13. Available online at
http://news.bbc.co.uk/2/hi/south_asia/8513849.stm, accessed on 25 February
2010

Hoh, Matthew (2009) Letter of resignation, 10 September. Available online at http://www.washingtonpost.com/wp-srv/hp/ssi/wpc/ResignationLetter.pdf?sid=ST2009102603447, accessed on 25 February 2010

Independent (2010) Leading article: A multi-track approach to Afghanistan, 17 February. Available online at http://www.independent.co.uk/opinion/leading-articles/leading-article-a-multitrack-approach-to-afghanistan-1901549.html, accessed on 25 February 2010

Mostrous, Alexi (2010) Business big shot: Richard Sambrook, Edelman PR, The Times, 16 February. Available online at http://business.timesonline.co.uk/tol/business/movers_and_shakers/article7028335.ece, accessed on 9 June 2010

Oppel Jr., Richard A. (2010) Tighter rules fail to stem deaths of innocent Afghans at checkpoints, *New York Times*, 26 March. Available online at http://www.nytimes.com/2010/03/27/world/asia/27afghan.html, accessed on 27 March 2010

Porter, Gareth (2010a) Offensive in Marja directed at US public opinion, 17 February 2010. Available online at http://therealnews.com/t2/index.php?option=com_content&task=view&id=31&Itemid=74&jumival=4829&updaterx=2010-02-17+04%3A07%3A05, accessed on 25 February 2010

Porter, Gareth (2010b) Marja offensive aimed to shape U.S. opinion on war, IPS, 23 February. Available online at http://www.ipsnews.net/news.asp?idnews=50434, accessed on 25 February 2010

Starkey, Jerome (2010a) Nato admits that deaths of 8 boys were a mistake, *The Times*, 25 February. Available online at http://www.timesonline.co.uk/tol/news/world/afghanistan/article7040166.ece, accessed on 26 February 2010

Starkey, Jerome (2010b) Assault force killed family by mistake in raid, claims Afghan father, *The Times*, 25 February. Available online at http://www.timesonline.co.uk/tol/news/world/afghanistan/article7040216.ece, accessed on 26 February 2010

Starkey, Jerome (2010c) Nato "covered up" botched night raid in Afghanistan that killed five, *The Times*, 13 March. Available online at http://www.timesonline.co.uk/tol/news/world/afghanistan/article7060395.ece, accessed on 14 March 2010

Travis (Alan) Support for war falls to new low, *Guardian*, 21 January

Urban, Mark (2010) Why Moshtarak might succeed where Soviet army failed, War and Peace: Mark Urban's blog, *Newsnight*, BBC Online, 15 February. Available online at http://www.bbc.co.uk/blogs/newsnight/markurban/2010/02/the_joint_natoafghan_offensive.html, accessed on 25 February 2010

Walsh, Declan and Bates, Stephan (2010) Nato rockets kill 12 Afghan civilians, *Guardian*, 14 February. Available online at http://www.guardian.co.uk/world/2010/feb/14/nato-rockets-kill-afghan-civilians, accessed on 25 February 2010

Note on the authors

David Edwards is co-editor of Media Lens (www.medialens.org). He is the author of *Free to be Human* (Green Books, 1995) and *The Compassionate Revolution* (Green Books, 1998). He is also co-author with David Cromwell of *Guardians of Power* (Pluto Press, 2006) and *Newspeak in the 21st century* (Pluto Press, 2009).

David Cromwell is co-editor of Media Lens and a researcher at the National Oceanography Centre, Southampton. He is author of *Private Planet* (2001), co-author of two Media Lens books, *Guardians of Power* (2006) and *Newspeak in the 21st Century* (2009), and co-editor of *Surviving Climate Change* (2007).

"Can't talk now, mate": New Zealand news media and the invisible Afghan war

Donald Matheson argues that the reporting of New Zealand's special forces in Afghanistan, by far the country's most significant military commitment outside of peacekeeping for 20 years, has been largely hidden under a blanket of secrecy

Introduction

New Zealand's involvement in the US-led military campaign in Afghanistan is small, comprising in 2010 a group of about 70 Special Air Service (SAS) troops and twice as many other soldiers involved in what is called 'provincial reconstruction'. Their activities are of wider interest, however, because the deployment has been conducted under a cloak of secrecy and lack of scrutiny, accompanied at times by quite overt management of news media personnel. New Zealand journalism has allowed this to be done to itself, reproducing the stories of heroic soldiers it has been offered and failing, for the most part, to ask critical questions about the legitimacy of these troops on Afghan soil, about their role in human rights abuses or about military and political strategy.

Why that is the case cannot be answered simply. But the chapter suggests that part of the reason can be found in the country's journalism culture. New Zealand has almost no tradition of critical foreign correspondence. Its news organisations have over many years failed to invest in overseas postings for journalists, so that newsrooms lack expertise on foreign affairs and, perhaps, also lack confidence in reporting on the country's military and diplomatic activities. In particular, the stories found elsewhere of journalists holding the state to account for its activities overseas and standing to one side of the space of patriotic nationalism, from Kate Adie in Tripoli in 1986 to Anna Politkovskaya in Chechnya in 1999, have no exemplars in New Zealand. In addition, for historical reasons, the military is reported less as a political and more as a national cultural object, something to be proud of rather than critiqued.

Creating heroes

New Zealand is not a militarist nation. The defence budget and resources are small – the navy, for example, possesses two frigates. What the country does have, however, is a strong cultural attachment to a version of military history in which the New Zealand soldier is a heroic figure who embodies many of the characteristics of an ideal New Zealand male. The country, along with Australia, remembers World War One not primarily on Armistice Day (a day of peace) but on ANZAC Day, commemorating the botched British-led campaign to take the Gallipoli Peninsula in Turkey. For almost a century, the day has been an important symbol of national identity formation for New Zealanders and Australians, so that up to 10,000 of them can be found on that date each year at Gallipoli. Fighting prowess is a celebrated element in Māori culture, commemorated in the likes of tales of heroism among the Māori Battalion during the bloody 1944 battle for Monte Cassino, Italy. Military history has provided important cultural reference points and, in particular, ones that give support to key national discourses of self-determination, harmony between Māori and the dominant white culture, and a particular version of masculinity (Phillips 1996, Hucker 2010).

The New Zealand Defence Force (NZDF) tapped into these tropes of national identity when, in 2007, it invited a Television New Zealand crew to produce a fly-on-the-wall documentary about the awarding of a Victoria Cross to an NZSAS soldier, Willie Apiata, who had saved another soldier's life during an ambush in Afghanistan in 2004. *The Reluctant Hero*, which had the head of the SAS as one of its producers, was screened a year later on ANZAC Day and followed Apiata's return home for the medal ceremony, along with his welcome on to his home marae (tribal meeting ground) as a hero, and a poignant visit to war graves in Belgium. Other voices, particularly army officers, commented on his bravery, humility and quintessential New Zealandness. The film was a success in the country, garnering little criticism – indeed, to do so at the time would have attracted charges of churlishness – other than some debate about the appropriateness of the NZDF spending $35,000 on media training for Apiata.

The film contained shadowy reconstructions of the 2004 ambush, but provided no other details on what Apiata and his fellow SAS troops had been doing in Afghanistan. Indeed, to this day no information has been released on who shot at Apiata's patrol and where the incident took place, and no New Zealand journalists have shone any further light on the events. Nor is much known about the fighting that the SAS has taken part in. The lionisation of this one soldier, then, took place in something of a vacuum. The decision to deploy the NZSAS to support the US-led Operation Enduring Freedom in 2001 was only made public the year after the first rotation of SAS troops had arrived home from Afghanistan (Espiner 2010). More information, in fact, was released about their activities by the White House, when in 2004 they were among special units to receive a US presidential award. The citation stated that the troops had neutralised Taliban and al-Qaeda forces "in extremely high risk missions" in late 2001 and early 2002 that included "destruction of multiple cave and tunnel complexes", "apprehension of military and political detainees" and "identification and destruction of al-Qaeda training camps" (US Navy 2004).

Deaths of thousands of fighters and civilians – yet no public debate

It can only be guessed how far New Zealand soldiers were involved in the deaths of thousands of fighters and civilians in Afghanistan during that period, or in the torture, summary killings and other human rights violations recorded by later investigations of the US and its allies (e.g. Human Rights Watch 2004). One incident they have been linked to was the Blitzkrieg bombing of the Shah-i-Kot area in March 2003 (Hager 2003), although it was one of the murkier events in the war, with claims of hundreds of Taliban and al-Qaeda fighters killed but little evidence (O'Neill 2002). Because the SAS were covert soldiers, there was no public debate beforehand about the legitimacy of New Zealand state involvement in that fighting.

After the deployments began, there has also been little news to juxtapose with the government line that the military involvement was helping to "stabilise" Afghanistan and make the world safer. The government has, until recently, observed a rule of complete secrecy on the SAS, ostensibly to protect its soldiers and their families who might be targeted by terrorists. New Zealand news organisations send almost no reporters to Afghanistan, the few instances being almost always short trips organised by the NZDF or other state agencies to visit the military engineers involved in reconstruction and the soldiers protecting them. The exception, Jon Stephenson, who has financed many of his trips to the country himself and published mostly in one Sunday newspaper, the *Sunday Star Times*, stands out.

Instead, most coverage of Afghanistan aired or published in New Zealand is taken from US or UK news outlets or from international agencies, in which New Zealand's troops are not mentioned. The Apiata documentary, then, was disconnected from any political debate, slipping easily and without complication into the ideas of the heroic soldier. The longest-running military campaign in the country's history, longer now than its participation in the war in Vietnam, and possibly the first deployment of troops in anger since the Gulf War of 1991, is largely invisible.

Secrecy breached

On 20 January 2010, New Zealand suddenly recalled that its soldiers were fighting. The *New Zealand Herald* reported that *New York Times* correspondent Dexter Filkins had identified New Zealanders as among troops involved in heavy fighting in Kabul, in which at least 13 people had been killed (Young 2010). The Prime Minister, John Key, in response was tight-lipped, saying only he had been advised the New Zealand soldiers' involvement had been "very limited" and that they were "not involved in particular instances that caused harm" (ibid). The next day the newspaper published an image taken by a French photographer in Kabul, showing two NZSAS soldiers in full battle gear walking down a street. One of the soldiers was identified after publication as the famous Apiata himself, as he had removed his helmet and sunglasses.

The image created a storm of controversy, with Key, "rebuking" the newspaper for breaching the long-standing "gentleman's agreement" that SAS personnel should not be identified, and the military expressing its disappointment, claiming that Taliban could use the image to garner intelligence about the soldiers' clothing and weaponry. Another newspaper republished the image the next day, although with the second soldier's identity further concealed. Both newspapers defended their publication on public interest grounds: these soldiers were walking in a public place with no attempt at concealment and the public had a right to know what its forces were doing, said one (*New Zealand Herald* 2010); New Zealanders would want to see their hero, said the other, and besides the NZDF had only itself to blame for making Apiata's face so widely known (*Dominion Post* 2010). For journalism commentators, the incident suggested New Zealand journalism was becoming more assertive. One, Jim Tully, said the media would not have published photos of the SAS five to 10 years earlier (cited in Harding 2010).

The larger point, however, was the rare snippet of information revealed about New Zealand military activities, something that was often lost sight of in the arguments over the identification of the individual SAS soldier in the photograph. This was a rare moment when the battle for control of Afghanistan and the deaths of Afghans could be connected to New Zealanders, and the first direct evidence for three years that the troops' own lives were at risk. The *New York Times'* Filkins expressed himself amused:

> The attack on the Central Bank in downtown Kabul this week revealed many things about Afghanistan. But one of the more surprising things it brought to light was that New Zealand is at war.
>
> New Zealand? At war?
>
> Who knew?
>
> Not a lot of New Zealanders, apparently. The news – first reported in my story – that a team of commandos from New Zealand had joined Afghan soldiers at the scene caused a sensation in the little country off the coast of Australia.
>
> I spotted the team of New Zealanders as they moved into Pashtunistan Square, the site of the Taliban attack, which killed five people and wounded at least 70. All seven militants died or killed themselves. The city was paralyzed for hours.

"Get out of here," one of the New Zealanders said to me. I saw the patch on his arm announcing his country.

Others were more friendly. "Can't talk now, mate," another said with a smile (Filkins 2010).

A few journalists noted that Filkins' account, and that of the photographer Philip Poupin, was at odds with the version given by the Prime Minister and the chief of the NZDF, Lieut. Gen. Jerry Mataparae, which had placed the troops far from the action. Poupin saw the soldiers enter buildings in which he later saw dead fighters. Their accounts also cast doubt on PM Key's assurances made the year before that the latest deployment would be involved in the training of Afghan special troops (the CRU) and not in actual combat (Stephenson and Hubbard 2010). These half-truths and evasions were allowed to stand by other journalists, however, and the Prime Minister at his press conferences was not challenged when he evaded questions with vague generalities. More importantly, there was almost no discussion in New Zealand news media about the reasons for the country's participation in this war. Critical voices, such as the Green Party, the third largest party in parliament, or Amnesty International were buried in stories on the topic, if quoted at all.

"Operating under the strictest censorship in the Western world"

Where journalists did push this story further was in reacting against the Prime Minister's "rebuke" by questioning the secrecy surrounding the SAS and other military activities and, in particular, the tendency of the government to release information about its activities only when it suited it. One noted that PM Key announced a new SAS deployment – well after they had arrived there – on the eve of a visit to Washington in September 2009, presumably as a "news bump upon his arrival in the US" (Watkin 2009). A number of journalists noted how little was known about the SAS's deployment. Watkin wrote: "Never has New Zealand committed to a war for so long with so little public coverage" (Watkin 2010). Another observed:

Our media seem to operate under some of the strictest censorship in the Western world when it comes to the operations of the military, and the SAS in particular…The public is entitled to know what is being done and who is being shot at in its name (Espiner 2010).

Commentators observed too that the few snippets about the SAS's operations had come almost entirely from overseas sources, such as Filkins above, or the Norwegian defence minister, who had told journalists there in 2009 that New Zealand SAS troops would be taking over from Norwegians in training the CRU in Kabul. The willingness of the Norwegians, Australians, US and other officials to discuss their special forces' operations after missions were completed, in contrast to New Zealand policy, was also noted (e.g. Beatson 2010a). This criticism, possibly in combination with a reappraisal from within the government of the publicity value of a little more information about the troops, led to a decision a week after the photograph was published, that the NZDF would hold occasional press conferences in relation to the SAS's activities. Certainly, the idea that publishing photographs of soldiers could allow the Taliban to gain sensitive information from studying their clothes and weapons was hard to sustain when the military's own website contained images of these soldiers in combat gear.

Yet these are relatively superficial issues, a matter of asking for more publicity handouts and of defending the right to show a dramatic photograph of a war hero. Critical questions of the military campaign have not followed this slight opening up of public information on the topic. A key question that remains unaddressed by the New Zealand government is over the protocols associated with the handover of prisoners from NZSAS to US and Afghan detentions centres. Longstanding concerns about this question were substantiated in 2009, when the independent correspondent, Jon Stephenson, gathered testimony from former SAS soldiers that they had in 2003 handed over prisoners to a US detention centre in Kandahar, known as "Camp Slappy" for its widespread use of beatings, and done so without recording their captives' identities, contravening the Geneva Convention (Stephenson 2009).

Another journalist has written about the refusal of the NZDF to let him see the standard operating procedures used by the SAS for detaining and processing captives, and reported Amnesty International's call on the SAS to refuse to hand captives over until there was no risk of torture or other ill-treatment (Beatson 2010b). Perhaps because of the absence of hard information about the SAS's share of responsibility for the torture and ill-treatment of captives, these stories have only very sporadically been tackled by other journalists. As noted above, the same is the case on the involvement of SAS troops in doing much more than train Afghan special forces, but fight alongside them. While denied by the government, interviews with Afghan officers suggest they are indeed doing so (Stephenson 2010).

This failure by all but a few journalists to probe the country's military involvement further is very convenient for a government which has much to gain in trade from helping out the US but little to gain from public debate of that. Why journalists have acceded to that situation, however, is another question, no doubt related to journalism's chronic lack of time and possibly related to direct requests from officials to journalists to drop the story. Martin Hirst suggests that journalists are allowing themselves to be shaped by the general myth that "the news media MUST take the side of the nation state in matters of national interest" (Hirst 2010). One further example, discussed below, suggests that the dependence on overseas sources of news, combined with the powerful discourse of the Kiwi soldier as the quintessential Kiwi male, makes it difficult for a more critical, combative journalism on Afghanistan to take root here.

The kind of hero that war makes

On 9 March 2010, Television New Zealand's main news programme began: "Tonight we salute a war hero. You'll hear how a Kiwi soldier saved his comrades' lives." Correspondent Paul Hobbs, based in London, reported that a 29-year-old New Zealand soldier, James McKie, serving in the British army, had the week before saved the life of his commanding officer in Afghanistan by tossing away a grenade a second before it exploded. Hobbs described the story as "one of those heroic stories that comes out of a war zone." Back in New

Zealand, his colleague Catherine Wedd interviewed the soldier's father, Andrew McKie: "Did James show any early signs of bravery as a child?"

As with the Apiata story, the New Zealand media quickly and easily located the story within the discourse of the Kiwi male. One newspaper described McKie as a gentle man, an avid sports fan and a loyal friend, qualities that had turned him into a hero (Capital Times 2010). Jon Stephenson, interviewed on Radio New Zealand's *MediaWatch* programme, lamented the way the story was covered. Heroism, he suggested, could also be found among the Afghan people suffering under waves of invasion and insecurity, yet was almost never reported:

> We don't really get to hear anything about Afghanistan unless one of those soldiers has done something heroic or is involved in the capture of some Taliban leader or is involved in some sort of ambush or attack, so I think it's very sad that most of our coverage seems to be towards the entertainment end of the spectrum rather than towards the informative and enlightening (interviewed on *MediaWatch* 2010).

Indeed, as the *Mediawatch* team revealed, the story was taken directly from the Helmand Blog, written by Major Paul Smith of the UK forces' "Media Ops" department, prompting the programme to suggest that New Zealand news media were being led by the nose by military public relations. The photographs of a blood-stained McKie used on television and in newspaper accounts were taken directly from the website. As with the other cases discussed above, the problem here is not so much in what was said but in what was absent. The coverage of McKie contained no mention of whom he was fighting against, what the larger battle was or why both sides were there. As with the previous cases, that is largely because the New Zealand news media were in a dependent position with little knowledge, reporting on Afghanistan without having any correspondents there and reporting on the war without experienced and senior staff able and willing to critique what they were being told.

Conclusion

The BBC's world news editor Jon Williams described Afghanistan in January 2010 as the most important story for the broadcaster. "If we, and other news organisations, are to report it accurately, then doing so from the front line is vital," he wrote (Williams 2010). The contrast with New Zealand is stark, and a reminder of the consequences of reducing the country's foreign correspondent corps down to a total of half a dozen individuals. Although New Zealand is widely regarded as a country with a high degree of openness and press freedom, there is a high degree of restriction on the news media in relation to military matters.

The reporting of its special forces in Afghanistan, by far the country's most significant military commitment outside of peacekeeping for 20 years, has been covered in a piecemeal and often uncritical way that at times has bordered on hagiography. Most news about the country's military involvement has come from overseas media. The half-truths and omissions of the government have been given little scrutiny. Without a lively tradition of foreign correspondence, there have been only a few reporters, most prominently the freelancer Jon Stephenson, who have been able and willing to ask the difficult questions and thereby to hold the government to account.

On one level, the country's military commitment is so small that this failure to force the actions of the military into the sphere of legitimate public debate has few consequences. Similarly, the human rights abuses committed by allied forces could be seen as a moral issue but not one that New Zealand is likely to have much purchase on. But on another level, the lack of scrutiny of the New Zealand military is of wider significance for the country's political direction. In mobilising certain historic ideals of the Kiwi male, the government and the military have successfully aestheticised politics, aligning New Zealandness with loyalty to a Western world order through nostalgic appeal.

There are, however, competing discourses of the nation, particularly ones that arose in the 1980s as New Zealand forged a nuclear-free foreign policy and a South Pacific identity. Within that latter discourse, questions were raised about the need of this small country for an offensive military capability and for participation in the United States' security, intelligence and military network. Those questions should be asked again. In allowing the only stories about New Zealand soldiers in Afghanistan to be stories of individual heroism, journalists have allowed the important political debate about the country's place in the world to be elided away and have, therefore, allowed themselves to be used in that wider politics.

References

Beatson, D. (2010a) SAS: Now you see them, now you don't, pundit, 10 March. Available online at http://www.pundit.co.nz/print/1149, accessed on 20 June 2010

Beatson, D. (2010b) Key lifts the SAS veil – a little bit, pundit, 1 February. Available online at http://pundit.co.nz/content/key-lifts-the-sas-veil—-a-little-bit, accessed on 22 June 2010

Capital Times (2010) Medal citizen, Capital Times, 17 March. Available online at http://www.capitaltimes.co.nz/article/2859/Medalcitizen.html, accessed on 20 June 2010

Dominion Post (2010) Editorial: Apiata's cover was already blown, *Dominion Post*, 26 January. Available online at http://www.stuff.co.nz/dominion-post/opinion/3260264/Editorial-Apiatas-cover-was-already-blown, accessed on 20 June 2010

Espiner, C. (2010) The secret army, On the House blog, www.stuff.co.nz, 27 January. Available online at http://www.stuff.co.nz/the-press/news/politics/blog-on-the-house/3267587/The-Secret-Army, accessed on 20 June 2010

Filkins, D. (2010) Kiwis in Kabul, At war: Notes from the front lines blog, *New York Times*, 20 January. Available online at http://atwar.blogs.nytimes.com/2010/01/20/kiwis-in-kabul/, accessed on 24 June 2010

Hager, N. (2003) Our secret war, *Sunday Star Times*, 16 February. Available online at http://www.nickyhager.info/our-secret-war/, accessed on 22 June 2010

Harding, E. (2010) Clark blamed for SAS exposure, *Southland Times*, 23 January

Hirst, M. (2010) Soldiers in harm's way: Don't ask, don't tell, Ethical Martini blog, 22 January. Available online at http://ethicalmartini.wordpress.com/2010/01/22/soldiers-in-harms-way-dont-ask-dont-tell/, accessed on 20 June 2010

Hucker, G. (2010) A determination to remember: Helen Clark and New Zealand's military heritage, *Journal of Arts Management, Law, and Society*, Vol. 40, No. 2 pp 105-118

Human Rights Watch (2004) *US: Systematic abuse of Afghan prisoners*, press release. Available online at http://www.hrw.org/english/docs/2004/05/13/afghan8577.htm, accessed on 22 June 2010

MediaWatch (2010) *Mediawatch*, Radio New Zealand National, 14 March, 9 am

New Zealand Herald (2010) Editorial: Public right to know more about SAS, *New Zealand Herald*, 23 January. Available online at http://www.nzherald.co.nz/nz/news/article.cfm?c_id=1&objectid=10621788, accessed on 22 June 2010

O'Neill, B. (2002) The strange battle of Shah-i-Kot, spiked-online, 22 March. Available online at http://www.spiked-online.com/articles/00000006D851.htm, accessed on 24 June 2010

Phillips, J. (1996) *A man's country? The image of the pakeha male, a history*, Penguin Books, Auckland

Stephenson, J. (2009) Kiwi troops in "war crimes" row, *Sunday Star Times*, 2 August. Available online at http://www.stuff.co.nz/national/2712026/Kiwi-troops-in-war-crimes-row, accessed on 20 June 2010

Stephenson, J. (2010) SAS HQ: Walk right in, *Sunday Star Times*, 2 May. Available online at http://www.stuff.co.nz/national/3647775/SAS-HQ-Walk-right-in, accessed on 20 June 2010

Stephenson, J. and Hubbard, A. (2010) Key "broke pledge" on Kiwis in battle, *Sunday Star Times*, 24 January. Available online at http://www.stuff.co.nz/national/3257154/Key-broke-pledge on-Kiwis-in-battle, accessed on 24 June 2010

US Navy (2004) Enduring Freedom task force earns presidential unit citation, press release, 12 October. Available online at http://www.navy.mil/search/display.asp?story_id=16216, accessed on 22 June 2010

Watkin, T. (2009) SAS deployment: Is the government making it up as it goes along? pundit, 22 September. Available online at http://www.pundit.co.nz/print/870, accessed on 22 June 2010

Watkin, T. (2010) Willie Apiata: The photo the army published, pundit, 22 January. Available online at http://www.pundit.co.nz/content/willie-apiata-the-photo-the-army-published, accessed on 24 June 2010

Williams, J. (2010) Death of British journalist in Afghanistan, The Editors' blog, 11 January. Available online at http://www.bbc.co.uk/blogs/theeditors/2010/01/death_of_british_journalist_in.html, accessed on 24 June

Young, A. (2010) SAS involved in Kabul defence: Key, *New Zealand Herald*, 20 January

Note on the author

Donald Matheson is Senior Lecturer in Media and Communication at the University of Canterbury, New Zealand. Among his publications are *Media Discourses* (2005) and *Digital War Reporting* (with Stuart Allan, 2009). He co-edits the journal *Ethical Space* (with Richard Keeble and Shannon Bowen). He writes on journalism practices, with particular emphasis on news discourse and the communicative ethics of the news, interests that have led him to study weblogs and other digital media. He previously worked at Cardiff and Strathclyde universities in the UK and as a journalist in New Zealand.

Thanks to Mike Anstee for research assistance on this chapter.

Index

Clinton, President Bill 104, 152, 196
CND (Campaign for Nuclear Disarmament) 249
CNN 152
Coburn, Philip 58
Cockburn, Patrick 71, 231, 249
Cook, Jonathan 271, 272

D
Daily Chronicle 90, 91
Daily Express 90, 91, 98
Daily Herald 96
Daily Mail 90, 91, 123, 148, 149, 209, 218, 220, 221, 243, 246
Daily Telegraph 31, 91, 218, 222, 244, 246
Daily Times (Pakistan) 182
Democracy Now! (radio station) 240
Dimbleby, Richard 50, 65
Drudge Report 203

E
Engelhardt, Tom 249
Evans, Harold 67, 68
Evening Post 90
Evening Standard, London 231

F
Falklands War 50, 86, 214, 231, 235
Farrell, Stephen 12, 98
Filkins, Dexter 279, 280, 281, 282
Fisk, Robert 97, 243, 249
Fox News 30
Frontline Club 5, 48
Fox, Robert 72, 73, 74, 79

G
Gall, Carlotta 180
Galtung, Johan 130, 135, 138, 145
Gardner, Frank 75, 264, 265
Gellhorn, Martha 65, 93
Gibbs, Philip 91, 92
Gillard, Frank 50
Goldenberg, Suzanne 130, 139, 140
Gopal, Anand 230, 240
Gowing, Nik 113
Greste, Peter 269, 270

Los Angeles Times 194
Loyn, David 48

M
Mailer, Norman 65
Marcus, Jonathan 51-53
McChrystal, Stanley 141, 142, 233, 244, 248, 268
McCormick, Cami 59
Media Lens 14, 204, 261, 270, 275
MediaWatch (New Zealand) 284
MI6 230, 232
Military Covenant 203, 206-227
Miller, Jonathan 147
Milne, Seamus 245, 246
Morenatti, Emilio 59
Morning Star 231, 247
Moshtarak, Operation 16, 17, 31, 44, 50, 53, 140, 229-260, 262, 263, 265, 266, 267
Mullah Abdul Ghani Baradar 240, 264
Mullah Omar 111, 121, 239
Murray, Craig 265

N
Nato 12, 15, 16, 17, 19, 21, 56, 57, 76, 85, 86, 87, 88, 89, 98, 105, 106, 110, 111, 131, 136, 140, 146, 147, 148, 161, 168, 170, 177, 178, 179, 183, 186, 187, 188, 192, 193, 194, 195, 197, 233, 237, 241, 243, 244, 247, 248, 262, 263, 264, 266, 268, 269, 270, 271
Newsinger, John 231
News of the World 208, 222
New York Times 12, 16, 95, 98, 113, 131, 177, 233, 279, 280
New Zealand Herald 279, 280
New Zealand Defence Force 277, 279, 280, 281, 282, 283
Nightingale, Mary 265
Norton-Taylor, Richard 179, 217, 229, 238, 248

O
Obama, President Barack 108, 139, 180, 231, 233, 242, 244, 248
Observer 217, 246
O'Kane, Maggie 65
Operation Enduring Freedom 4, 147, 148, 149, 152, 153, 158, 159, 161, 163, 278
Oppel, Richard 146, 192, 195, 268
Orwell, George 65, 96, 236

Lightning Source UK Ltd.
Milton Keynes UK

178116UK00001BA/8/P